SHIPS TO REMEMBER

SHIPS TO REMEMBER

1400 YEARS OF HISTORIC SHIPS

WRITTEN BY RORKE BRYAN & PAINTINGS BY AUSTIN DWYER

The History Press

First published 2016

The History Press
The Mill, Brimscombe Port
Stroud, Gloucestershire, GL5 2QG
www.thehistorypress.co.uk

British Library Cataloguing in Publication Data.
A catalogue record for this book is available from the British Library.

ISBN 978 0 7509 6590 3

Typesetting and origination by The History Press
Printed in China

CONTENTS

Acknowledgements   6
Forewords   7
Introduction   8

1   The *Brendan*, the Saint and the Island of the Blessed   9
2   The Royal Ship *Vasa* and a Meddling Monarch   15
3   USS *Constitution*: the Saga of 'Old Ironsides'   21
4   Nelson, HMS *Elephant* and the 'Battle Won by a Fish'   26
5   HMS *Beagle* and the Voyage that Shook the World   32
6   *An Górta Mór* and the Irish Emigrant Ship *Jeanie Johnston*   37
7   The China Tea Trade and the Great Rival Clippers, *Thermopylae* and *Cutty Sark*   44
8   *Yavarí*: the First Steamer at the Roof of the World   65
9   Yukon Sternwheelers and the Lure of Gold   70
10 The *Charles W. Morgan*: Last of the Sailing Whalers   76
11 *Nimrod*: a Veteran Sealer's Moment in the Sun   82
12 A Tale of Two Boats   87
13 SMS *Emden*: the Swan of the East and the Twilight of Chivalry   93
14 *Pamir* and the Cape Horners' Farewell   115
15 RMS *Lusitania*, the Blue Riband and the Fortunes of War   120
16 *Bluenose* and a 'Race for Real Sailors'   126
17 The Northwest Passage and the RCMP Schooner *St Roch*   132
18 *Altmark*: the 'Hell Ship' That Wasn't   138
19 HMCS *Sackville* (K 181) and the Battle of the Atlantic   143
20 The Tanker SS *Ohio* and the Relief of Malta   148
21 USS *Indianapolis* (CA-35) and the Sacrifice of a Scapegoat   152
22 SS *Flying Enterprise*: the Fight for Survival that Mesmerised Two Continents   157
23 RRS *John Biscoe*: Antarctic Workhorse   178
24 The SS *Edmund Fitzgerald* and the Gales of November   182
25 Sisters of Mercy: the Tugs *Yelcho*, *Foundation Franklin* and *Turmoil*   186

ACKNOWLEDGEMENTS

This book obviously relies on information from a very wide range of sources. Many of these are listed in the references, which follow each chapter, but we would also like to acknowledge the role of Wikipedia for verification of countless details. The book would never have been completed without the constant support and advice of our wives, Ingrid and Mig. In Ingrid's case this involved continual patience during many hours spent visiting old ships and maritime museums around the world and incisive comments on the manuscript. John Cook and Conrad Pilditch also made valuable comments on several of the earlier chapters. Austin would like to acknowledge the enthusiasm and support of Russ Kramer, Robert Semler and Christine Diehlmann. The expert help of Leena Baumann of the University of Basel, Switzerland, who drew all the maps, was particularly invaluable. Danny Fraser helped greatly by relaying images between authors separated by some 4,000 kilometres. We would like to acknowledge Nimbus Press, Halifax, Nova Scotia, for permission to quote from books by Benjamin Doane and by Heather-Anne Getson. We are also grateful to Tim Severin for permission to use his image of the *Brendan*, to Rosemarie Speranza of the University of Alaska Archives for permission to use the image of the *Clifford Sefton* in Miles Canyon and to Joseph Lonergan of Irish Heritage Quebec for advice related to the quarantine station at Grosse Île, Quebec.

FOREWORDS

Rorke Bryan has chosen twenty-five historic vessels and to each name has added an intriguing note. His subjects have little in common, which adds to their appeal: they provide an eclectic look at matters maritime.

Three names are, of course, familiar to me, *Nimrod, James Caird* and *Yelcho. Nimrod* was the ship of my grandfather Ernest Shackleton's British Antarctic Expedition (1907–1909). Shackleton's next expedition, The Imperial Transantarctic Expedition (1914–1916) produced the most iconic vessel associated with him: the tiny *James Caird* in which Ernest Shackleton made possible the rescue of his twenty-two men marooned on Elephant Island. This rescue was completed by the Chilean naval tug, *Yelcho,* Shackleton guiding her into a fog-bound Elephant Island.

Rorke Bryan tells these stories well; I look forward to reading more of his tales of the sea.

Hon. Alexandra Shackleton
President, The James Caird Society

Rare is the artist whose paintings can command your attention, transport you to a time and place where something extraordinary is happening … and make you *feel* it. This is the true gift of the master storyteller and visionary artist whose paintings of these great ships are also of the great men who worked them. Through Austin's feel for the dramatic moment, compelling compositions and mastery of light and atmosphere, we too are able to experience human peril, or duty, or wonder.

Our shared interest in painting maritime history and service to the American Society of Marine Artists brought us together as kindred spirits. Through the Society, Austin has been instrumental in supporting budding young talents. Those who one day are inspired themselves to capture on canvas adventures at sea will undoubtedly salute, as we all do, and celebrate Austin Dwyer for his unique talent to stir something within us.

Russ Kramer
American Society of Marine Artists, President, 2011–2015

INTRODUCTION

What lies beyond the horizon? On coasts all around the world young men and women have gazed out to sea, dreaming of setting out 'beyond that angry or that glimmering sea' to find out, or have wondered about the stories each ship moored along the quays could tell. The magic of ships is easily lost in the din of a modern container port, as massive steel boxes are shuffled around by giant cranes or stacked high on some of the least graceful vessels ever launched, but it is quickly restored by wandering amongst the salt-bleached pilings of old harbours, smelling evocatively of tarred ropes and seaweed. What dramas have played out along the weathered quays and what dreams, hopes, fears and despair have they witnessed? For many, ships have promised adventure, freedom from stiflingly boring societies, escape from squalid industrial cities or grinding rural poverty: the cocky young crewman Orient-bound on a crack tea clipper; the fierce plunder-lust of the Norseman on his dragon-headed long ship; the impoverished emigrant dreaming of New World prosperity. For others, ships have promised nothing but greater misery, fear or danger: the terrorised shackled slave whipped aboard a squalid 'blackbirder' for the terrible Middle Passage to plantations in the West Indies; the angry, resentful convict, deported for trivial pilfering, facing the lengthy, dangerous voyage through the Roaring Forties to Van Diemen's Land; the sleep-deprived skipper of a tanker laden with aviation fuel, running the gauntlet of the torpedoes of Nazi U-boats across the Atlantic to wartime Britain.

For more than three and a half millennia, since long before Tutankhamun's treasure-laden barges dropped down the Nile from Nubia, ships have silently observed a full spectrum of human emotions. They have stimulated innumerable authors and artists: Joseph Conrad, Herman Melville, Joshua Slocum, Alan Villiers, Basil Lubbock, C.S. Forester, Patrick O'Brien, Jan de Hartog, Tim Severin, Bjorn Landström, Jack Sparling and Winslow Homer, to name only some of the best. Perhaps even more evocative have been 'ship poets' like James Elroy Flecker and the master of them all, John Masefield.

All ships have stories to tell. Some, like the *Marie Celeste* and the *Titanic*, are now an indelible part of the lore of the sea, and have even passed into everyday language, but most have ended their careers in obscurity as rotting hulks on mudbanks, in undignified dismemberment on a distant Asian beach or, far too often, disappearing at sea with all hands. It is not possible here to recall more than a handful of accounts, or to do justice to their varied, colourful or prosaic careers, let alone probe all the emotions they evoked. Nevertheless, all these ships should be remembered, if only through the stories of a few. Total agreement on even a handful of representatives would be impossible to achieve, but this collection of essays and paintings, and the limited cross-section of maritime history they provide, represents our attempt to express our personal fascination with ships, our love for everything to do with the sea, and our immense admiration for the countless generations of mariners who 'have gone down to the sea in ships and done business in great waters'.

The vessels chosen span nearly 1,500 years of maritime history; some are famous, familiar even to those with few maritime connections; others pursued their careers in almost complete obscurity without public attention. Nevertheless, all have stories that are interesting or significant. In most cases we have tried to choose ships that also represent a much wider range of vessels or maritime issues. We have employed some licence and have included several ships whose careers were spent entirely on lakes or rivers, and we have also told the stories of two 'honorary' ships, small open rowing boats that, in extreme emergency, completed two of the most extraordinary voyages in maritime history.

1 THE *BRENDAN*, THE SAINT AND THE ISLAND OF THE BLESSED

Brendan (original):	'curragh' or 'naomhóg' built Co. Kerry, Ireland, probably around AD 570.
Size:	uncertain, but large enough to fit fifteen monks with stores under a half deck.
Construction:	willow ribs and gunwales, wickerwork sheathed with oak-tanned hides sealed with resin; lug or square sail on two (?) masts, eight oars + steering paddle; bronze cauldron + turf for cooking.
Career:	used by St Brendan of Adfert for pilgrimage voyages to Scottish islands, Faroes, Iceland and possibly Newfoundland.

Brendan (replica):	Kerry-pattern naomhóg, built at Crosshaven, Cork in 1976 for Tim Severin.
Length:	11.07m
Beam:	2.44m
Construction:	oak gunwales plus frames, ash stringers covered by tanned ox hides.
Sails:	two flax square sails on two masts, 18.93m².
Oars:	four 3.66m sweeps, steering paddle on starboard quarter.
Career:	17 May 1976: Left Brandon Creek, Kerry, with six-man crew, sailed via Scotland and Faroes to reach Reykjavik, Iceland, on 17 July.
	7 May 1977: left Reykjavik, reaching Peckford Is., Newfoundland, on 26 June 1977.

There are days when you can forget that they are there at all. Crisp and sharp like cut diamonds on a clear day, when fog blankets the coastal cliffs and misty rain blends with spray above a storm-wracked Atlantic, the islands fringing the west coast of Ireland may seem like imaginary shadows. Mysterious, and possibly magical, the islands – the Blaskets, the Skelligs, Inishmór, MacDara's Island, Omey, Inishturk, Inishshark, Inishboffin and a hundred more – form the westernmost ramparts of Europe that for centuries lay at the edge of the known world. Even now when you can fly to the great continent to the west in five hours, the surly winter Atlantic can be fearsome; it is difficult to fathom how dangerous it must have seemed to those who gazed westwards from the cliffs, 2,000 years ago. It is no wonder stories were woven about its hazards and magical islands that seemed to come and go without pattern.

Even today courage and faith are needed to set out to the west across the Atlantic; it would have taken much more to set out in tiny skin-covered boats without any modern safety measures. And yet, we now know that nearly 1,000 years before Columbus's carracks and caravels reached the Caribbean, and 500 years before Leif Erikson's lithe Viking knorrs drew up to the Newfoundland coast, Irish priests – the *peregrini pro Christo* – regularly embarked on lengthy, hazardous voyages to spread Christianity and found monasteries on remote Atlantic islands.

Prince Henry the Navigator, the fifteenth-century Portuguese patron of exploration, only set foot a ship once but is usually regarded as the founder of modern navigation who established the celebrated Sagres school in 1418. However, the title also belongs to an earlier explorer who personally undertook many voyages. St Brendan the Navigator was a revered Irish monk who founded many monastic settlements in Ireland, Scotland, Brittany and many of the Atlantic islands. According to Adomnán, Columcille's eighth-century biographer, he was 'the greatest founder of monasteries of them all'.

St Brendan was born in AD 484 near Fenit on the Shannon estuary, where sea travel is strongly embedded in the local culture. In the fifth century Ireland was a sanctuary of tranquillity from the violent turbulence that roiled Europe after the Roman Empire collapsed. Christianity was spread rapidly throughout the island by apostolic monks who arrived as slaves or refugees. Strongly influenced, Brendan was ordained in AD 512 and soon founded a monastery at Ardfert in Kerry. Many others followed throughout Ireland, but he was soon roaming the western islands, travelling with fellow monks in 'naomhógs', enlarged versions of the traditional skin-covered curraghs.

Nobody is certain how many monasteries St Brendan personally founded, but his name survives all over the north-western islands of Europe. Most monasteries would have been quite large, secular communities, but some were tiny groups of hermit monks seeking isolated tranquillity in primitive stone 'beehive' cells like those of Skellig Michael, off the Kerry coast. Around AD 550 Brendan returned to Ireland and in AD 558 founded his most famous monastery at Clonfert, Co. Galway. This community of some 3,000 monks would become one of the greatest monastic abbeys in Ireland; suppressed by Henry VIII, it became Protestant in 1571, but the church with its magnificent Romanesque doorway, flanked by 1,000-year-old cedars, remains an active place of worship today, 1,457 years after it was founded by St Brendan.

St Brendan's powerful influence on North Atlantic history resulted from an extraordinary manuscript, *Navigatio Sancti Brendani Abbatis* (The Voyage of the Holy Abbot St Brendan), which appeared at least 200 years after his death. This became extremely popular throughout Europe and more than 120 Latin manuscripts and hundreds of vernacular translations appeared during the early Middle Ages. The *Navigatio*'s origin is obscure; it is not certain if it was written in Ireland, but it probably dates from before AD 786. It has a complicated relationship with the *Vita Brendani,* probably written around the same time, *De Reise van Sint Brandaan* (The Journey of St Brendan), which appeared in the Rhineland during the twelfth century, and with the early Irish 'immrama' and 'echtrae', which tell of sea voyages and journeys to the 'Otherworld'. Many researchers have attempted to disentangle the discrepancies and common elements in the accounts; which version borrowed from which, or do all originate in earlier documents, now lost; were the discrepancies caused by years of oral repetition and embellishment before they were finally written down? St Brendan apparently made two very long voyages far out into the North Atlantic, perhaps even to North America, but it is often unclear which events occurred on which voyage, and whether the voyages took place before St Brendan founded Clonfert abbey, when he was already 74, or between then and his death in 577.

Despite such questions, reports of St Brendan's voyages steered the history of Atlantic exploration. They were searches for *Terra repromissionis sanctorum* – the Promised Land of the Saints, the Land of Paradise, the Island of the Blessed, or in Gaelic, Hy-Brasil – enduring elements in Irish folklore. Hy-Brasil appeared on many medieval charts: on Cortesão's 1424 nautical chart it is a round island to the west of the Blaskets, but on the 1367 Pizzigani chart and the 1424 Weimar chart it was linked to Madeira, and on others is confused with the Canaries.

Belief in the island was sufficiently strong to encourage merchants in Bristol to fund a search for Hy-Brasil, 400km south-west of Ireland in 1480, and at the University of Pavia, Columbus would certainly have known of Brendan's voyages. It appeared on many maps during the eighteenth century, sometimes as far west as Newfoundland, and did not finally disappear until 1865.

St Brendan's first voyage resulted from meeting Barrindus, a monk who spoke of an oceanic 'island of Paradise' his son Mernóc had found while seeking solitary refuge as a monk. Brendan decided to seek this paradise and set out with fourteen fellow *deóraidhthe* (wanderers) for Kerry. There they camped near Mt Brandon and built a boat – a great curragh or *naomhóg* – to fit the fifteen men and their stores. The *Navigatio* specifies that its gunwales and ribs were of willow, filled between with wickerwork, and covered by three layers of oak-tanned hides with joints sealed by holly resin and tar. Spare hides were shipped for repairs and butter to re-waterproof them. Sails (a triangular lug or a square sail) were made of more pliable hides from stag, wolf, pine marten or fox, and the mast, which could be unshipped, was lashed to the mast-thwart. A carving on a stone pillar at Bantry shows a naomhóg resembling a present-day Inuit umiaq; like modern curraghs it would have had four long bladeless sweeps per side on thole pins, rowed by two sets of oarsmen. A steering paddle would be mounted on the raised stern and a half deck would protect stores, including dried fish, grains, seaweeds and mosses, and water carried in earthenware jars or skins. Cooking would be in a riveted bronze cauldron over smouldering turf in a shallow metal brazier, as in Kerry curraghs fifty years ago.

The naomhóg was launched at Brandon Creek, the mast was stepped and, after a prayer, the monks, joined by another three who begged St Brendan to take them, set out westwards with a fair wind. They sailed for fifteen days then were becalmed and had to row. After more than a month, almost out of supplies, they reached a tall rocky island with steep cliffs (Rockall?). Landing, they found food in a deserted hall, but met no one until just before they set out again, when a man brought them more food. Next they reached a large island overrun with wild white sheep (the 'Island of Sheep') where they stayed until Easter Saturday. An islander (the 'Steward') brought them food, and said that they would move to another island for Easter Sunday, then return to a nearby island (the 'Paradise of Birds') until Whitsun (Pentecost).

The monks moored the naomhóg at a stony, barren third island, and landed to cook over a driftwood fire, but as the water boiled, the island began to move. Hurriedly re-embarking, the terrorised monks watched it move off with the fire still burning. St Brendan explained that the 'island' was the biggest fish in the sea, called 'Jasconius'.

After this startling encounter, the monks sailed back to a small vegetated island close to the Island of Sheep and hauled the naomhóg up to a waterfall surrounded by trees covered with perched white birds. One bird told St Brendan that these were the spirits of men, and that the monks would search for seven years before reaching the 'Promised Land of the Saints'. They were then visited again by the Steward who brought a lot of food for the long voyage they started at Whitsun.

Now the naomhóg was at sea for many weeks 'driven here and there' in foggy weather, before reaching a craggy island with steep cliffs lashed by pounding waves. Half-starved and exhausted, they drifted round the island ('for 40 days') before entering a very narrow strait. On landing they met a white-haired elder who brought them to an abbey (the Community of St Ailbe) with twenty-four monks where they stayed until Epiphany. Setting out again, they rowed and sailed until Lent, becoming 'very distressed' with lack of food before reaching another island where they found plants, roots and a well where the water sent them to sleep. Sailing on northwards for three days, they reached a calm, 'coagulated' sea where they lay becalmed for weeks before a westerly wind blew them back to the Island of Sheep.

The same travel cycle would be repeated over the next six years, fulfilling the bird's prophecy: Easter would be spent on the long-suffering Jasconius's back, Whitsun at the Paradise of Birds and Christmas at the Community of St Ailbe, before returning to the Island of Sheep. At the mercy of winds, storms and tides, with little ability to beat or tack, the monks experienced many new marvels. All their adventures are of allegorical and religious significance, but several appear to be geographically significant. Once they encountered a 'pillar' of 'bright crystal' in the sea, which appeared close, but took three days to reach. This seemed harder than marble, and St Brendan measured each of its four sides to be about 700m.

The naomhóg then ran for eight days before the wind, before approaching a 'very rough, rocky' island, 'full of slag, without trees or grass, full of smiths' forges'. They tried to stay clear but were blown close and 'heard the sound of bellows blowing, as if it were thunder'. A shaggy 'savage' threw 'a lump of burning slag of immense size and heat' at the monks, which fell short; 'the sea where it fell, began

to boil, as if a volcano were erupting.' Many more 'savages' then appeared throwing lumps and 'it looked as though the whole island was ablaze … and the stench of fire assailed their nostrils'. Some days later, a high mountain appeared through the clouds 'very smoky on top'. The cliffs were very high, the colour of coal and perpendicular. One of the crew landed but 'was carried off by a multitude of demons to be tormented' and set on fire. When they looked back the mountain was 'spouting flames … the whole mountain from the summit right down to the sea looked like one big pyre'.

After another 'forty-day' journey, they were enveloped in such a dense fog that they could scarcely see themselves. The Steward, who this time accompanied them, told St Brendan that 'fog encircles the island for which you have been searching for 7 years'. After an hour the boat 'rested on the shore' and, disembarking, they saw 'a wide land full of trees bearing fruit as in autumn time', which they could explore without night falling. 'Forty days' later they came to a great river, which they could not cross, where a 'youth' told them 'before you lies the land which you have sought for a long time'. After gathering precious stones and fruit, the pilgrims returned swiftly to Ireland and their abbey.

According to most accounts, St Brendan's voyage in the naomhóg occurred after the founding of Clonfert, and he died not long after his return, but in some versions, he did not reach the Paradise of the Saints on this voyage but later in a much larger ship. For this St Brendan went into Connaught and built a 'great marvellous ship and it was distinguished and huge, and he embarked in her with his household and people and they carried with them various plants and seeds, and wrights and smiths'. Unlike the naomhóg, there is little information about this ship, but Little suggests that she was wooden and tar-caulked with a deck supported by wooden stanchions, though iron spikes were used and she had an iron anchor. Her sail was of woven material, there were no oars and she was big enough to house a crew of sixty with stowage for cargo and provisions. Lacking direct evidence, Little suggested a plausible design based on early Breton craft described by Julius Caesar: robustly built of oak planks fastened by iron spikes, with high prows and freeboard, and shallow keels for negotiating shallow tidal waters. Adomnán wrote that Colmcille's ships, like Roman warships, were built of oak and pine. Little's book shows a conjectural model of this ship, and the 'Phillips ship' – a bluff-bowed, beamy naomhóg with high freeboard, big enough to fit thirty men, with a single mast, large reinforced square sail and a killick. This is significant because it was sketched live by Thomas Phillips, an Admiralty engineer, in 1685.

What to make of the tales and circumstantial evidence? Whether the ships were skin-covered or wooden, it is clear that Irish seamen embarked on lengthy ocean voyages from the earliest years of the first millennium and Irish religious settlements dotted most of the western islands. Monks certainly reached Iceland before the Norsemen arrived in AD 870 and are embedded in Icelandic folklore; Nobel Laureate Haldor Laxness describes Icelandic mothers threatening recalcitrant children with 'the Devil Kolumkilli', just as English mothers did with 'Boney' during the Napoleonic wars. Most tales of St Brendan's voyages are clearly allegories, full of details of monastic life, but some have been plausibly linked to geographic locations: the Faroes are islands of sheep, with cliffs covered by clouds of birds like the Paradise of Birds; the Island of Smiths resembles the volcanic islands off southern Iceland, like Vestmannaeyar (Irishmen's Islands), and the high mountain, a large volcano in southern Iceland, like Hekla. The 'congealed' sea must describe pack or frazil ice and the crystal pillar an iceberg. Rather more controversially, the island surrounded by dense fog sounds like Newfoundland and the un-crossable river could represent the St Lawrence or the Straits of Belle Isle.

That Irish monks travelled along the islands to reach Iceland has been accepted for years, but the possibility that they crossed the North Atlantic to the New World was regarded as sheer fantasy, despite the fact that Norsemen, using ships very like those of the Irish, settled at L'Anse aux Meadows in Newfoundland around AD 1000. This was before a British explorer, Tim Severin, changed perceptions in the 1970s. Severin has since become famous for daring voyages in many parts of the world, but when, inspired by the *Navigatio*, he planned to sail a naomhóg like St Brendan's to North America, many regarded him as somewhat unhinged. His fascinating book *The Brendan Voyage*, which describes the meticulous research, the quest for authentic materials, the gradual conversion of the skeptics and the final triumphant voyages of the *Brendan*, is amongst the most extraordinary modern adventure stories.

The *Brendan* was designed by Colin Mudie with the hull shape of a traditional Kerry curragh as a two-masted 11.07m long by 2.44m beam vessel. Pat Lake built her frame at Crosshaven in Co. Cork using well-seasoned 2.5 x 15.25cm oak gunwales and 5 x 1.58cm frames,

with a lattice of 6.4 x 1.58cm 80-year-old ash stringers, lashed with leather thongs 'tawed' (an ancient Egyptian method of tanning to produce stiff, white leather) with alum, then soaked in sea water. This was covered by forty-nine oak-tanned Cornish hides, stitched together with waxed flax thread under the supervision of master Cork harness-maker, John O'Connell, by Severin and volunteers. The skin was treated with wool grease and lashed to the lattice with strips of leather, and a protective oak keel skid was attached with copper rivets. The two ash masts, 3.72 and 4.93m long, fixed to oak mast steps on the keelson, carried a 13.3m^2 square mainsail and a 5.7m^2 square foresail of woven flax, which could be extended with laced bonnets. The naomhóg had four 3.7m ash sweeps and a large steering paddle at the stern, lashed to an H-frame, while a large leeboard was lashed near the foremast to reduce leeway. The few concessions to comfort and twentieth-century safety ideas included covered shelters abaft the mainmast and at the bow and stern, survival suits, lifelines, an inflatable eight-man life raft and a solar-powered transceiver.

On 17 May 1976 the five-man crew rowed the *Brendan* out of Brandon Creek, Co. Kerry, into the Atlantic swells, set her sails and started northwards. (Map, see p. 50) Severin gives a taut account of their journey north along the Irish coast, gradually learning to sail a vessel unlike any seen there in 400 years. A crew member was put ashore for medical treatment at Malin Head, but a replacement was picked up at the monastic island of Iona before *Brendan* ran north through the Minches at more than 12 knots before a strong wind to Stornoway in the Hebrides. Past Cape Wrath, *Brendan* felt the full fetch of the North Atlantic and despite adverse winds, damage to the stern and provisions destroyed by seawater, covered the 320km to the Faroes in a week.

The approach to the storm-beaten cliffs of the Faroes in a half gale and dreadful visibility with the *Brendan* tearing through a narrow sound in a powerful tide race at 20 knots was daunting, but the clouds lifted enough to reveal the swarms of sea birds that made the islands a likely candidate for the Paradise of Birds. Another crew member, a Faroese from Brendansvik, joined and, after repairing the steering and flax ropes, they set off towards Iceland. On this leg they met hundreds of curious whales and, nervous about their rather palatable vessel, had some disturbingly close encounters with killer whales. In continuing heavy weather, a course was intentionally set to give a wide berth to the hostile southern coast of Iceland, but they had difficulty rounding

The *Brendan*, Tim Severin's replica of the naomhóg used by St Brendan for his sixth-century North Atlantic voyages. (Tim Severin Archives)

the south-west corner against the wind to enter Reykjavik on 17 July, two months after leaving Brandon Creek.

The *Brendan* needed overhauling, so after three weeks of contrary winds, Severin decided to halt the voyage in Reykjavik until the following summer. On 7 May 1977, the *Brendan* was towed out of Reykjavik and, in light airs and mild temperatures, the four-man crew set off westwards, escorted by curious whales. After a week, mild weather changed to south-westerly gales, which drove them back on their tracks. Despite using oil bags to calm the waves, with the wind rising to force 9, the heavily laden boat shipped a lot of water. Pumping constantly, they were swamped several times by waves coming over

the stern before an awning was rigged from some spare hides then, as the gale subsided, they fought towards the east Greenland coast in search of a favourable wind. (Map, see p. 50)

On 25 May, the wind veered north-east at last and helped by the current *Brendan* made good progress south-west towards Cape Farvel, which it rounded four days later before heading west past ice floes and occasional icebergs into the Labrador Sea. Gradually the pack ice thickened, seriously threatening the *Brendan*'s leather hull and limited manoeuvrability. Eventually a floe punctured the leather, and the bilges quickly flooded. The hole couldn't be traced until the next day and hours of work in freezing conditions were needed before a leather patch could be stitched on and the bilges pumped dry. On 23 June, finally clearing the ice, they caught sight of the Canadian Coastguard ship *John Cabot* and could confirm their position 192km off Newfoundland. Entering a typical Newfoundland fog, as they drew closer they were joined by humpback whales and dolphins before the *Brendan* finally grounded on the rocky shore of Peckford Island, near Musgrave Harbour, at 8 p.m. on 26 June.

The *Brendan*'s arrival in Newfoundland did not prove that Irish monks landed the New World, but it certainly proved that they could have. Despite heroic efforts by some archaeologists to demonstrate that stone carvings in West Virginia are written in the old Irish Ogham script, no direct evidence of such a landing has been found. St Brendan certainly existed, but he may not have personally carried out the voyages described. The *Navigatio* could be an amalgam of the experiences of many seafaring monks, embroidered by imaginative seanchaithe. However, there is increasing agreement amongst scholars, including the distinguished Finnish maritime historian, Bjorn Landström, that the exceptionally wide circulation of the Brendan legend must reflect real voyages, and with the prevailing winds and currents west of Iceland, it is likely that at least some of the monks did reach North America.

References

De Courcy Ireland, J., 1986, *Ireland and the Irish Maritime History,* The Glendale Press, Dun Laoghaire.

Donnchada, G.Ó., 2004, *St Brendan of Kerry, the Navigator,* Four Courts Press, Dublin.

Little, G.A., 1946, *Brendan the Navigator,* M.H. Gill & Son, Dublin.

Mackley, J.S., 2008, *The Legend of St Brendan: A Comparative Study of the Latin and Anglo-Norman Versions,* Brill, Leiden and Boston.

Morison, S.E., 1971, *The European Discovery of America: The Northern Voyages, AD 500–1600,* Oxford University Press, New York.

O'Meara, J.J., 1976, *The Voyage of Saint Brendan: Journey to the Promised Land,* The Dolmen Press, Dublin.

Severin, T., 1978, *The Brendan Voyage,* Hutchinson, London

Strijbosch, C. (trans. T. Summerfield), 2000, *The Seafaring Saint: Sources and Analogues of the Twelfth-Century Voyage of St Brendan,* Four Courts Press, Dublin.

Wooding, J.M. (ed.), 2000, *The Otherworld Voyage in Early Irish Literature,* Four Courts Press, Dublin.

2 THE ROYAL SHIP *VASA* AND A MEDDLING MONARCH

Royal Ship *Vasa*:	launched in Stockholm as flagship of King Gustaf Adolf's fleet, 1627.
Tonnage:	1,210t displacement
Length:	47.5m
Beam:	11.7m
Draught:	4.8m
Sails:	1,275m^2 on three masts.
Armament:	sixty-four guns (forty-eight 24lb, eight 3lb, two 1lb, six howitzers) on two gun decks.
Crew:	145 sailors, 300 soldiers.
Career:	10 August 1628: sank after voyage of 1.3km with loss of about fifty lives. 1956: rediscovered by marine archaeologist, Anders Franzén. 1961: refloated and moved to shore for preservation and installation as museum ship in Vasamuseet, Stockholm.

On the afternoon of Sunday 10 August 1628, the massive new royal warship *Vasa* cast off from Lodgården quay, just below the Tre Kronor palace in Stockholm and, with Captain Söfring Hansson at the helm, was warped out into the harbour. The departure of the new Swedish flagship to join the fleet at Älvsnabben was no ordinary event but a vital piece in King Gustav Adolf's political strategy. No expense had been spared to make *Vasa* one of the largest and most heavily armed warships afloat. Displacing 1,210t and 69m in overall length, *Vasa* looked magnificent as she fired a two-gun salute, with her brightly painted fo'c'sle and poop, lavishly ornamented with gilded sculptures. The surrounding quays and wharves were crowded with onlookers as the splendid ship, with open gun ports, flags and pennants whipping in the breeze and gilded ornamentation glittering in the summer sunshine was drawn slowly across the harbour. By the Södermalm heights the crew swarmed aloft to set the foresail, the foretopsail, the main topsail and the mizzen, before turning eastwards towards the sea. As *Vasa* gained way and emerged from the shelter of the rocky cliffs, she suddenly heeled to port in a gust of wind. She momentarily righted

herself, then rapidly heeled over completely as water rushed into the open lower gun ports, and sank to the bottom in more than 30m of water, some 100m off the small island of Beckholmen. Her mast tops were still above water (the main topgallant mast was 57m high) and many of the 133 crew (her contingent of 300 soldiers were probably not yet aboard) were able to escape but it is believed that about fifty people were drowned.

Since gaining independence from Denmark in 1524, Sweden had become increasingly powerful and prosperous, extending its territory to include much of the region surrounding the Baltic (apart from southernmost Sweden). In 1611, when he ascended the throne, Gustav Adolf inherited three wars and adopted a policy of territorial expansion that would make Sweden dominant in the Baltic region for 100 years. The king was not in Stockholm to watch *Vasa*'s departure but was in Poland fighting a war that had already lasted nearly a decade, and would draw Sweden, the leading northern Protestant country, into the devastating pan-European Thirty Years War. Gustav Adolf's foreign policy demanded a powerful navy and, under Admiral Klas Fleming, a major programme to construct additional heavy warships was started in 1620. Between 1620 and 1625, when the contract to build *Vasa* was signed, twenty-five large ships were added to the navy. However, fourteen ships had been lost in the same period, ten in a storm in the Gulf of Riga in 1625 and two (the flagship *Tigern* and the *Solen*) in the Battle of Oliva with Polish forces in 1627, while Admiral Fleming's own flagship *Kristina* had been wrecked in the Gulf of Danzig in early 1628. *Vasa*'s launch was particularly critical as it was the first of five much larger ships designed to strengthen the navy as Sweden's role in the Thirty Years War expanded (the other four, *Äpplet*, *Kronan*, *Sceptre* and *Göta Ark*, were duly launched and served successfully for several decades).

The *Vasa* cost more than 40,000 dalers and its sinking after a maiden voyage of less than 2km was a national disaster. Gustaf Adolf, who received the news two weeks later, was furious, claiming

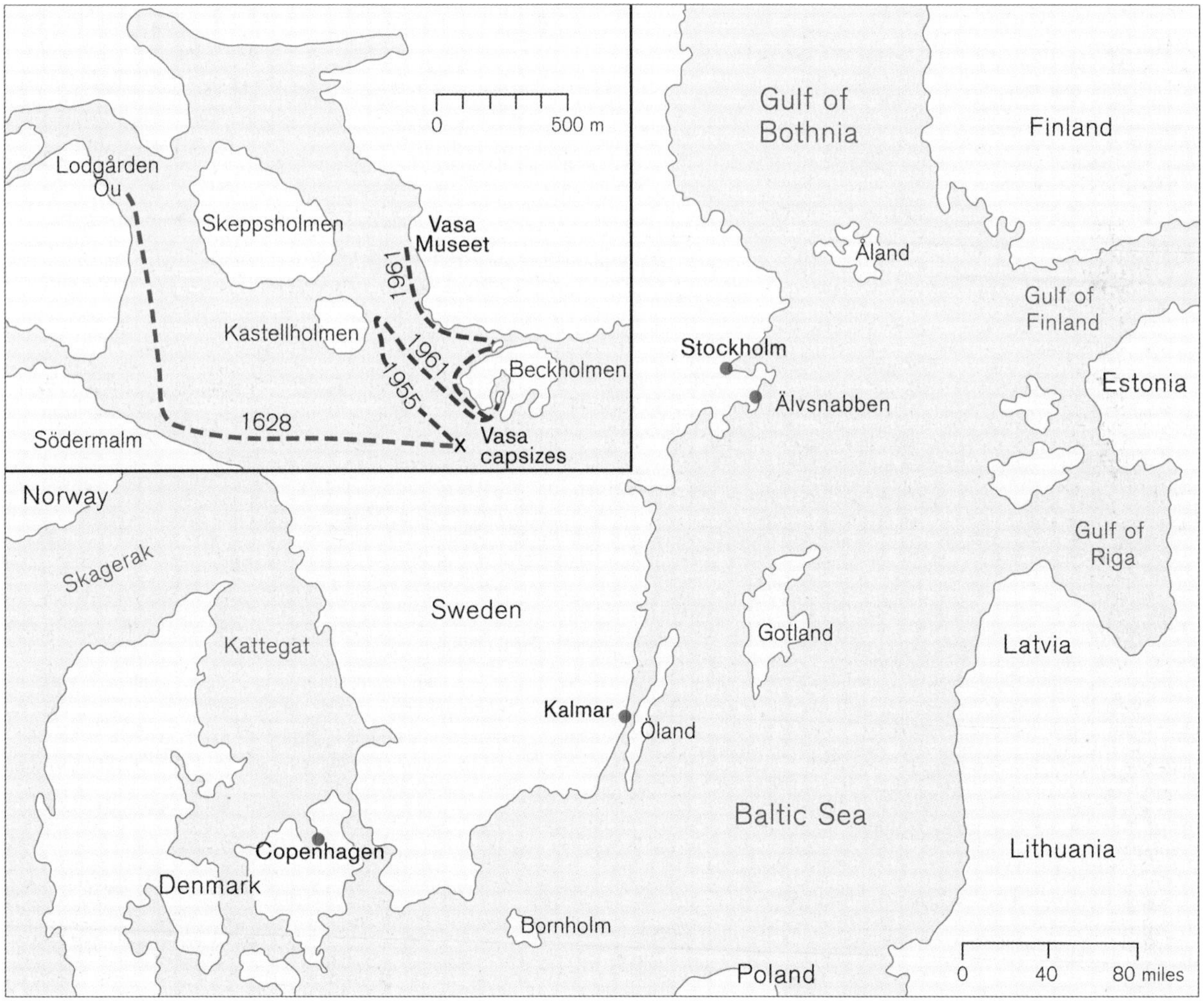

Map labels:

Lodgården Öu

Skeppsholmen

Vasa Museet

1961

1961

1955

Kastellholmen

Beckholmen

1628

Södermalm

Vasa capsizes

Norway

Skagerak

Sweden

Kattegat

Kalmar

Öland

Copenhagen

Denmark

Bornholm

Poland

Baltic Sea

Gotland

Stockholm

Älvsnabben

Gulf of Bothnia

Finland

Åland

Gulf of Finland

Estonia

Gulf of Riga

Latvia

Lithuania

0   500 m

0   40   80 miles

'ignorance and carelessness' and demanding an immediate enquiry and punishment of the guilty. Inevitably suspicion rested first with Captain Hansson, who was arrested and jailed but managed to convince the court of enquiry led by Admiral of the Realm, Karl Gyllenhielm, that his seamanship was not negligent and that the ship's sixty-four cannon were properly secured. The next suspects were the shipwrights who designed and built the *Vasa*. Warship design had evolved rapidly in northern Europe during the sixteenth century as warring monarchs strove for supremacy with increasingly powerful and heavily armed ships, but when the *Vasa* was laid down, it was still more of an art than a science. Rules were gradually emerging to calculate contours of the main frame, which would be drawn full scale with chalk on timbers and would largely determine the hull shape, but detailed line drawings did not appear until the mid-seventeenth century. In their absence, a ship's stability and seaworthiness depended greatly on the individual builder's instinct and experience. There were many successes but also notable failures and the *Vasa*'s fate was not too uncommon; Henry VIII's *Mary Rose* had capsized in the Solent in 1545 and in 1782 Rear-Admiral Kempenfeldt's HMS *Royal George* would be lost the same way off Portsmouth with the loss of some 800 lives.

There were several 'schools' of ship design by the end of the sixteenth century, but the most highly respected shipwrights were Dutch, particularly noted for their careful design below the waterline. By the early seventeenth century they had a long record of successful shipbuilding; Dutch ships had rounded Cape Horn and there were regular commercial voyages by the Dutch East India Company ships to Batavia (Java) in Southeast Asia. Links between Sweden and Holland were strong and the Dutch master shipwright initially responsible for the *Vasa,* Hendrik Hybertszoon, had worked at dockyards in Stockholm, Kalmar and Nyköping since the start of the century. By 1620 he was in charge of the Stockholm dockyard at Skeppsgården and in January 1625, with his brother Arendt de Groote, received a contract to maintain the complete Swedish fleet and construct four new ships. The first two, *Tre Kronor* and *Vasa*, were intended to be the same size, about 33m keel length and 10m beam, with a single gun deck and thirty-two 12lb cannon. The *Tre Kronor*, launched first in summer 1626, was a stable and successful ship. One key puzzle about the *Vasa* is why she was built so differently, with a keel length of 38.3m and slightly wider beam at 11.68m, but, crucially, with two gun decks.

As soon as the contract was signed, work would have started to collect the vast amount of timber required. All the mature oaks from at least 40ha of forest would be needed, and part of the shipwright's skill was careful selection of strong, naturally grown limbs to match the shapes of frames and knees required. The timber used in the *Vasa*'s construction came from forests south of Kalmar where large oaks were preserved for this purpose as the property of the Crown. Collection and sawing of timber was completed in early 1626 and construction probably started immediately. This followed the Dutch method with outer hull planking erected around three frames, rather than the English method in which the complete framework was built before hull planking was started.

It is not certain if the decision to add a second gun deck was taken by then or was a later modification. This fundamental change posed major problems and certainly would not have been undertaken without the king's personal authorisation. The decision was possibly influenced by the need to maintain the Baltic balance of power by matching the powerful two-decked *Sancte Sophia* with twenty 24lb cannon then being built in Copenhagen. It may not have been decided until August 1626, when the king ordered seventy-two 24lb cannon for the ship, which could not fit on a single deck. By then part of the hull would have been completed. The master shipwright could not seriously contest the king's instructions, though some concerns were clearly expressed. By then Hybertszoon was seriously ill (he died in early 1627) and his assistant, Hendrik Jacobsson, had taken over responsibility for the *Vasa*. The problem he faced was the added height of the hull and the great weight of the additional deck with the guns and ammunition (the sixty-four bronze cannon alone weighed 71t). The *Vasa* was already narrow and the higher transom required for the new deck would fundamentally change the lines of the hull, dangerously increasing the height-to-beam ratio. To provide adequate stability she would need to be significantly wider, with her maximum beam further above the waterline. Jacobsson's concern was shown by his court testimony that, on his own initiative, he increased the beam by 43cm, but he couldn't raise the height of maximum beam. Also, as the *Vasa* had a shallow draught (only 4–4.8m) and a flat floor, there was very little ballast space on the lowest deck, close to the keel; the

Vasa Prow.

Vasa uniforms.

gun was salvaged in 1683, but after that the *Vasa* was allowed to sink into the mud of Stockholm harbour and was gradually forgotten. In most parts of the world her timbers would have rotted swiftly or been chewed to pieces by the marine boring worm, *Teredo navalis*. However, the borer cannot survive in the Baltic's low salinity and though exposed iron rusted away quickly, anything covered by mud or the then heavily polluted harbour water was preserved in the anoxic environment.

Some 270 years later a young amateur marine archaeologist, Anders Franzén, who was interested in Baltic shipwrecks learned about the *Vasa*. By then, records about the exact location of the wreck were confused, but Franzén patiently spent years exploring Stockholm harbour, sounding from a small boat with a grappling iron and a core sampler. In August 1956 the sampler brought up a plug of blackened oak and soon afterwards divers confirmed that the *Vasa* had been found. There was considerable damage to the upper decks caused by earlier salvage efforts, dredging and by generations of ships' anchors, and most of the elaborate sculptures had fallen off the hull as nails rusted away, but most of the hull was remarkably well-preserved. The persistent Franzén then mounted a national campaign to raise the ship to the surface.

There was no precedent for recovering such an ancient vessel and a wide range of complicated methods were proposed, including freezing her in an immense block of ice, or filling her with table tennis balls, but eventually fairly orthodox methods were used in what was still a difficult and dangerous operation. Using powerful compressors, a team of divers led by Per Edvin Fälting blasted six 18m-long tunnels through the mud under the massive hull, continually alert to the danger that the wreck might shift or the walls of the tunnels could collapse and bury the divers. Cables were then passed under the hull and attached to two massive pontoons on either side. In August 1959 the pontoon buoyancy tanks were filled and slowly the huge hull was dragged from its cradle of mud and suspended just above the sea bed. Very gradually, in tiny stages, the *Vasa* was then moved to shallower water near Kastellholmen where the holes left by rusted bolts could be plugged and gaps planked over to make the hull watertight. Eventually, on 24 April 1961, the final lift could take place and slowly, before an excited crowd of onlookers, the *Vasa*'s great blackened oak frames emerged into the sunlight for the first time in 333 years.

The difficult and dangerous salvage operation was complete, but this was just the start of a lengthy restoration, which continually faced

Vasa could fit only 130t of stone ballast, regarded by experts at the enquiry as far too little, though it was claimed to be considerably more than Admiral Fleming wanted.

The *Vasa* was clearly 'crank', a dangerously unstable ship. This was known even before her departure; stability tests carried out at Lodgården involving thirty men running to and fro across the deck caused her to heel so alarmingly that after the third pass Admiral Fleming ordered the tests to cease. Recent studies at Tekniska Högskolan in Stockholm have shown that with her hull design the *Vasa* could not have safely heeled more than 10° and could not have carried the sails hoisted in a wind stronger than 4m/s (less than 8 knots). It is difficult to assign responsibility precisely after more than 300 years; there seemed to be plenty of blame to spread around, but the court exonerated everyone. Very likely this was a diplomatic decision taken to obscure the role of the king's interference.

Salvage attempts started almost as soon as the ship sank. An English engineer, Ian Bulmer, attempted to raise her with anchors and lines suspended between pontoons but only managed to right her list. In 1663–64 Albrecht von Treileben and Andreas Peckell successfully salvaged more than fifty of the valuable bronze cannon (probably worth much more than the ship itself) using a primitive diving bell in which a diver could work submerged for thirty minutes. One more new and technically challenging conservation problems. The saturated timbers would decay rapidly if allowed to dry out, so the *Vasa* had to be sprayed continuously with polyethylene glycol to progressively replace salt water in the pores. It took seventeen years before the spraying could be halted. It was then dried for nine years before the *Vasa* could be moved into a permanent museum building where temperature and humidity are carefully controlled (18–20°C, 55 per cent humidity). Despite immense care, other problems have arisen; during the long burial sulphides from the surrounding mud penetrated the timbers, which when exposed to oxygen first turned into sulphuric acid and then to sulphate salts, which can expand and crack the timbers. More than 2t of sulphuric acid have already formed and it is estimated that the timbers contain enough sulphides to produce another 5t, probably sufficient to destroy the ship completely. It also now appears that treatment with polyethylene glycol in an acidic environment can produce formic acids, which can eventually liquefy the wood. The nails also present problems: the original iron nails, long rusted away, were originally replaced by galvanised nails covered with epoxy resin, but these have now started to rust, damaging the surrounding timber. Research is continuing to develop methods to counter deterioration by replacing these nails with titanium, carbon fibre or fibreglass fastenings, and possibly bathing the ship with basic solutions to counteract acidity.

Preservation of the ship itself has been the continual central focus, but there have been many other challenging research and conservation tasks. During diving and salvaging operations more than 24,000 fragments were collected from the surrounding seabed, which had to be identified and preserved. These formed an immense jigsaw puzzle to be solved during the fifty years since the *Vasa* was brought to the surface, without any plans or original illustrations. More than 700 are sculptures, intended to impress Sweden's foes by the power and majesty of King Gustaf Adolf, which fell off the hull as the retaining iron bolts rusted away. Many are elaborate, important examples of Renaissance and Baroque art carved by identifiable Swedish, German and Dutch sculptors, though some, badly eroded by the strong currents in Stockholm harbour, have been difficult to identify. In each case, identification was one challenge, while establishing their original location on the ship for restoration was another. Numerous bits of the upper hull, masts and long beakhead also had to be pieced together before they could be restored to the ship. Without contemporary paintings of the ship, it has been very difficult to determine the original colours from surviving flecks and fragments on the timbers. It now appears that gilding was not nearly as extensive as originally believed and many different colours were used on decorations.

After years of careful research, most of the puzzle has now been solved, the pieces restored to their original locations, and the *Vasa* can be seen much as it must have appeared in 1628. When raised she was 137 years older than the oldest ship previously individually identified, Nelson's HMS *Victory*. She has provided invaluable information on the

EARLY STOCKHOLM
DUTCH GABLE ENDS.

THUMBNAIL
FOR VASA

development of ship design during the critical transition from Renaissance galleons to the powerful, scientifically designed ships-of-the-line of the eighteenth century and has clarified many features of ship construction previously only inferred from paintings and drawings. Apart from the ship itself, a treasure trove of artefacts was found on board – clothing, remnants of foodstuffs, pipes, medical and navigational instruments – which have provided extraordinary insight into maritime life and social conditions in seventeenth-century Sweden. While his subjects may not have been appreciative, the meddlesome interference of a powerful monarch, which probably caused the *Vasa* disaster, eventually produced benefits greater than any of his foreign wars.

References

Cederlund, C.O., and Hocker, F., 2006, *Vasa I: The Archaeology of a Swedish Warship of 1628,* Vasamuseet, Stockholm.

Franzén, A., 1974, *The Warship Vasa: Deep Diving and Marine Archaeology in Stockholm,* Norstedts/Bonniers, Stockholm.

Hedin, M., 2011, *Vasa: The Story of a Swedish Warship,* Bonnier Fakta, Stockholm.

Hocker, F., (trans.K. Helmersson), 2011, *Vasa*, Medströms, Stockholm.

Kvarning, L-Å., Barkman, L., and Soop, H., 1972, *Vasa*, P.A. Norstedt and Sons, Stockholm.

Kvarning, L-Å., and Ohrelius, B., 1998, *The Vasa, The Royal Ship,*

Landström, B., 1980, *Regelskeppet Vasa,* Stenströms Interpublishing, Stockholm.

3 USS *CONSTITUTION*: THE SAGA OF 'OLD IRONSIDES'

USS *Constitution*:	one of six large nominally forty-four-gun frigates authorised by US Congress in 1794; launched at Edmund Hartt's shipyard, Boston, October 1777.
Tonnage:	2,200t displacement
Length:	53.35m
Beam:	13.26m
Draught:	6.4m forward, 7m aft
Sails:	3,968m², ship-rigged on three masts
Speed:	13 knots
Hull:	53cm-thick live oak, white oak and pine
Armament:	nominally forty-four guns but usually carried fifty-two to fifty-five (thirty 24lb, twenty 32lb, two 24lb bow chasers).
Crew:	450, including 55 marines, 30 boys.
Career:	action against Barbary States, Mediterranean; several actions in Atlantic during 1812–15 war, notably defeats of HMS *Guerriére*, HMS *Java*, HMS *Cyane* and *Levant*. Subsequent long career in US Navy. 1940: Commission made permanent. Currently moored at Boston Naval Shipyard, Massachusetts.

With the exception of the wreck of the RMS *Titanic*, lying 3,841m below the surface on the floor of the Atlantic, 650km south-east of Cape Race, Newfoundland, the USS *Constitution* is the most famous ship in the western hemisphere. She is only thirty years younger than the oldest commissioned naval ship, HMS *Victory*, in dry dock in Portsmouth, but the *Constitution* is afloat and seaworthy, while *Victory* hasn't sailed in nearly 100 years.

Soon after the War of Independence, the new government of the United States realised the need for a national navy to protect American interests on the high seas. During the war Royal Navy ships habitually intercepted American ships to search for deserters and to obtain crew for His Majesty's ships. Nevertheless, it took George Washington nearly ten years to persuade Congress to allocate the necessary funds. The immediate trigger was the capture and ransoming of the crews of eleven American merchant ships in 1793 by Algerian pirates. The Navy Act (1794) authorised construction of six heavy frigates, *United States, President, Constitution, Constellation, Congress* and *Chesapeake*, as capital ships to provide protection against pirates from the Barbary States, and from aggressive action by European powers such as Britain or revolutionary France.

The key figure in the frigate-building programme was the well-known Philadelphia shipbuilder, Joshua Humphreys. The young nation could not afford to build and equip a fleet to compete with the great battle fleets of Great Britain and France, so Humphreys promoted a different philosophy. The new ships would be rated as frigates but fitted with unusually heavy guns (24lb rather than 18lb), they would be powerful enough to outfight any vessel they couldn't outsail, and fast enough to outrun any vessel they couldn't outfight. The new ships were expensive, originally projected to cost $688,882. *Constitution* alone cost $302,718, so Congress stipulated in the Act that the ships would be cancelled if a peace treaty were reached with the Dey of Algiers.

The *Constitution* was laid down at Edmund Hartt's Boston shipyard in November 1794. Humphreys was responsible for the overall frigate programme, but the detailed design of *Constitution* was completed by William Doughty and Josiah Fox, while other designers were responsible for the frigates built in different shipyards. *Constitution* was bluff-bowed with a marked tumble-home, and was unusually long with a low profile to enhance her speed. At 62m overall, she was longer both than contemporary British and French forty-gun frigates and many ships of the line, including Nelson's flagship at the Battle of Copenhagen, HMS *Elephant,* and, displacing 2,200t, she was sometimes described as a 'disguised 74'. Her three-layered hull, with a core of southern live oak, sandwiched between layers of white oak, was immensely strong, 53cm in total width and 63.5cm at the waterline. Massive frames of southern live oak were spaced 5cm apart, compared with 10–20cm on British and French frigates. Long ships tend to hog, particularly with very heavy guns, so the hull was reinforced with six heavy diagonal riders on each side, while, to support the large number of guns, deck beams were massive and planking was lock scarfed. She was rated as a forty-four-gun frigate, but usually carried fifty-two to fifty-five guns, with thirty 24lb long guns on the gun deck, twenty-two 32lb carronades on the spar deck and two 24lb chasers at the bow and stern. She also had very large fighting tops on the tall masts (mainmast: 67m), which marksmen could man in battle.

Constitution's construction progressed slowly and the Navy Act plan was overtaken by events. In 1796 peace was signed with the Dey of Algiers, who received $1 million, $21,600 in naval stores per year and a frigate. However, President Washington persuaded Congress to allow the three vessels closest to completion, Constitution, Constellation and United States, to be finished. The other three were eventually completed in 1799 and 1800 after Congress added a further $715,833, bringing the total cost of the frigates to $1,394,915. United States and President were the same dimensions as the Constitution, while Constellation was a thirty-eight-gun ship of 1,265t, Congress a thirty-six-gun ship of 1,286t, 50.5m long, and Chesapeake, rated at thirty-six guns, was 1,244t and 47.1m long.

Constitution was launched in September–October 1797 in several stages as her great weight caused the slipway to sag. She put to sea on 22 July 1798 and was soon responsible for a diplomatic incident by arresting a French-crewed twenty-four-gun ship, Niger, acting under Royal Navy orders, which resulted in an $11,000 restitution payment to Britain. Several years later in the West Indies, she again ruffled diplomatic feathers by capturing the French privateer, Sandwich, from a neutral port in Santo Domingo. When peace was reached between the United States and France in 1802, she was laid up for nine months before returning to active service. Despite peace with the Dey of Algiers, the situation in the Mediterranean had not settled down and in 1801, Tripoli's ruler, Yusuf Karamanli, jealous of the generous terms provided to Algiers, demanded $250,000 in protection money to leave American merchant ships in peace. Two squadrons of frigates led by USS President and USS Chesapeake were immediately ordered to escort American ships in the Mediterranean and to negotiate with the Barbary States. The Chesapeake's captain, Richard Morris, seems to have been particularly inept and he was soon replaced and dismissed from the Navy.

In August 1803 a third squadron left Boston, commanded from Constitution by Edward Preble who was made of sterner stuff than Morris. As soon as he reached Gibraltar, he got two American ships held by Sultan Slimane of Morocco released, but his next action was much more challenging. In October, while pursuing a vessel, the frigate USS Philadelphia (a smaller frigate built by municipal subscriptions) ran aground off Tripoli, was captured and moved into Tripoli harbour where the 307 crew members were imprisoned. Constitution was too deep to enter the harbour and recapture Philadelphia, but in February 1804 Preble sent in the captured ketch, Intrepid, commanded by Lieutenant Stephen Decatur to burn her. Six months later, Preble led another attack on Tripoli with Constitution together with Argus, Scourge, Syren and Enterprise, supported by six gunboats and two bomb ketches. These wreaked havoc on the Tripoline gunboats, while Constitution bombarded the land fortifications from deeper water. Shortly afterwards, Preble and Constitution were replaced by Samuel Barron with Constellation and President and retired to Malta to refit. In April 1805 she returned to the blockade of Tripoli captained by John Rodgers, and in June Karamanli signed a peace treaty and released the prisoners from Philadelphia. Constitution then joined a powerful American fleet of nine ships and eight gunboats off Tunis, where a further peace treaty was extracted after a short blockade, before eventually returning to Boston in October 1807 after more than four years.

Unfurling the jib.

In Boston, *Constitution* underwent an expensive refit, which cost nearly $100,000. By early 1812, relations with Britain had become very strained and on 18 June war was declared. *Constitution*, now commanded by Isaac Hull, was sent to sea to join a squadron under John Rodgers on the *President*. Off New Jersey, she met a squadron of five British frigates, HMS *Shannon, Aeolus, Africa, Belvedera* and *Guerrière*. Clearly outgunned, *Constitution* had no option but to flee. There was no wind and she was at a disadvantage against the lighter British frigates, but in searing summer heat, *Constitution*'s boats kedged her for a marathon fifty-seven hours before she drew sufficiently far ahead for the Royal Navy frigates to abandon the chase. Safely back in Boston, *Constitution* took on supplies, and then left to prey on British shipping lanes near Halifax, where she quickly captured and burned three British merchantmen. In mid-August, Hull heard of a British frigate to the south and decided to give chase. On 19 August he sighted HMS *Guerrière*, 720km south-east of Halifax at 41°42′N, 55°33′W and set in train the first of the three major sea-fights which made *Constitution* famous.

HMS *Guerrière* was a fifth-rate frigate displacing 1,092t, rated as a thirty-eight-gun frigate though she actually carried sixteen 32lb carronades, thirty 18lb long guns, two 12lb chasers and an 18lb carronade. Originally French, she had served in the West Indies in an assault on Sainte Domingue in 1803, where she had a brief engagement with the seventy-four-gun HMS *Elephant*. Returning to Europe she narrowly escaped Sir Edward Pellew's squadron off north-western Spain and reached Corunna after being mauled by Troubridge's seventy-four-gun HMS *Culloden*. In 1806 she was sent with a French frigate squadron to attack British and Russian whalers off Greenland but was intercepted by the British frigate HMS *Blanche*, captured and commissioned into the Royal Navy. She saw action against privateers in the West Indies and, commanded by Captain James Dacres, was on the Halifax station when the 1812 war broke out.

Constitution and *Guerriére* exchanged broadsides ineffectively at long range for thirty minutes while manoeuvring for advantage, before *Constitution*, running down with the weather gauge in the 18-knot wind, closed to within 25m of *Guerrière*'s starboard beam and engaged her with a double-shotted broadside of round and grape shot. (Map, see p. 53) This wrought havoc on *Guerrière*, bringing down her mizzen mast (possibly due more to a rotten mast than accurate marksmanship; the badly-decayed *Guerrière* was en route to Halifax for a refit). Nevertheless, *Constitution*'s broadsides were devastating while most of *Guerrière*'s shots simply bounced off *Constitution*'s massive sides. An exulting American sailor remarked that 'her sides are made of iron', christening her with her indelible nickname. With her mizzen mast trailing over the side, *Guerrière* had difficulty steering and collided with *Constitution*, her bowsprit becoming entangled with the American ship's mizzen shrouds and shattering, wrecking all her rigging. Both crews tried to board but were prevented by the heavy swell. As the ships parted, *Constitution* raked *Guerrière* from the port bow, bringing her foremast and mainmast crashing down. The British ship was now an unmanageable hulk, wallowing deeply in the heavy swell, with waves washing over the guns on her main deck. Captain Dacres and the master were both severely wounded and with *Constitution*'s withering broadsides inflicting heavy casualties and, unable to fight most of her guns, the British frigate eventually hauled down her colours. She was too badly damaged to be brought back to Boston as a prize, so the survivors were transferred and she was then burnt. Isaac Hull was cheered as a hero in Boston but within a week was replaced as *Constitution*'s captain by the more senior William Bainbridge; he never held another fighting command. Dacres faced a court martial for surrendering his ship but was exonerated because of *Guerrière*'s advanced state of decay and the much lighter construction of French frigates.

Several months later *Constitution* faced a much tougher fight against another fifth-rate British frigate, HMS *Java*. *Java* was also French-built, launched in 1805 as *Renomminée*, but was in much better repair than *Guerrière*. Although also rated as a thirty-eight-gun frigate, *Java* was actually a forty-six-gun Pallas-class ship displacing 1,073t, which had been captured at the Battle of Tamatave in 1811 while ferrying troops for a French attack on Mauritius. She carried eighteen 32lb carronades, twenty-eight 18lb long guns, two 12lb chasers and one 24lb carronade. Commissioned in July 1812 under Captain Henry Lambert, she was on her way back from Bombay with supplies when she met *Constitution*, which sailed from Boston in October with the 440t brig-rigged sloop-of-war, USS *Hornet*.

Constitution had reached San Salvador, Brazil, in December, hoping to find prizes along the British shipping lanes. Bainbridge was particularly interested in HMS *Bonne Citoyenne* sighted in the harbour, which was carrying close to $2 million in currency, but he was unable to goad her into leaving the safe neutral harbour, and set off to look for other prizes. When *Constitution* met *Java* on 29 December, almost immediately her rigging was damaged and her wheel shot away by a

British broadside. Over the next two hours the ships circled one another like fencers, each trying to get into a position where they could rake the other. (Map, see p. 53) Although more powerful, *Constitution* was slower and less manoeuvrable than the light *Java*, particularly as she now had to be steered by lines from the tiller. The ships continued to exchange broadsides for hours but *Java's* bowsprit eventually became entangled with *Constitution's* rigging and her foremast was shot away. *Constitution* drew away for repairs but then closed again to bow rake *Java*. Like *Guerrière*, *Java* was now unmanageable and with her captain and twenty-one others dead, and 102 wounded, she surrendered. With more than thirty holes below her waterline, she was too badly damaged to be taken as a prize, so after transferring the British prisoners and taking her wheel to replace the one shattered on *Constitution*, she also was burnt. After transferring the prisoners to the *Hornet, Constitution* returned to Boston for comprehensive replacement of timbers and rigging. Later in 1814, she had a brief encounter with the British frigates, HMS *Junon* and HMS *Tenedos,* but her mainmast split and she had to retreat to Boston where she was blockaded until mid-December. Then, with Charles Stewart now in command, she escaped for Bermuda, pursued by a British squadron led by Captain Sir George Collier on the fifty-gun HMS *Leander.*

Under Charles Stewart, *Constitution* set off across the Atlantic towards Spain, and captured several British merchant ships before intercepting the British sixth-rates, HMS *Cyane* and *Levant,* which were accompanying a convoy off Cape Finisterre on 20 February 1815. The Treaty of Ghent, ending the war, had been signed on 24 December 1814, but was not ratified by Congress until 15 March 1815. Although much smaller than *Constitution,* the 464t, twenty-gun Cyrus-class *Levant* and the 539t, thirty-two-gun Banterer-class *Cyane* together mounted a heavier broadside of forty 32lb carronades. *Cyane* also had an expert crew with an outstanding record of action in the Mediterranean. The British ships exchanged broadsides with *Constitution* for thirty minutes but then were outmanoeuvred by Stewart, who managed to isolate *Cyane* when *Levant* drew away to carry out repairs. (Map, see p. 53) With her rigging badly damaged, five loose carronades rolling along her deck and nearly 2m of water in her hold, *Cyane* soon became unmanageable and had to strike her colours. *Levant* returned to the fray, and when *Cyane* surrendered, she attempted to escape, but was soon overtaken and forced to surrender. *Constitution* suffered very little damage, but after

the action was found to have no less than a dozen 32lb carronade balls embedded in her massive sides.

After repairs, *Constitution* set sail with the two prizes for the Cape Verde Islands, where the prisoners were landed. She was nearly caught there by Sir George Collier on *Leander. Constitution* and *Cyane* made good their escapes, but *Levant* was recaptured. Returning to the United States, *Cyane* was commissioned into the Navy and started an effective career in anti-slavery and anti-pirate patrols, once capturing six of seven slavers intercepted. Of Humphreys' six original heavy frigates authorised by the 1794 Navy Act, four survived the war; USS *President* was captured by HMS *Pomone* and HMS *Tenedos* after being badly damaged by grounding while escaping blockade in New York, followed by an engagement with HMS *Endymion*. She was commissioned into the Royal Navy as HMS *President*, but she was in such bad condition that she was scrapped in 1818. USS *Chesapeake,* with a novice crew, was defeated in a famous fight against the crack British frigate, HMS *Shannon*, off Cape Ann, Massachusetts, on 1 June 1813. She was also commissioned into the Royal Navy, before being sold and broken up at Portsmouth in 1820.

Constitution was laid up ('placed in ordinary') in Boston until 1820 and played no role in the Second Barbary War. She was comprehensively refitted and for a short time was fitted with experimental manually operated paddles, which were removed before she left on a three-year tour of duty in the Mediterranean in May 1821. Her long subsequent career was rather prosaic, and lacked any further high-profile single-ship actions, but she was saved from the usual fate of elderly naval ships by patriotic sentiment. When she returned from Mediterranean service, she was already old for a wooden ship and rot was well established. Repairs of $137,000 were needed but the rumour that she was to be scrapped caused such public outcry that these were carried out. Her less-fortunate sister and member of the 'original six', *Congress,* was scrapped in 1834. *Constitution* returned to active service as flagship in the Mediterranean and the Pacific, and to diplomatic flag-waving missions around South America. In 1843 she carried the new American ambassador to Rio de Janeiro, then continued into the Indian Ocean to East Africa, carried out a minor action off Vietnam (then Cochin China), before visiting Canton and the Philippines, and finally rounding Cape Horn to reach the United States in 1846. Six years later she used her guns for the last time in a minor action off Liberia.

Constitution was converted into a training vessel for the United States Naval Academy at Annapolis in 1860 but during the Civil War was moved to New York, then to Rhode Island to prevent capture by Confederate forces (which happened to her remaining sister frigate, *United States*). She returned to Annapolis in 1865, carrying out training cruises until 1870. By then she had deteriorated so much that she was retired and towed to the Philadelphia Naval Yard to be overhauled to take part in the 1876 Independence Centenary celebrations. This was not completed in time, but she was used to carry displays to the 1878 Paris Exposition. She ran aground off Devon on the way back and spent some time under repair near HMS *Victory* in Portsmouth, then her rudder was damaged in severe storms in the North Atlantic.

The repairs for the Centenary were botched and by 1881 she was deemed unfit for service, decommissioned and transferred to the Portsmouth Naval Yard, Boston, as a barracks ship. A building structure was installed above her spar deck, but she deteriorated rapidly. In 1905 the Navy's proposal to use her as a gunnery target generated such a public outcry that Congress had to allocate funds for a partial restoration in 1906, after which she became a museum ship. By 1925 she was so rotten that she was in danger of falling to bits, but over $600,000 was raised by public subscription and the balance of $945,000 need for comprehensive restoration was provided by Congress. Most of her timbers were replaced and in 1931, she was recommissioned. During the next three years she visited ninety ports from Maine to Seattle, towed by the minesweeper *Grebe*, then returned through the Panama Canal to again become a museum ship in Boston. In 1940, President Roosevelt made her commission permanent, and in 1970, after further reconstruction, she was able to lead a ship parade during the 1976 Independence Bicentennial celebrations. In 1993 she was restored to 1812 specifications at a cost of $12 million and money was collected to reproduce six sails. These allowed her to sail to Marblehead, Massachusetts, and back on her 200th anniversary in July 1997, when she achieved speeds of up to 4 knots in light winds. After this she returned to her role in Boston as a museum ship, but every summer she makes a short 'turnaround' cruise in the harbour to ensure that her restored hull weathers uniformly and that she remains a living national naval icon.

References

Brodine, C.E., Crawford, M.J., & Hughes, C.F., 2007, *Interpreting Old Ironsides: An Illustrated Guide to USS Constitution*, Naval Historical Center, Department of the Navy, Washington, D.C.

Chapelle, H.I., 1949, *The History of the American Sailing Navy: The Ships and Their Development*, W.W. Norton & Co., New York.

Gardiner, R., 2006, *Frigates of the Napoleonic Wars*, Chatham Publishers, London.

Gillmer, T.C., 1993, *Old Ironsides: The Rise, Decline and Resurrection of the USS Constitution*, International Marine, Camden, Maine.

Magoun, F.A., 1928, *The Frigate Constitution and Other Historic Ships*, Bonanza Books, New York.

Marquardt, K.H., 2005, *The 44-gun Frigate USS Constitution, 'Old Ironsides'*, Conway Maritime Press, London.

Martin, T., 2003, *A Most Fortunate Ship: A Narrative History of 'Old Ironsides'*, Naval Institute Press, Annapolis.

Smelser, M., 1959, *The Congress Founds the Navy, 1787–1798*, University of Notre Dame, Notre Dame.

Toll, I.W., 2006, *Six Frigates: The Epic History of the Founding of the United States Navy*, W.W. Norton & Co., New York.

Winfield, R., 2008, *British Warships of the Age of Sail, 1793–1817: Design, Construction, Careers and Fates*, Seaforth Press, Barnsley.

4 NELSON, HMS *ELEPHANT* AND THE 'BATTLE WON BY A FISH'

HMS *Elephant*:	third-rate Arrogant-class ship of the line designed by Sir Thomas Slade, launched at George Parsons shipyard, Bursleden, Hampshire, August 1786.
Tonnage:	1,604t displacement
Length:	51m
Beam	14.25m
Draught:	6.12m
Rig:	three-masted ship-rigged two decker
Armament:	upper gun deck twenty-eight 18lb guns, lower gun deck twenty-four 32lb guns, quarter deck fourteen 9lb guns, fo'c'sle four 9lb guns.
Crew:	550
Career:	1790: struck by lightning, mainmast destroyed: 1801; Admiral Horatio Nelson's flagship at the Battle of Copenhagen; 1803: involved in capture of the French privateers *Poisson Volante, Superieure*, West Indies; 1803: participated in the blockade of Sainte Domingue; 1818: reduced to a fifty-eight-gun fourth-rate ship; 1830: broken up.

As Nelson's captains gathered under a cold blanket of cloud on the deck of his flagship, HMS *Elephant,* at 8 a.m. on 2 April 1801, the muddy green waters of Øresund were dotted with small ice floes. The water looked menacing and was miserably cold but the real menace was invisible; beneath the featureless waters lay many complicated shallows and shifting, irregular muddy shoals, separated by narrow, sinuous channels. Normally the shoals and channels were marked by buoys to allow ships safe entry to Copenhagen harbour, but in preparation for the British fleet, Danish authorities had removed every buoy and even useful seamarks on the adjacent flat coast of Amager island. British seamen led by Nelson's close friend, Captain Thomas Hardy, had been out all night in small boats sounding to determine the location of the shoals, but there were no buoys to guide the British ships heading northwards into the King's Deep to engage the well-prepared Danish forces.

By 1801, Britain had been at war with France for eight years, as a member of various coalitions. Alliances varied, but two constants were domination by the brilliantly successful French army on land, and the mastery at sea of the weather beaten ships of the Royal Navy. Britain's sea dominance, underlined by Nelson's crushing victory of the French fleet at the Battle of the Nile in Aboukir Bay in 1798 enabled Britain to blockade ports under French control. Search, control and seizure of merchant ships by the Royal Navy, which drastically hampered profitable trade, had made the blockade intensely unpopular amongst neutral countries. Denmark was particularly outraged when Royal Navy ships captured the Danish frigate *Freya*, escorting six merchant ships in the English Channel in July 1800. The following December under pressure from Tsar Paul I, Denmark, Prussia and Sweden joined Russia in a League of Armed Neutrality to resist British blockades. This was a serious challenge to British sea power, which depended on Baltic countries to supply naval stores, particularly mast timbers. Three hundred British merchant ships in Russian ports were seized, while Denmark placed an embargo on all British ships and, entering Hamburg, closed the Elbe to British ships. The British government, faced with the most serious threat encountered during the entirety of the Napoleonic wars, decided that it had to send a strong fleet into the Baltic to free their ships, deter the League and, if necessary, destroy their navies.

Following his actions at Cape St Vincent and Aboukir Bay, Nelson was the toast of England and was created a viscount and promoted to Vice Admiral of the Blue in January 1801. He was an immensely popular hero, but his tumultuous private life and adulterous liaison with Lady Emma Hamilton ruffled many feathers and drew demonstrated disapproval from King George III. Nelson's courage and naval brilliance were beyond question, but he was a political and diplomatic liability, as a peaceful resolution was still possible. So it was the cautious Sir Hyde Parker who was appointed commanding admiral of the Baltic squadron assembling at Yarmouth. Nelson, who had hoisted his flag

Hardy sounding the shoals.

ninety-eight-gun three-decker second-rates, *London* and *St George*, each carrying twenty-eight 32lb guns on the main gun deck, thirty 18lb guns on the middle gun deck and thirty 12lb guns on the upper gun deck. The second-rates were not very successful ships of the line; they were tall for their short length, slow and tended to make a lot of leeway. (Ten years later *St George* was wrecked with the loss of more than 1,000 lives near Ryssenstaen on the west coast of Denmark when she was unable to claw off a lee shore during a gale.) However, the ninety-eights drew only 7.7m and were more suitable for the shallow Baltic, compared to the longer, more manoeuvrable first-rates like *Victory* which drew 8.86m. Perhaps more important were the third-rate seventy-four-gun two-deckers, which formed the core of the Royal Navy and most other European navies. Developed in France in the early eighteenth century, seventy-fours first appeared in the Royal Navy in 1755. They provided the most useful combination of firepower, seaworthiness and cost (in 1789 a seventy-four cost £43,850 compared with £57,120 for a second-rate). By 1801, fifty-one of the Royal Navy's 180 ships of the line were seventy-fours, but they varied considerably in design. There were only seven with the Baltic squadron as it left Yarmouth, though three more, *Elephant*, *Defiance* and *Invincible*, were expected to join before the Baltic was reached. The remaining seven ships of the line were third-rate sixty-fours, usually regarded as too weak for the line of battle, one old fifty-gun fourth-rate and the experimental fifty-four-gun *Glatton* commanded by William Bligh of *Bounty* notoriety. Built for the East India Company, this was slow and beamy but was bought by the Royal Navy in 1795 and converted to carry twenty-eight 68lb carronades on her lower deck and twenty-eight 48lb carronades on her main deck, which gave her a devastating short-range broadside.

Nelson's frustration with the delay was increased by the squadron's lethargic zigzagging across the North Sea as the cautious Parker, afraid of running aground on the coast of Jutland, repeatedly hove to for soundings. Still in a huff, he largely ignored his second-in-command at first, but Lieutenant Layman of the *St George* improved relations by catching a turbot, which Nelson immediately sent to Parker: 'I know the Chief is fond of good living and he shall have the turbot.' This thawed Parker's disdain and earned a warm note of thanks; Layman later claimed that it was the fish that persuaded Parker to give Nelson the freedom of action that made victory possible:

in the powerful first-rate ship of the line 104-gun *San Josef* (which he captured as the *San José* at the Battle of Cape St Vincent), was ordered to join the squadron, transferring his flag to the ninety-eight-gun second-rate, *St George,* which was lighter and more suitable for the shoal waters of the Baltic. The combination of Hyde Parker with Nelson inevitably caused problems. Nelson, anxious for swift action, realised that the Baltic mission would become much more difficult once the ice thawed at the Reval base, releasing the Russian fleet. However, the lethargic, bureaucratic Parker was in no hurry to leave his new 18-year-old bride to rush off to the Baltic; he had not even left London when *St George* arrived at Yarmouth on 6 March. Nelson was left to supervise the assembly of the squadron, and it was only a letter he wrote to Thomas Troubridge at the Admiralty Board, and a direct order from the First Sea Lord, St Vincent, that goaded Parker into action. He complied resentfully as his wife had to cancel the ball she was organising, but early on 12 March the squadron weighed anchor.

The squadron that left Yarmouth was large but lacked the most powerful ships of the line. It was headed by Hyde and Nelson's

I well recollect your great desire to catch a turbot and your astonishing many by insisting on its being immediately sent to Sir Hyde who condescended to send civil note, without which opening your Lordship would not have been consulted in the Cattegat, without such intercourse your Lordship would not have got the detached squadron, without which there would not have been any engagement and consequently, no victory.

(Lieutenant Layman, cited in Mahon, 1897)

The fleet took a week to reach the Kattegat round the long Skagen spit. Despite its erratic course, two of the missing seventy-fours, *Elephant* and *Defiance*, managed to catch up, but in bad weather the third, *Invincible*, ran aground off Norfolk and sank with the loss of 400 lives. The fleet anchored near Kullen on the Swedish coast on 20 March, waiting to find out if Denmark would agree to the demand to withdraw from the League of Armed Neutrality within forty-eight hours as stipulated in a diplomatic note sent to Copenhagen.

It was three days before the Danish refusal was received. Though Parker's orders specified immediate hostile action he still lingered indecisively, worried about passing through the narrow strait under the guns of Kronborg fortress and by reports of the strength of the Copenhagen defences. (See map, p. 54) Ignoring the urgency of acting before the Russian fleet arrived and refusing to pass Kronborg into Øresund, he waited in the Kattegat, hoping that the enemy would emerge. Nelson was itching for action, but it took five hours before he could cajole Parker to take any decision (to take the fleet through the Great Belt, to isolate Russian or Swedish reinforcements and attack Copenhagen from the south). After further persuasion the following day, Parker eventually agreed to take the direct route into Øresund. By then the wind had backed to the south-west and it was another six days before the fleet could enter the sound (suffering no damage from the 270 guns of Kronborg) to anchor 8km north of Copenhagen on 30 March.

Denmark started preparations for war in December 1800 but if the British fleet had arrived in early March it would have found the defences far from ready. Fully trained fighting seamen were scarce and most of the Danish battle fleet lay unrigged, unballasted and without stores in Copenhagen dockyard and could not be made battle-ready in time. The entry to Copenhagen was protected by the Sixtus and Quintus batteries on land, the Tre Kroner and Lynetten batteries on artificial islands, armed with 24lb guns, and, to the south on Amager, the small Stricker's battery with six 36-pounders and two mortars. Emergency defences would link these batteries with eighteen floating batteries or ships moored as static batteries along Refshalen Shoal to prevent the British ships bombarding the city from the deep channel (the King's Deep), which separates the city from the shallow Mittelgrund Shoal. (See map, p. 55) Most of the ships were unrigged elderly hulks saved from the breaker's yard, but they were reinforced by a few more powerful newer ships like the seventy-four-gun *Sjaelland*. Few of these ships were in place at the beginning of March, but the Danes used the delay well and, with a massive volunteer effort, all were warped out and moored fore and aft by the time Parker's fleet appeared. Finally all channel markers were removed and seamarks at Dragør were dismantled.

Any attack on Copenhagen would require delicate manoeuvring in shallow, constricted waters. Nelson's flagship *St George* was quite unsuited, so he shifted his flag to the seventy-four-gun third-rate HMS *Elephant*, which was more manoeuvrable and drew only 6.12m. This was one of twelve Arrogant-class seventy-fours in the Royal Navy designed by William Slade, which first appeared in 1861. Built by George Parsons in Bursleden, Hampshire, *Elephant* displaced 1,604 tons burden (Builder's Old Measurement) and was launched in 1786. She was commanded by Thomas Foley, one of Nelson's 'band of brothers' from the Mediterranean, who as captain of *Goliath* led the attack on the French line at Aboukir Bay, raking *Guerrier* with a broadside. Nelson's very close friend, Thomas Hardy, captain of the *St George*, also transferred to *Elephant* as a volunteer.

Still nervous about an attack on Copenhagen, on 30 March Hyde Parker reconnoitred the defences on a small lugger, *Lark*, together with Nelson and Rear Admiral Graves from *Defiance*. He found the defences 'far more formidable than we had reason to expect', but Nelson felt that 'with ten sail of the line I think I can annihilate them; at all events I hope to be allowed to try'. He offered to lead an attack from the south with his ten ships of the line, six frigates, the seven bomb vessels and two fire ships. Parker eventually agreed with Nelson's plan on 1 April and even added the seventy-fours *Ganges* and *Edgar* from his own division to Nelson's force.

Nelson planned to take his ships south through the narrow Hollander Deep, round the Mittelgrund Shoal to attack the Danish line in the King's Deep from the south. While he was with Parker aboard

London, men from the frigate *Amazon* replaced the marker buoys along the Hollander Deep channel. With a fair northerly wind, Nelson now hurried to move his force south through this channel. Returning through the fleet to *Elephant* in a gig, he stopped to visit each ship personally ordering them to weigh anchor immediately. Thanks to the new buoys and with smaller ships as guides, the move was successfully completed and by 6 p.m. his force was anchored just south of the Mittelgrund Shoal, just beyond the maximum range of Stricker's battery on Amager.

Nelson then called all captains for a dinner conference aboard *Elephant.* Some captains had been with him in the Mediterranean, but as the fleet was recently assembled he had to ensure that everyone understood his complicated plan of attack. The Danish force including the artillery on land was superior in firepower and precise manoeuvring under fire in the narrow King's Deep would be essential. Each ship would enter the King's Deep in succession, led by the seventy-four-gun *Edgar,* firing as they went to anchor abeam a specific enemy ship or floating battery, which they would engage at 250m range. *Agamemnon* and the frigate *Desirée* would engage *Provøsten, Isis* and the frigate *Jamaica* would attack *Wagrien,* while the gun brigs and the remaining ships would pass to starboard of *Edgar,* leap-frogging one another to reach their allotted targets. *Elephant* would be anchored right in the centre to engage the most powerful Danish ship, *Sjælland.* As each ship subdued her target, her cables would be cut, allowing her to pass north to reinforce the attack on the stronger defences to the north, while five of the slow bomb vessels would anchor to starboard of *Elephant* to bombard the city, while the other two would attack the Tre Kroner battery. Finally, five frigates commanded by Captain Edward Riou on the thirty-eight-gun *Amazon* would operate independently at Riou's discretion. This was very unusual, particularly as Nelson had only just met Riou, but showed the excellent impression the young frigate captain had made on his commander.

When the dinner ended, most captains returned to their ships to clear for battle, but Riou remained with Nelson and Foley to finalise details. This took hours and eventually the exhausted Nelson, never in very good health, had to participate from his cot. The biggest problem was the precise location of the shoal water at the edge of the King's Deep: were the Danish ships moored right at the edge of the Refshalen Shoal and exactly where did the Mittelgrund Shoal start? Meanwhile, Thomas Hardy set out in an open boat to take soundings and bearings. The Danish forces were fully alert, so this had to be done surreptitiously, with muffled oars and without lights, using a long pole rather than a sounding lead. It was 6 a.m. on 2 April before clerks completed detailed written orders for each captain. By then the northerly wind had veered to the south-west and was fair for entry to the King's Deep. Despite Hardy's soundings, navigation was still a concern when the captains assembled again on *Elephant*; to Nelson's frustration, none of the pilots accompanying the fleet (mainly from merchant ships with trading experience in the Baltic) agreed to guide the large ships of the line into the channel. Exasperated, Alexander Brierly, master of *Bellona,* eventually volunteered to join the *Edgar* to lead the fleet.

At 9.30 a.m., *Elephant,* with her distinctive yellow hull, red gun ports and a broad black stripe separating the lower and middle gun decks, and flying Nelson's Blue Ensign, signalled to weigh anchor. Almost immediately *Agamemnon* was in trouble, unable to weather the Mittelgrund shoal against the south-west wind. Drifting leeward she had to re-anchor before being laboriously kedged away from the shoal. She was far out of range and unable to play any part in the battle. Nelson had to improvise by ordering *Polyphemus* to take her place and engage *Prøvostenen.* At 10.30 a.m. *Prøvostenen* opened fire on *Edgar,* but her captain saved his opening double-shotted salvo until her target, *Jylland,* was reached. Nelson's plan soon fell into further disarray as *Bellona,* passing to starboard of *Isis* ran aground on the soft mud of Mittelgrund. She could still engage the enemy, but at 700m range her broadside's impact was greatly diminished. The *Russell* following was blinded by gun smoke and, steering by *Bellona's* topmasts, followed her onto the shoal.

Within thirty minutes of the opening shots, Nelson had lost one quarter of his ships of the line. Despite dense gun smoke, which obscured signals, the complex order of battle had to be urgently rearranged. The pilots were still giving trouble, ignoring Hardy's soundings, insisting that the deepest channel lay close to Mittelgrund, and refusing to anchor the British ships close to the enemy. Despite the accuracy and rapidity of the British fire, the Danish guns were being served with skill and determination; it was clear that the Nelson's fleet was in for a serious slogging match. Some British ships were being raked both fore and aft by ships outside their cannons' arc of fire, and all found the low-lying floating gun batteries difficult to hit. At the southern end of the line, casualties on both sides were severe;

Polyphemus and *Isis* were intensely engaged with *Wagrien* and *Prøvosteenen*, which was also being raked by *Desirée*, which in turn was under fire from Stricker's battery. Just to the north *Bellona* was seriously damaged when two double-shotted 32lb guns on her lower gun deck blew up, wrecking the deck above and killing many men; eighty-three men were killed or wounded during the battle. *Ardent*, engaging *Kronborg*, also suffered heavily, with ninety-four killed or wounded, while *Monarch*, abeam *Holsten* and under fire from the Tre Kroner battery, lost 163 wounded and fifty-seven killed, including the captain. Further north, Riou had anchored his frigates ahead of the British line and was engaging several ships as well as the Tre Kroner battery. Intense fire continued for hours with serious casualties and damage mounting on both sides. Some of the Danish ships had lost their rigging and with their cables cut by gunfire drifted out of position, but most continued to maintain fire, with replacements for their casualties being continuously rowed out from Copenhagen.

No Danish ship gave up easily, but by 1.30 p.m. several had been forced to surrender and others were about to be captured. Four of the bomb ketches had reached their positions abeam *Elephant* and started to shell the city with their mortars. Meanwhile Hyde Parker's ships, continuing to beat slowly southwards against the wind and the tide, were still 6.5km away. It was difficult to see through the dense gun smoke, but the battle had lasted much longer than expected and Nelson was clearly encountering very strenuous defence. At 1.15 p.m., convinced that defeat was imminent, Parker, in the most famous incident of the campaign, ordered signal number thirty-nine 'discontinue the action' to be hoisted. This required all ships to obey, but Nelson insisted that signal number sixteen 'engage the enemy more closely' remain hoisted on *Elephant*, remarking to Foley beside him 'you know, Foley, I have only one eye' and placing his telescope to his blind left eye said: 'I really do not see the signal.' This flagrant breach of discipline could have resulted in court martial and hanging, but withdrawal while many Danish guns still firing would have been disastrous. As it was, the signals caused considerable confusion; most ships followed *Elephant* and continued action, but Riou's frigates could not see Nelson's signal in the dense smoke and ceasing action, turned north-east towards Parker's ships. As their gun smoke cleared, the Tre Kroner battery was able to stern-rake them; the frigates escaped, but as they turned, a cannonball crossed *Amazon*'s quarterdeck, cutting Edward Riou in half.

Gradually Danish resistance was being broken down; Commodore Olfert Fischer, who had to move to *Holsteen* early in the action when his flagship *Dannebroge* was set on fire by *Elephant*'s guns and incendiaries from *Glatton*, now had to move again to the Tre Kroner battery. Most Danish ships had lost their rigging so coherent signalling was nearly impossible and, in the dense gun smoke, it was difficult to see which had struck their colours. By 2 p.m. most Danish guns had been silenced, five ships had drifted out of action and at least four ships had struck, but the batteries were still hammering the British ships so Nelson decided to offer a truce. Standing at *Elephant*'s rudderhead, he wrote a short, ambiguous letter to Crown Prince Frederik offering to spare the Danish vessels if the firing ceased. He claimed that his sole motive was to avoid further slaughter, but many have interpreted it as a *ruse de guerre* to extract his ships from a very dangerous situation. Although most Danish ships were effectively out of action, the batteries were still intact and, with little wind and badly damaged rigging, it would have been very difficult for the British ships to escape safely. Both *Elephant* and *Defiance* later ran aground on the Mittelgrund and, if the Tre Kroner battery had still been firing, would certainly have been destroyed.

Nelson entrusted the wax-sealed letter to his Danish-speaking *aide-de-camp*, Frederick Thesiger, who was rowed north under a flag of truce in the lee of the British ships, around the Tre Kroner battery to the Danish block ship *Elefanten*, moored in the main channel to Copenhagen. At 3 p.m. he reached the Crown Prince at the Sixtus battery and almost immediately, the Crown Prince sent his English-speaking *aide-de-camp*, Thomas Lindholm, back with Thesiger to clarify Nelson's truce offer. Soon afterwards, the batteries ceased firing and at 3.15 p.m. a flag of truce was hoisted on *Elephant*.

Nelson's adroitly timed naval and political tactics, and refusal to follow Parker's order, turned 'the severest and most doubtful' battle he ever fought into a major naval triumph. He had won, but like the Battle of Waterloo, it was a very close-run thing. All the British ships were still in action, though many were badly damaged, and the casualties on each side were almost equal. The Danes lost 367 dead and 635 wounded, of whom 106 soon died, while the British lost 254 dead and 689 wounded. Nelson's success was in no way diminished by the fact that the battle turned out to have been completely unnecessary, as on 24 March Tsar Paul I had been assassinated in St Petersburg, and his successor, Alexander I, dissolved the League of Armed Neutrality.

At about 4 p.m., moments before the burning *Dannebroge* finally exploded, *Elephant* set sail to join Parker but almost immediately grounded on the Mittelgrund. Soon afterwards, Nelson left for the *London* by boat to continue discussion of terms with the Danish emissaries. *Elephant*'s moment in the limelight was almost over. It was 9.30 p.m. before she could be kedged off the shoal; by then the exhausted Nelson, despairing of sleep on the damaged seventy-four, had returned to his flagship, *St George*. He returned to *Elephant* next morning then inspected all the prizes. The Danes were still quibbling about the truce terms, so at Parker's request, Nelson, having shed his old green coat for full dress uniform resplendent with his decorations, was rowed to Copenhagen to negotiate directly with the Crown Prince. Negotiations continued for days, but on 8 April the news of Tsar Paul's death finally convinced the Danes to sign the armistice and withdraw from the League of Armed Neutrality. A prolonged voyage to Karlskrona and Reval with Nelson replacing Parker as commander-in-chief was still needed to complete the Baltic mission and allow the Royal Navy to concentrate again on Napoleon, but thanks to the timely gift of a turbot and Nelson's victory, the critical gateway to the Baltic would remain open.

References

Bennett, G., 1972, *Nelson the Commander,* B.T. Batsford Ltd, London.

Blake, N., and Lawrence, R., 1999, *The Illustrated Companion to Nelson's Navy,* Navy, Chatham Publishing, London.

Bradford, E., 1977, *Nelson, the Essential Hero,* Macmillan London Ltd, London.

Feldbæk, O. (tr. T. Wedgwood), 2002, *The Battle of Copenhagen 1801: Nelson and the Danes,* Danes, Leo Cooper, Barnsley.

Gardiner, R., 1992, *The Line of Battle,* Conway Maritime Press, London.

Lambert, A., 2000, *War at Sea in the Age of Sail, 1650–1850,* Cassell & Co., London.

Lavery, B., 1983, *The Ship of the Line, Volume I. The Development of the Battle Fleet, 1650–1850,* Conway Maritime Press, London.

Mahan, A.T., 1897, *The Life of Nelson: the Embodiment of the Sea Power of Great Britain,* Britain, London.

Pope, D., 1972, *The Great Gamble: Nelson at Copenhagen,* Weidenfeld and Nicolson, London.

Tushingham, E., and Mansfield,C., 2001, *Nelson's Flagship at Copenhagen: The Men, The Ships, The Battle,* The Nelson Society, London.

5 HMS *BEAGLE* AND THE VOYAGE THAT SHOOK THE WORLD

HMS *Beagle*:	Cherokee-class ten-gun brig designed by Sir Henry Peake, launched Woolwich dockyard, London, 1820.
Tonnage:	297t displacement
Length:	25.5m
Beam:	7.47m
Draught:	3.5m forward, 3.9m aft
Armament:	eight 18lb carronades, two 6lb long guns
Crew:	65
Career:	1820–25: laid up. 1825: re-rigged as a barque. 1826–30: hydrographic survey of Straits of Magellan and Tierra del Fuego under command of Pringle Stokes. 1830: modified then 1830–36: circumnavigation under command of Robert Fitzroy with extensive research in South America and Galápagos by Charles Darwin. 1837–43: survey of northern Australia under command of John Wickham. 1844–70: coastguard watch vessel, Essex coast.

When HMS *Beagle* was launched at Woolwich dockyard on 11 May 1820 no one could have foreseen that, nearly 200 years later, she would be amongst the most famous of world ships. She started life as one of an unprepossessing class of ships, which had gained little respect in a service enthralled by great glamorous ships of the line like Nelson's HMS *Victory*, or dashing frigates like Sir Edward Pellew's HMS *Indefatigable*, 'the eyes of the fleet'. *Beagle* was a simple, small brig, a sturdy two-masted square-rigger, the like of which were the backbone of commercial shipping along every coast of Europe and North America. Brigs lacked the public appeal of larger ships, but from the late eighteenth century onwards they were responsible for most routine naval tasks like carrying despatches and resupplying fleets at sea. Simple and cheap, their handling was familiar to those merchant sailors press-ganged into the Royal Navy during the Napoleonic Wars. They were too small to carry large cannon but could still give a good account of themselves in combat, thanks to carronades, developed in Scotland in 1779. These powerful guns were only accurate at very short range but were much lighter than long guns and gave even small vessels serious firepower.

Brigs were small, typically less than around 45m in length, but *Beagle* was particularly small with a displacement of 297t, and only 25.5m from stem to stern. Designed by surveyor to the Navy, Sir Henry Peake, she carried eight 18lb carronades and two 6lb long guns. She was flush-decked without a raised fo'c'sle or a poop and had six gun ports on each side and two in the transom stern. There were no deck skylights and the 'tween decks were poorly ventilated and dark, with only 1.35m headroom and light only from hatches, companion ways and glass 'bull's eyes' let into the deck. With a crew of sixty-five, accommodation was extremely cramped and she could carry only 6.5t of provisions and 19t of water together with carpenter's and gunner's stores, spare canvas and fuel for the galley. This limited her range of operations to about three months.

Cherokee-class brigs were introduced in 1808 when thirty-one were commissioned. They were immediately unpopular, soon earning an unenviable reputation for sinking; by 1815 nine had sunk and of 107 built between 1808 and 1845, twenty-six were wrecked or sank. As a result they were nicknamed 'coffin brigs' or 'half-tide rocks'. They were simple and robust but could be tricky to handle and were very wet, deep-waisted ships whose high gunwales prevented water draining quickly. Prone to 'deep, quick rolling', they often shipped water over the sides and without a raised fo'c'sle, waves often came over the bow. If water from one wave did not drain before the next arrived, they could be seriously destabilised and a third wave could cause broaching and capsizing. This problem was exacerbated if the gun ports were sealed; some ships were saved only by alert crew members breaking open the gun ports. Despite their lack of comfort and evil reputation, when well handled they were safe and seaworthy and many survived for very prolonged naval careers.

Because of their dubious reputation, Cherokee-class brigs were nearly abandoned when the naval establishment was rapidly reduced after the Napoleonic Wars ended in 1815. Very few were built in the first years of the peace and Beagle was mothballed for five years after her launching in 1820. With no threat of imminent invasion national priorities changed; few large capital ships were needed, but Britain was now responsible for managing a worldwide empire. Trade and imperial administration both depended on safe, predictable navigation. Merchant ships along far-flung shipping routes needed accurate charts of coastlines, identification of navigational hazards and safe harbours and anchorages where supplies of food and fresh water could be obtained. The Navy's Hydrographic Office, established in 1795 under Alexander Dalrymple to survey and prepare nautical charts, was now given a much more far-reaching mandate for exploration. This required many small, nimble ships that, in the depressed post-war economy, also had to be cheap; Beagle was built and commissioned for £7,703. Apart from their limited range and despite their poor reputation, ten-gun brigs were suitable and the class received a new lease on life. The Navy also changed to meet its peacetime role and in 1817 the Admiralty established a new Surveying Service whose officers were expected to carry out wide-ranging scientific research.

The first major expeditions for ten-gun brigs were the 1826–30 hydrographic voyage by the Beagle to the Straits of Magellan and Tierra del Fuego under Commander Pringle Stokes and the 1828–31 'Pendulum' voyage under Captain Henry Foster in HMS Chanticleer, which carried out hydrographic surveys across the South Atlantic and gravity and magnetic observations south to Deception Island in Antarctica. The deficiencies of Cherokee-class brigs on long voyages in notoriously stormy, dangerous waters had been noted and both Beagle and Chanticleer were modified before their missions in 1825. They were re-rigged as barques with the mainmast moved forward, the big main spanker with its very long boom eliminated and a mizzen mast with a small sail added close to the transom. Their seaworthiness and ability to sail close to the wind were significantly improved. This was particularly important for Beagle in the Straits of Magellan where she had to force her way through very narrow, difficult channels against strong prevailing winds and contrary currents which run at up to 6 knots. Two other important modifications were the addition of a low poop extending 6.1m forward from the stern and a raised fo'c'sle. The fo'c'sle provided more storage space and a sick berth, and gave some protection from waves, while the poop protected the helmsman and also provided a room for drafting charts, well lit by a deck skylight.

Surveying the Straits of Magellan and Tierra del Fuego was extremely challenging, requiring prolonged work in small open boats in atrocious weather conditions. It was very difficult to obtain fresh provisions and many health problems were encountered; the constant stress was too much for the seriously ill Pringle Stokes who shot himself at Port Famine in August 1828. Back in Montevideo, he was replaced by 23-year-old Robert Fitzroy, an outstanding seaman and a fine scientist, who was destined to play an important role on the voyage that made Beagle famous. Fitzroy had to complete the difficult survey and also restore the morale of the depressed crew, who believed that the ship was haunted by Pringle Stokes' ghost. The start was inauspicious as violent 'pamperos' hammered Beagle onto her beam ends off Rio de la Plata, killing two crew members, but Fitzroy managed to complete the survey south to Cape Horn successfully before returning to Plymouth in October 1830. He brought with him with four Fuegian hostages, which he planned to 'civilise', Christianise and bring back to Tierra del Fuego as missionaries.

The new charts, so laboriously surveyed, were of limited navigational use unless linked to a standardised global meridianal grid. A key priority for the Hydrographic Office, now directed by the redoubtable Irish Admiral Beaufort, inventor of the Beaufort Wind Scale, was a circumnavigational chronometric survey to establish precise meridianal locations. This was originally to have been carried out by Chanticleer under Henry Foster, a brilliant mathematician who served as astronomer with Sir William Parry in his search for the Northwest Passage and had received the Royal Society's Copley Medal for scientific contributions. Unfortunately Foster was drowned in a canoe on Chagres River, Panama, just before Chanticleer returned to England. A new commander was needed and Chanticleer was found to be in too bad condition for the proposed five-year mission, so Beagle was assigned with Fitzroy as commander.

Before departure, Beagle was modified yet again at Devonport dockyard. Fitzroy was a perfectionist and the expensive, comprehensive refit cost £7,583, almost as much as Beagle's original construction. Many original timbers, now rotten, were replaced and a triple sheath of fir, felt and copper was added to her bottom. New innovations included a windlass to replace the capstan, a patent Fraser stove, an oven in the galley, and Harris patent lightning conductors on spars and masts. Rigging was strengthened with heavier crosstrees, and chains replaced some ropes. The upper deck was raised by 20–30cm, improving 'tween decks comfort by raising the headroom to 1.83m. The 'large' (2.6 x 5.49m) poop cabin became more habitable but was still very cramped; it had a large table for drawing charts and preparing specimens, but two people would sleep there, and the mizzen mast passed through. Fitzroy's cabin was also large and lit by a skylight, but the other officers were housed in dark, tiny (1.83 x 1.22m) cells around a cramped, central 3.05 x 2.44m gunroom. The bulwarks were not raised with the upper deck, so *Beagle* became less deep-waisted and drier, but decks were still very congested with guns and boats. Fitzroy insisted on brass guns, which would not interfere with the compasses, and when the Admiralty provided only seven he added two at his own expense. Seven boats were carried: a 7.93m yawl amidships with a slightly smaller cutter stowed inside, two 8.54m whale boats on quarterdeck skids, two 7.62m whale boats on the quarters, and a 3.96m dinghy on davits at the stern. *Beagle* was also equipped with twenty-two chronometers, a barometer (Fitzroy pioneered the use of atmospheric pressure for weather forecasting) and a patent sounding winch.

Apart from *Beagle*'s refit, the most important change for the new mission was the addition of a new member to the crew. After the first voyage Fitzroy had pledged that he would 'carry out a person qualified to examine the land' while the naval personnel would look after the hydrography. It was this person that would make *Beagle*'s voyage famous. Fitzroy wanted a good naturalist but also an intellectual peer to act as his companion, share meals (the captain ate in the gunroom only by invitation) and alleviate his lonely isolation during the prolonged mission. He approached the Reverend John Henslow at Cambridge University, a leading botanist, and on his advice offered the position to one of Henslow's students, Charles Darwin.

Although only 22, Darwin was already an experienced natural scientist who had been tutored by Henslow for three years, and before that had studied marine biology and geology at Edinburgh University where he had been enrolled as a 16-year-old. He had unusually broad scientific interests but regarded himself primarily as a geologist with first-hand experience of geological field research methods. He was clearly an intellectual match for Fitzroy, though he was nearly rejected because Fitzroy believed that he could judge character by features and 'he doubted whether anyone with my nose could possess sufficient energy and determination for the voyage'. Unsurprisingly, their relationship suffered some strain during the following five years, but nevertheless they developed deep mutual respect. Two particular

areas of contention were political and religious; Fitzroy was a Tory and Darwin a Whig, placing them on opposing sides in Wilberforce's then controversial campaign to abolish slavery. Fitzroy was also an orthodox creationist; Darwin started the voyage with similar views, but as evidence mounted along the way, these gradually changed.

Darwin joined *Beagle* in Plymouth on 28 October 1831, assisting Fitzroy to resurvey the stone longitude reference point used for the previous voyage to adjust the twenty-two chronometers. He found it difficult to adapt to the cramped poop cabin and sleeping in a hammock and, when *Beagle* first put to sea on 10 December in the teeth of a gale, he became violently seasick: 'I suffered most dreadfully … nothing but misery; such a whistling of the wind and a roar of the sea.' This was a taste of things to come, and he continued to suffer from seasickness throughout most of the voyage. However, this time *Beagle* put back to Plymouth and did not finally depart until 5 January 1832, when the crew had sobered up after a very drunken Christmas.

The voyage south was eventful. Unable to land at Madeira and Tenerife, Darwin did his first collecting on the volcanic St Paul Rocks. Rio do Janeiro followed, where existing longitude figures were found to be incorrect by 4° (about 440km), then Buenos Aires where *Beagle* had a confrontation with a guard ship (related to ownership of the Falkland Islands), and finally Montevideo where Fitzroy led Darwin and fifty-two of the crew in helping to suppress a military revolution. By contrast, scientific observation was almost mundane, but at Punta Alta, near Bahía Blanca, Darwin made an important discovery of huge bones of fossilised giant sloths and a large extinct ungulate *Toxodon,* formerly extremely widespread through South America. Sent back to Britain, these made him famous long before his return. The fossils triggered his curiosity about their relationship to present-day species, the cause of their extinction, the fixity of species, and subversive questions about how such large animals could fit into Noah's Ark.

Darwin was an obsessive collector who observed every facet of natural history, so the poop cabin was crammed with skins, plants, rocks, snakes and microscopic marine organisms. In view of the subsequent results, it is easy to forget that the primary objective of *Beagle*'s voyage was still hydrographic. There were long intervals when the ship remained anchored while comprehensive surveys were carried out along the Patagonian and Tierra del Fuegan coasts. Darwin took full advantage to explore on land, and his diaries include many detailed reports on native Fuegians. Surveying was frequently interrupted by bad weather and on several occasions, *Beagle* was saved only by timely shortening of sail in response to Fitzroy's barometric forecasts. At the end of the year, they rounded Cape Horn and *Beagle* nearly foundered after being struck successively by three huge waves. Darwin was disturbed by the navigational uncertainties – 'it has an awkward sound to hear the officers … telling the lookout to look well to leeward'. In mid-January 1833 Fitzroy landed the three surviving Fuegian hostages, together with a missionary, Richard Matthews, to spread Christianity. However, the mission was plundered by 'cannibalistic' Fuegians, and Matthews had to be rescued three weeks later.

The *Beagle* then moved to the Falkland Islands, which Darwin was astonished to find had been claimed by Britain. He was not impressed, 'the whole landscape … has an air of extreme desolation … we have never stayed so long at a place with so little for the journal', and was pleased to return to Patagonia (which also provided some respite from seasickness). He was able to enthusiastically explore a great swath of Argentina on horseback before rejoining *Beagle* at Montevideo in November 1833. When the charts of the Patagonian coast had been completed, *Beagle* left again for the Straits of Magellan, spending Christmas at Port Desire to finish surveying before continuing into the Pacific to reach Valparaiso in July 1834. Darwin again took the opportunity to leave the ship for long journeys into the Andes, partly for relief from Fitzroy's company – the captain was suffering acute depression (perhaps an early indication of the mental instability that would later plague him and lead to his suicide).

Darwin's stay ashore was extended for three months when he was laid up, possibly with Chagas' disease contracted from a bite from a Benchuca bug. By November he was able to rejoin *Beagle*, which then headed south again to finish surveying the Chilean coast. He was fascinated by the damage caused by the violent earthquake (believed to be of 8.5 magnitude) which devastated Concepción in February 1835. This strengthened his growing appreciation of the power of forces causing instability in the earth's crust and his scepticism about orthodox creationist views. *Beagle* soon had to return to Valparaiso having lost most of her anchors, allowing Darwin to again depart on journeys right across the Andes to Mendoza in Argentina, and to fill his diary with observations on geology, locust swarms, copper mining, indigenous communities and social conditions in post-colonial Chile and Peru. He rejoined *Beagle* in Lima and sailed for the Galápagos Islands in early September and the most momentous part of the voyage.

The fourteen islands of the Galápagos archipelago straddle the Equator, 973km west of the Ecuador coast in a geologically extremely active area where three tectonic plates join. (Map, see p. 58) The very recently formed volcanic islands lie above a hotspot where the earth's crust is melted by an ascending mantle plume, and volcanoes are still very active on the youngest islands. Despite their equatorial location, moderate temperatures are maintained by the cold, nutrient-rich Humboldt current, which supports extraordinarily diverse marine and terrestrial fauna. It is a biologically fascinating area, which is home to an extraordinary diversity of endemic species including the Galápagos penguin, giant tortoises, marine and terrestrial iguanas, frigate birds, wavy albatrosses, blue and red-footed boobies and numerous smaller bird species such as Darwin and vampire finches, as well as highly unusual vegetation like the Opuntia cactus forest on Santiago Island. They were discovered by one of Pisarro's captains, Fray Tomás de Berlanga in 1535 and subsequently used by pirates preying on Spanish bullion galleons and then by whalers attracted by sperm whales in the nutrient-rich waters. The Galápagos were unpopulated until 1807 when an Irish seaman, Patrick Williams, was marooned there. The islands were annexed by Ecuador in 1832, shortly before the arrival of Darwin and the *Beagle*.

From the moment *Beagle* dropped anchor on 15 September 1835, Darwin was fascinated. The highly active landscape supported his growing understanding of the origins of volcanic oceanic islands and the continuous dynamism of the earth's crust. His diary for the next month was filled with observations about the diverse fauna, notably the marine iguanas, which he found repellent, 'the most disgusting, clumsy lizards'. However, his stay in the Galápagos is associated particularly with the endemic species of giant tortoises, mockingbirds and Darwin finches. These species are spread throughout the islands, but subtle differences have evolved on different islands with species adapting closely to the slightly different environmental conditions. It is not clear how soon Darwin recognised the significance of these differences. He certainly observed the four different species of mockingbirds and the differences in giant tortoises pointed out to him by the acting governor, Nicholas Lawson, and noted that 'such facts would undermine the stability of species'. However, he did not recognise the significance of beak gradations in the Darwin finches until they were examined by the celebrated ornithologist John Gould once *Beagle* returned to Britain. Darwin failed to record the island on which each of his finch samples was collected, but fortunately Syms Covington, the cabin boy he appointed as his assistant, and Captain Fitzroy also made parallel collections with the originating islands identified.

When *Beagle* sailed from the Galápagos on 20 October, Darwin must have been physically and intellectually exhausted and, despite seasickness, he welcomed the respite during the 5,000km voyage to Tahiti. Though the remainder of *Beagle's* voyage lasted nearly a year and Darwin recorded many observations from visits to Tahiti, New Zealand, Australia and South Africa in his diary before reaching Falmouth on 2 October 1836, the momentous portion that would make *Beagle* famous was already complete. Darwin certainly had plenty of time to reflect on the significance of his observations during the long voyage, but although he published *The Voyage of the Beagle* in 1839 (volume 3 of the *Narrative of Surveying Voyages* edited by Robert Fitzroy), it would be twenty-three years after he stepped ashore in England before the publication of *On The Origin of Species* would shake the foundations of society. By then one of his most vociferous opponents was Robert Fitzroy who, after his marriage, increasingly adamantly believed in the literal truth of the Bible and interpreted the variations in Darwin's finches as 'one of those admirable provisions of Infinite Wisdom by which each created thing is adapted to the place for which it was intended'.

Publication of *On The Origin of Species* secured the fame of both *Beagle* and Darwin, but *Beagle's* career was not yet finished. Leaving Falmouth, she continued to Plymouth where the circle of meridianal observations was completed at the same stone from which it started; three of the original twenty-two chronometers were still working. *Beagle*, still in excellent condition, continued to the Thames where she was laid up until October 1837. She then left for her third great six-year voyage to survey the northern and north-western coasts of Australia under command of John Wickham, first mate on Darwin's voyage. After being laid up again for nearly two years after she returned, she was moored permanently at Pagelsham, on the Essex coast, as a coast guard service watch ship. In 1870 her decaying hulk was sold, probably to be scrapped.

References

Barlow, N. (ed.), 1933, *Charles Darwin's Diary of the Voyage of HMS Beagle,* Cambridge University Press, Cambridge.

Darwin, C., 1845, *The Voyage of the Beagle,* J.M. Dent & Sons., reprint 1975, London.

Darwin, F., 1887, *The Life and Letters of Charles Darwin, Including and Autobiographical Chapter,* John Murray, London.

Fitzroy, R., 1839, *Narrative of the Surveying Voyages of His Majesty's Ships Adventure and Beagle Between the Years 1826 and 1836 Describing the Shores of South America and the Beagle's Circumnavigation,* 3 Vols. Henry Colburn, London.

Keynes, R.D. (ed.), 1988, *Charles Darwin's Beagle Diary,* Cambridge University Press, Cambridge.

Marquardt, K.H., 1997, *Anatomy of the Ship HMS Beagle: Survey Ship Extraordinary,* Conway Maritime Press, London.

Moorehead, A., 1971, *Darwin and the Beagle,* Penguin, London.

Thomson, K.S., 1995, *HMS Beagle: The Story of Darwin's Ship,* W.W. Norton, New York/London.

6 AN GÓRTA MÓR AND THE IRISH EMIGRANT SHIP JEANIE JOHNSTON

Jeanie Johnston:	three-masted barque built by John Munn at Quebec in 1847.
Tonnage:	408t
Length:	32.3m
Beam:	7.38m
Draught:	5.49m
Crew:	17
Passengers:	194–253 emigrants
Career:	maiden voyage with timber to Liverpool, then sold to merchants J. & N. Donnellan, Tralee, Ireland. Employed as emigrant ship between Kerry and Québec; under Captain James Attridge and Dr Richard Blennerhassett carried over 2,500 passengers without loss of life. 1855: sold to W. Johnston, North Shields. 1858: foundered in the Atlantic, crew and passengers rescued without loss of life.

Jeanie Johnston (replica):	three-masted barque launched at Blennerville, Co. Kerry, 2002.
Tonnage:	510t displacement
Length:	37m
Beam:	7.9m
Draught:	4.5m
Hull:	larch on oak frames
Sail:	645m^2 on three masts
Engines:	two 280hp diesel engines; two 105KVA generators
Crew:	11 permanent, 29 sail trainees
Career:	2003: sailed to the United States and Canada. Currently moored as museum ship and famine memorial on River Liffey, Dublin.

The summer of 1845 started well in Ireland and hot dry weather at the beginning of July promised a bumper potato crop. No people in Europe, and probably in the world, were so dependent on the well-being of a single crop. Centuries of warfare and systematic dispossession, culminating in Cromwell's promise to send them 'to hell or Connacht' and the vicious Penal Laws, had driven most of the Gaelic-speaking Catholic population away from more fertile lands to the wet acidic soils of the western counties. The land was too poor for most crops, but potatoes, introduced by Sir Walter Raleigh more than 200 years earlier, thrived in the cool moist climate. Most of the rural population lived in desperate poverty on tiny plots of rented land, but potatoes allowed them to scratch out a living and raise enough money for their rent and other necessities of life. Even by the standards of the mid-nineteenth century, living conditions were appalling, but the population grew rapidly and in 1841 reached an all-time high (officially 8.2 million, but probably over 9 million) with one of the highest densities in the world. The promised bumper crop wouldn't change the poverty, but it would provide some security for another twelve months.

Then the weather changed. The sunny warmth was replaced by endless weeks of chilling rain and fog and in the continuous damp a new threat appeared. Nobody is quite sure where the potato blight came from or when it first appeared in Europe. The first well-documented case destroyed potato crops along the North American seaboard from Maine to Nova Scotia in 1842. The potato-blight fungus, *Phytopthera infestans*, is sensitive to heat and drought and cannot spread far through the air, but a diseased tuber must have made its way across the Atlantic and in August 1845 blight appeared in Kent. Its effects were dramatic: plants that looked vibrant and healthy in the evening would turn into a stinking, brown sludge by the following morning. Within weeks much of southern England and Belgium were affected and in September blight appeared near Dublin. In a country so heavily dependent on potatoes a disaster seemed to be taking shape. At first things didn't look too bad; most of the potatoes harvested looked fine and healthy, but within days they turned brown and rotten. By late October the failure was almost complete, not just in the west but over many of the central counties as well.

By late 1845 the disaster known in Gaelic as *An Górta Mór*, the Great Hunger, was well under way. It was an unparalleled catastrophe, which has left an indelible imprint of abandoned cottages and potato 'lazy beds' on the landscapes of western Ireland and an enduring scar on the Irish psyche. It is called the Great Hunger rather than the Great Famine for during the four years that starvation and disease stalked rural Ireland, there was food in Ireland, and exports of cereals and livestock continued to pour out of Irish ports to Britain and continental Europe. It would have been a disaster under any circumstances, but its effects were catastrophically amplified by the remote, inflexible, ill-informed government, reluctant to interfere in any way with the sanctity of private business. There were no profits or votes to be gained from starving, destitute peasants; public relief would just undermine free enterprise and encourage sloth. The pitifully inadequate public funds eventually provided would not be given freely but had to be earned by people on the edge of starvation, building walls and roads that were neither wanted nor needed.

The autumn of 1845 was desperate, but much worse was to follow. Many people still had something to eke out an existence through the winter in hope of a better harvest in 1846, some seed potatoes, a few hens and sometimes a pig. As winter turned to spring the situation grew progressively more desperate and by the summer of 1846, when crops failed again, many were struggling to survive by collecting blackberries, nettles and snails. Starvation was soon joined by disease; in the miserable, crowded damp cottages, typhus, dysentery, scurvy and tick-borne relapsing fever wiped out complete families. Without income, tenants couldn't pay their rents. A few landlords bent over backwards to help their tenants, but many grasped the chance to evict tenants from their tiny holdings to clear the way for more profitable sheep or cattle. Bailiffs supported by soldiers moved in, pulling down roof-trees so that cottages could not be reoccupied. By the 1846–47 winter, one of the worst in living memory, famine graveyards and desolate swathes of ruined cottages had appeared throughout the west, while starving, spectral swarms of survivors slept in ditches or 'scalps' and wandered the roads for help.

There weren't many choices left for survivors. Without their land, even the hope of a better 1847 harvest was gone; they could try to join the pitifully scarce public works, to find shelter in the disease-ridden hell of workhouses, or they could beg. For those who could reach the coast and scratch together money for the fare, there was also the last desperate resort: emigration. Some parishes took up collections for fares, and a few landlords even paid for their tenants so that the land could be cleared. Britain, detested and blamed for the tragedy, could be reached for a few shillings, all that many could afford. Some were even carried free as ballast on coal boats returning empty to Wales. Within months a tidal wave of impoverished Irish swamped towns in western Britain. In the first six months of 1847 more than 300,000 reached Liverpool, originally a city of 250,000 people, but everyone who managed headed west across the Atlantic to North America. Those who could went directly for the United States to evade vestigial British influence, but for most, only the much cheaper route to Canada (about £3) was possible.

Irish landlords were not the only ones who saw business opportunities in the disaster. British access to European timber supplies had been cut off in the war with Napoleon, potentially strangling shipbuilding and trade. The essential timber had to come from Canada and new vessels to carry it poured out of shipyards along the eastern seaboard from Halifax to Quebec. The timber trade was profitable but cargoes for the return journey were scarce. Most ships returned empty, in ballast, but ship owners soon realised that profits could be raised by carrying emigrants on the return journey. Costs were minimal; rough bunks in the hold and provision of fuel and water were sufficient; passengers had to bring their own food. The British government kept fares low to bolster population growth in Canada as protection against American

Emigrants on the dock.

annexation, demand was steady and by 1845 profits from the 'emigrant trade' exceeded those from timber.

Long before the famine there were concerns about conditions on emigrant ships; in 1834 alone, seventeen ships sank in the St Lawrence River with 731 deaths. Successive Passenger Acts had attempted to regulate the trade by insisting on lifeboats, medicines, minimal provisions and headroom of 1.23m in the hold, but as the famine entered its third year, the flood of emigrants made enforcement impossible. Some ships, like the most famous, the *Jeanie Johnston,* met or exceeded Passenger Act requirements, but the majority were old, ill-found hulks with ruthless, unscrupulous captains interested solely in packing in as many emigrants as possible for quick profits. Some owners were more interested in collecting inflated insurance claims than providing safe passage; the infamous English MP Edward 'Bully' Bates lost no fewer than six ships in one year. These were infamous 'coffin ships', which added further torment for the malnourished and often desperately ill emigrants.

Even on *Jeanie Johnston* conditions were pretty miserable, but she was incomparably better than most of the ships. *Jeanie Johnston* was a new vessel, the smallest of four barques built in 1847 by the well-known naval architect, John Munn, who launched more than 100 ships at his shipyard in Quebec between 1811and 1857, the second most productive of all Quebec shipbuilders. He was a humane man, well known for doing everything he could to help Irish emigrants by employing them as labourers in his shipyard. In fact, he apparently expedited the construction of *Jeanie Johnston* specifically in an attempt to alleviate the plight of the emigrants and the shortage of good ships. *Jeanie Johnston* was certainly a fine ship, surveyed to the highest Lloyd standards. However, no drawings of her exist and, like many ships of the period, she was probably built from a half model relying on Munn's expertise. She was a three-masted barque of 408t, 32.3m long, built of oak, rock elm, hackmatack and pine. Like all the timber ships, hatches were fitted on either side of her stem through which lengthy squared timber baulks could be loaded. The sixteen crew were housed in deck houses on the main and poop decks, but for the emigrants rough 1.85 x 1.85m wooden bunks like horse stalls, each to fit four people or a family, were set up in the hold. These housed between 193 and 254 emigrants. Even in good weather, when passengers could go on deck, it was congested. Complete families or groups of strangers were packed into the rough bunks, cooking food on a single stove on deck,

Entertainment in steerage.

and eating in the cramped hold. The only toilets were open buckets, and in bad weather, when the two hatches (the only ventilation) had to be closed and lights extinguished, conditions were appalling.

Jeanie Johnston sailed to Liverpool in late 1847 where she was sold for some £2,000 to Kerry brothers John and Nicholas Donnellan who ran a large hardware firm in Tralee. The Donnellans hired an experienced, compassionate captain, James Attridge of Castletownsend, Co. Cork, and went well beyond the Passenger Act in hiring an outstandingly well-qualified doctor, Richard Blennerhassett of Dingle. The full rations of medicines, food and water stipulated by the Passenger Acts were also provided. They couldn't do too much about the living conditions on *Jeanie Johnston* during the five or six weeks the voyage to Quebec lasted, but between them, Captain Attridge and Dr Blennerhassett were responsible for an exceptional record in the emigrant trade; on sixteen transatlantic emigrant voyages between 1848 and 1855, when she was sold to William Johnson of North Shields, England, *Jeanie Johnston* never lost a passenger. She even preserved her record when she foundered in the North Atlantic in 1858 en route with timber from Quebec to Hull; the crew clung to the sinking, water-logged ship for nine days but were all rescued by a Dutch brig, the *Sophie Elizabeth.*

There were a few other exceptions like the *Jeanie Johnston,* owned and run by ethical, compassionate men, but most vessels were

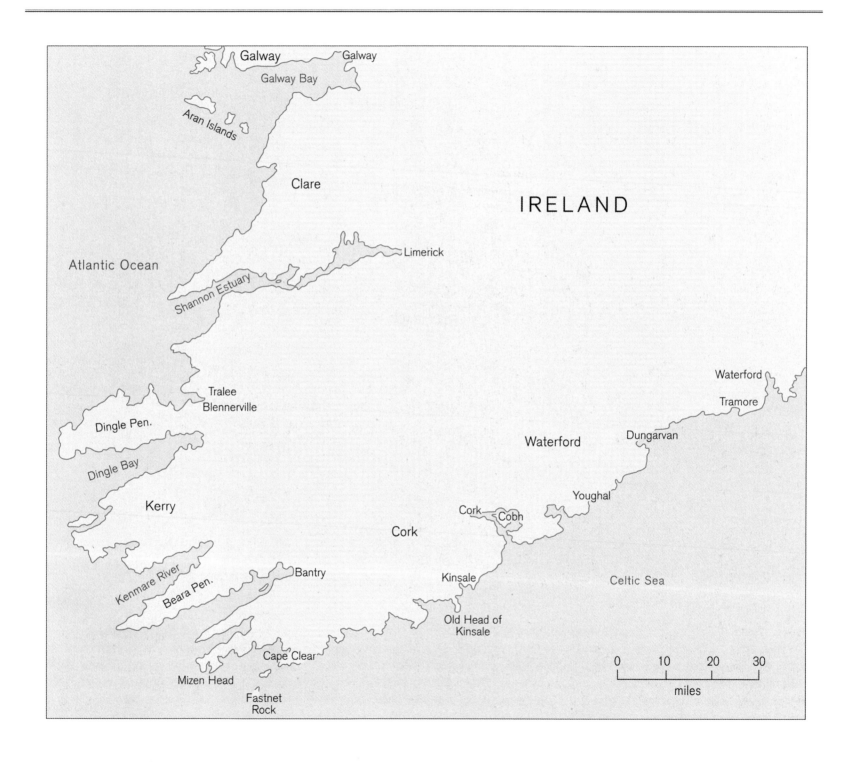

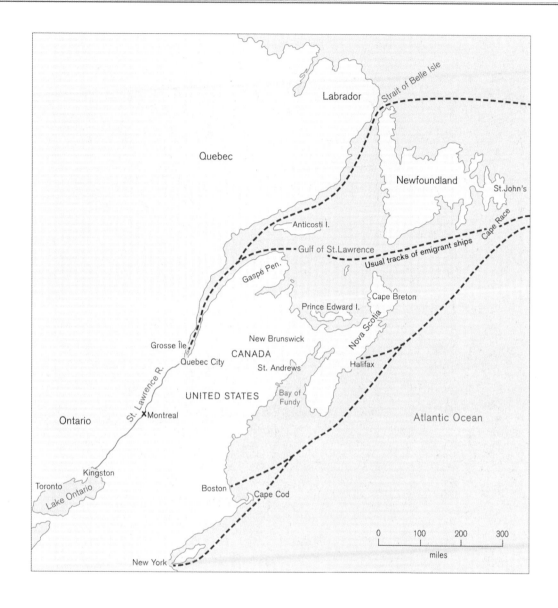

overcrowded hell ships – Gerald Keegan's Famine Diary (edited in a quasi-fictional version by James Mangan) describes more than 500 on the elderly barque *Naparima*, with capacity for only 300 during 1847. Passenger Acts stipulated 7lb of food per person per week, but often there were only mouldy ship's biscuits or nothing at all. Water was often foul, muddy and foetid. Many emigrants were already sick before they left and typhoid, dysentery, cholera, chickenpox and measles spread quickly in the cramped quarters; on *Naparima*, the first death occurred within two days. The 330t *Elizabeth and Sarah*, built in 1762, with a legal capacity of 165 sailed from Killala, Co. Mayo, in July 1846 with 276 passengers sharing thirty-two bunks. Only half the legal supply of water was carried and no food at all was issued during the eight-week journey during which forty-two passengers died. The *Syria*, the first ship to enter the St Lawrence in May 1847, arrived with 84 cases of fever amongst 241 passengers. The *Larch* left Sligo with 440 passengers and arrived in August 1847 with 108 dead and 150 sick. The *Sir Henry Pottinger* from Cork, with 399 passengers, arrived with 98 dead and 112 sick, the *Ganges* from Liverpool, with 393 passengers, anchored with 45 dead and 80 sick, and the *Virginius* sailed with 596 of whom 158 died on passage and 186 arrived sick, including the captain, mates and crew. On 30 October, just before the river froze, the *Lord Ashburton* arrived from Sligo with 477 passengers; 107 had died on the voyage and another 60 were ill.

The emigrants must have felt that things could not get any worse, but they could. Swarms of impoverished, sick, half-starved immigrants were welcome in neither the United States nor Canada. In both countries authorities were terrified that cholera would break out in their crowded, unsanitary cities and insisted on strict quarantine. Many, refused entry in New York, had to continue to Canada where conditions were much worse. The quarantine station set up on the 7.6km² Grosse Île in 1832, 51km downriver from Quebec City, had a capacity for 200 people, which was soon overwhelmed. In May 1847, seventeen ships arrived on a single day and by the end of the month thirty-six ships and more than 13,000 emigrants were waiting in a 3km queue down the St Lawrence. There were soon nearly 700 in the quickly erected rudimentary fever sheds and, without washing facilities, many of the sick had to lie outside without shelter, or remain aboard the filthy, cramped ships. There were few doctors or nurses; Dr Benson, an experienced fever doctor from Dublin, arrived on 21 May but died of fever six days later, and three other doctors followed him. Ships had to remain in quarantine for fifteen days; the *Agnes* arrived with 427 passengers, but only 150 survived the quarantine period. Eventually even a quarantine period was abandoned and desperately ill emigrants were landed at Quebec City or in Montreal. Nobody really knows how many of the 100,000 people who emigrated from Ireland in 1847 died during the journey. At least 5,294 died at Grosse Île, buried there in a mass grave.

Hundreds died while waiting on board ship for the medical examination. A great many died while being transported to shore and on the beach where they were laid. A large number, demented by fever or horror-stricken over the conditions of the fever-sheds escaped to the wooded areas of the island where they died. Corpses were found all over the island. The count of bodies … did not start till well on in June when almost half the victims were already buried … it is believed by some … that 15,000 would be a more accurate count.

(A. Béchard, 1902)

Probably at least as many died at sea, another 3,000 or so in Quebec, some 6,000 in the Point St Charles fever sheds at Montreal, and more in other cities throughout Upper and Lower Canada as immigrants spread out from Montreal and Quebec.

Three more years of blighted harvests would follow the dreadful 1847 Summer of Sorrows. By the time the famine sputtered out in 1850 more than one million people had emigrated to the United States, Canada and Australia planting the seeds of a diaspora that still continues. At least another million, probably more, had died in Ireland. Rural Ireland was devastated and complete villages had disappeared, while ruined cottages and famine graveyards littered much of the country. The coffin ships would continue for years until Samuel Plimsoll finally forced through acts to regulate the loading of ships through parliament in 1876. There are memorials to the desperate refugees from the famine in many countries, but none is more poignant than the gaunt statue of a three-masted emigrant ship at the foot of Croagh Patrick in Co. Mayo, or more haunting than the emaciated figures that line the quay along the Liffey in front of the Customs House in Dublin. A stone's throw away lies a living memorial, a replica of the *Jeanie Johnston*, built in Blennerville, Co. Kerry, near the original home port of Tralee, and launched in 2002. The replica, which sailed to Montreal in 2003, is equipped with diesel engines, electrical generators, water-tight bulkheads, navigational aids and lifesaving equipment, but it still evokes the hopes, miseries and fears of emigrants' voyages on even the best managed of ships during *An Górta Mór*.

References

Béchard, A., 1902, *Histoire de l' Île-aux-Grues et des îles voisines*, Imprimerie de 'La Bataille' Arthabaskaville.

Charbonneau, A., and Sevigny, A., 1997, *Grosse Isle: A Record of Daily Events, 1847*, Parks Canada, Ottawa.

Donnelly, J.S. Jr., 2001, *The Great Irish Potato Famine*, Sutton Publishing, Stroud.

English, M., 2012, *Jeanie Johnston, Sailing the Irish Famine Tall Ship,* The Collins Press, Cork.

Henry, W., 2011, *Famine: Galway's Darkest Years,* Mercier Press, Cork.

Keegan, G. (ed. James J. Mangan), 1991, *Famine Diary: Journey to a New World,* Wolfhound Press, Dublin.

Laxton, E., 1996, *The Famine Ships: The Irish Exodus to America,* Bloomsbury, London.

MacKay, D., 1990, *Flight From Famine: The Coming of the Irish to Canada,* McClelland and Stewart, Toronto, 1990.

Mangan, J.J., 1982, *The Voyage of the Naparima: A Story of Canada's Island Graveyard,* Carraig Books, Québec.

Miles, K., 2013, *All Standing: The Remarkable Story of the Jeanie Johnston, the Legendary Irish Famine Ship*, Free Press, New York.

O'Gallagher, M., 1984, *Grosse Île – Gateway to Canada, 1832–1937,* Carraig Books, Sainte-Foy.

Marcil, E.R., 2000, *On Chantait 'Charley-Man': La Construction de Grands Voiliers à Québec de 1763 à 1893,* Les Éditions GID, Sainte-Foy.

Whyte, R. (ed. James J. Mangan), 1994, *1847 Famine Ship Diary: The Journey of an Irish Coffin Ship,* Mercier Press, Cork.

Woodham-Smith, C. 1962, *The Great Hunger, Ireland, 1845–1849,* Hamish Hamilton, London.

7 THE CHINA TEA TRADE AND THE GREAT RIVAL CLIPPERS, *THERMOPYLAE* AND *CUTTY SARK*

Thermopylae:	three-masted, ship-rigged extreme composite clipper, designed by Bernard Waymouth, built by Thomas Hood, Aberdeen, for the Aberdeen Line; launched: August 1868.
Tonnage:	991t
Length:	64.6m
Beam:	10.97m
Draught:	6.4m
Career:	1868: record passage London–Melbourne, sixty-one days, including at least nine twenty-four-hour runs over 564km. 1869: Foochow–London, ninety-one days. 1872: Shanghai–London with *Cutty Sark*, 115 days. 1890: sold to Canada for Pacific rice and timber trade; cut down to barque. 1895: Sold to Portuguese Navy, renamed *Pedro Nunes*. 1907: Sunk at sea off Lisbon with full naval honours.
Cutty Sark:	three-masted ship-rigged, extreme composite clipper, designed and built by Scott & Linton, Dumbarton, for Capt. Jock Willis, specifically to beat *Thermopylae*; launched November 1869.
Tonnage:	963t
Length:	64.6m
Beam:	10.97m
Draught:	6.1m
Sail:	3,555m²
Career:	eight China tea voyages. 1872: Shanghai–London with *Thermopylae*, 122 days, after losing rudder in Indian Ocean. Australian wool trade, many record voyages: best passage 661km in twenty-four hours. Regularly overtook steam ships including 1889: P&O *Britannia* entering Sydney. 1895: sold to Com. Nacional de Navigacio, Portugal, renamed *Ferreira* and later *Mario do Amparo*. 1922: sold to Britain. 1938: Thames Nautical Training College. 1953: Museum ship on the Thames at Greenwich.

The sleek green ship with white yards and its gilded figurehead of Leonidas caused a stir as she coasted in to drop anchor in the muddy waters of the Min River's Pagoda Anchorage, off Foochow, in May 1869. *Thermopylae* wasn't just another ship waiting for tea to be brought down the narrow river from the hills to the southern Chinese port. She was the eagerly awaited newest challenger for one of the Victorian era's most demanding competitions, the 25,600km China Tea Race. Designed by Bernard Waymouth and launched in Aberdeen in August 1868 at Walter Hood's shipyard, *Thermopylae* had beaten all records on her maiden voyage, taking only sixty-three days from London to Melbourne, including nine daily runs of over 546km and one of 600km.

> The splendid and almost unprecedently rapid passage made by the new clipper ship *Thermopylae* to this port … seemed almost impossible and certainly never entered into the calculations of the most sanguine that a voyage to the antipodes could be accomplished by a sailing ship in 59 days (to first sight of Australian coast).
>
> (*The Melbourne Argus*, 13 January 1869)

After loading at Newcastle, NSW, *Thermopylae* made another record thirty-one-day voyage to the Whampoo River, Shanghai. Now she was ready to load tea for the most demanding and eagerly contested part of her journey, down the China Sea to the Sunda Strait, across the Indian Ocean to the Cape of Good Hope, then up the Atlantic to the English Channel. The prize was the premium price commanded by the first tea of the new season to reach the London market. Already, serious bets were being placed for a race that combined the excitement of the football World Cup, the America's Cup and the arrival of Beaujolais Nouveau, but was sustained over more than three months. Other fast clippers were waiting in Foochow; the 1867 winner *Sir Launcelot* was there, and *Ariel*, which had reached London in a dead heat with *Taeping* in 1866 after a ninety-nine-day voyage, and won again in 1868. As they watched from the Foochow waterfront, their captains spluttered with indignation at the golden cockerel carried arrogantly at *Thermopylae*'s masthead (soon 'borrowed' to be hoisted up *Taeping*'s mast).

China tea clippers were the culmination of an extraordinary period of evolution in sailing-ship design. At the end of the eighteenth century most ships, designed for cargo capacity or, like Nelson' ships of the line, to provide stable gun platforms, were ponderous sailers. The ships at the real cutting edge of design were fast, manoeuvrable schooners, brigs and brigantines, built to run rings around sluggish naval ships. These, the ships of choice for privateers, smugglers, Caribbean pirates and slave traders, were the grandparents of the sleek thoroughbreds anchored off Foochow. Great profits were to be made by fast, stealthy luggers smuggling brandy into England during the French wars, but the peak development occurred in American seaports around Chesapeake Bay. During the War of Independence, the threat that Royal Navy ships blockading American ports would strangle trade stimulated development of fast, agile blockade-runners known as Baltimore Clippers. Most were topsail schooners about 30m long, with fine lines, hulls rising in sharp 'deadrises' from their keels, slightly bluff convex bows, long bowsprits and two sharply raked masts. They could beat to windward like magic in light airs, allowing skilful, daring captains to evade waiting warships and earn huge rewards. One privateer captain, Thomas Boyle of the *Chasseur*, even carried the fight to the enemy, informing King George III that he had placed the whole of the British Isles under blockade!

The 1815 peace ended the heyday of privateers and smugglers in Europe and North America. Ship owners hurriedly had to scour the globe for new markets where fast ships and skilled crews could still gain handsome returns. The South China Sea was ideal. Trade with China, restricted for years, was monopolised by the large, heavily armed ships of the London East India Company sailing into Canton to purchase tea. It was difficult to find return goods of interest to the Chinese, but gradually the trade gap was filled by opium from the Company's Indian factories in Bihar, Patna and Benares. Chinese authorities reluctantly tolerated small-scale trade, but by the early nineteenth century it had expanded to undermine the complete Chinese society and economy with opium addiction. Increasingly restrictive new regulations imposed by Qing Dynasty officials did constrain the Company's trade, but triggered widespread smuggling along the poorly charted Chinese coast. By 1830, 30,000 cases of opium per year were arriving compared with 300 in 1729, and when the Company's monopoly ended in 1834, smuggling accelerated rapidly. The Qing Dynasty tried to impound the opium, but Britain enforced 'free trade' with a punitive modern warship fleet and the resulting Treaty of Nanjing opened most of the country to foreign traders in 1842.

Competition for the astronomical profits soon intensified, but the Chinese trade was not for the faint of heart. Ships had to thread their way through the narrow straits and passages of the Indonesian islands, and then dodge myriads of poorly charted islands, reefs and sandbanks in the shallow South China Sea. On outward voyages they had to beat against powerful winter north-easterly headwinds, and in summer had to fight back down the coast against south-easterly monsoons and violent typhoons, which could dismast and destroy the most seaworthy of ships. The route was infested by swift, heavily manned pirate junks ready to swoop on slow or becalmed vessels to relieve them of their valuable opium cargoes or their return freights of the silver they demanded as payment. Risks were high and the demands on ships and skilled seamanship intense; an ideal niche for fast privateer brigs and Baltimore Clippers with expert crews honed by years of smuggling and blockade running.

The need for speed and agility in the growing China trade spurred further innovation. For speed, hulls had to be as long and sharp as possible. In America John Griffiths achieved this with a radical, sharply raked concave bow. In Aberdeen Alexander Hall reached a similar result for a different reason. Before 1836 cargo capacity (registered tonnage) for payment of harbour dues was calculated as the hull length x breadth x depth, with depth assessed as ½ x breadth. This encouraged designers to evade dues by using very deep hulls. The 1836 New Measurement closed this loophole, requiring actual measurements of breadth x depth at three sections in the hull, while length was measured at mid-depth. Hall managed to reduce registered tonnage (and harbour dues) while maintaining cargo capacity by designing shallow hulls with narrow overhanging sterns and very long, narrow, overhanging, sharply raked bows (the 'Aberdeen bow'). The eventual result in both America and Britain was the characteristic tea clipper hull with its concave, 'hollow' bow and very sharp lines. For speed, clippers also had to be able to set vast areas of sail. They were all ship-rigged with square mainsails, topsails, topgallants and royals on three masts. They also set stunsails on most yards, an extraordinary array of staysails and jibs, and sometimes skysails and even moonsails above the royals. Such large areas of sail could be dangerous in sudden storms so very large crews also had to be carried so that sail could be simultaneously shortened on all three masts.

The Americans tested their ideas first in the China trade with Griffiths' 750t clipper *Rainbow,* launched in New York in 1845, which went from New York to Canton in ninety-two days and returned in eighty-eight. Her delighted captain, John Land, proclaimed her unbeatable, the fastest ship afloat. *Rainbow*'s career was very short; she foundered off Cape Horn in 1848, but she was followed by many fine ships, such as the magnificent 907t *Sea Witch,* built for the crack American skipper 'Bully' Waterman, a notorious driver of ships and men, who was reputed to padlock the sheets to prevent nervous crew shortening sail when he was below deck. *Sea Witch,* with her great gilded-dragon figurehead, ran from New York to Hong Kong in 105 days and from Canton back to New York in 81 days. She was one of the very fastest of the American clippers, matched only by the great clippers built in Boston by the brilliant Donald MacKay, until she was wrecked on the Cuban coast in 1856.

Attention in the United States was soon diverted by the 1848–49 Californian gold rush, which created a huge demand for fast passages to the west. Most American clippers were soon racing round Cape Horn to San Francisco before continuing across the Pacific, if they had been able to keep their crews from deserting to the gold fields. Meanwhile, British designers were beginning to respond to the American challenge. The 1849 repeal of the Navigation Act opened British ports to foreign ships. The first American clipper to reach the Thames, the 1,003t *Oriental,* caused a sensation when she ran from Hong Kong to the West India Docks in ninety-one days, and sold her tea cargo for £9,600, recouping three-quarters of her cost. British despondency increased when the schooner *America* whipped the pride of British yachts off the Isle of Wight in 1851 in what became the first America's Cup Race. The American Navigation Club rubbed salt in the wound by putting up £10,000 for a race between British and American ships carrying cargo from China to Britain, a challenge that was not taken up.

Alexander Hall developed splendid clippers in Aberdeen from his pioneer *Scottish Maid* launched in 1839, but they were too small to compete with the Americans for outright speed. The first British clipper big enough to seriously challenge the Americans was Hall's 1,000t *Cairngorm,* launched in 1852. By then British clippers had another advantage. American clippers were extremely fast, but, built lightly of softwoods, they deteriorated quickly under ceaseless driving by captains like Waterman. By the time *Sea Witch* was wrecked, she was already strained and waterlogged. British clippers, built of hardwoods, were much stronger and *Cairngorm*'s hull was also strengthened with iron deck beams. She was followed into the tea trade by some very fast clippers like the *Lord of the Isles* and Robert Steele's beautiful *Ariel* and *Sir Launcelot* built at Greenock. Public excitement grew rapidly and in 1856 when a £1 per ton premium was introduced for the first ship to reach London, the real tea races started. Designers worked tirelessly to gain the smallest edge by tweaking hull and rigging design, while the ships were polished and groomed like thoroughbred racehorses. Ship owners vied with one another to attract crack captains like John Keay of the *Ariel,* and semaphores were set up so that news of the arrival of ships in the Channel could be rushed to London. Excitement reached fever pitch with the extraordinary 1866 race when the *Ariel, Taeping* and *Serica,* which left Foochow on the same tide, arrived in the Thames on the same day, with *Fiery Cross* and *Taitsing* following two days later. Captain Keay shared the £100 prize and the traditional beaver top hat awarded to the winning captain with Captain McKinnon of *Taeping.*

This build-up set the scene for *Thermopylae*'s arrival in Foochow. An extreme composite clipper, she was the latest word in clipper design and a direct challenge from a new Aberdeen shipbuilder to Robert Steele's established supremacy. At 65.3m in length, she was bigger than Steele's yacht-like clippers and registered 991t compared with *Ariel*'s 853 and *Sir Launcelot*'s 847. She was a magnificent racer that many believe was the fastest sailing ship ever launched. Built of rock elm and teak over iron frames, with a pine deck and an extremely sharp hull, a long fine entry and with a 44.2m high mainmast, she set a vast cloud of sail, almost 2,000m^2. Sail on the new clippers was increased with very long yards; *Thermopylae*'s main yard was 24.4m long, and with stunsails set, sails stretched out over 36m. Such an array of sail required very careful handling and she was manned by a crack thirty-four-man crew. A splendid sea boat, she could run easily downwind in heavy seas at 13 knots, but her real edge was in light airs; she could reach 7 knots with so little wind that a man could walk round the deck with a lighted candle, and she 'went to windward like a witch'. She needed a captain who could trim her like a modern racing yacht and extract the last ounce of speed, and she had her match in Robert Kemball, a magician who knew the South China Sea like the back of his hand and could sail her to perfection in all conditions. *Ariel* was first down the Min River, but *Thermopylae,* leaving a day later, was ahead by Anjer in the Sunda Strait and reached the Thames in ninety-one days, eleven days ahead of *Ariel*. However, the year's bragging rights went to *Sir Launcelot* which arrived twelve days later, but only eighty-nine days out from Foochow.

While *Thermopylae* and Robert Steele's thoroughbreds were slugging it out up the Atlantic, a serious new challenger was being built for Jock Willis in Dumbarton, based on the lines of his famous ship *Tweed*. Willis, widely known as 'Old White Hat' for his elegant top hat, ordered *Cutty Sark* at a cost of £16,150 specifically to beat *Thermopylae*. Her dimensions were almost identical to those of *Thermopylae*; her hull was nearly 13cm longer but her lines were even sharper and she registered 27t less. She could also set more sail than any ship in the China fleet; she had 24m main yard, which stunsails on both sides stretched out to 48m. *Cutty Sark* was in China for the 1870 race, but she sailed from Shanghai more than a month before *Thermopylae* left Foochow and took four days longer to reach London. The racing was as keen as ever, but the kudos of carrying the first tea to London had disappeared. The Blue Funnel Line steamship *Agamemnon* from Liverpool brought tea from Foochow to London in 86 days in 1866 and the death knell of the tea races was sounded by the opening of the Suez Canal in 1869. Without the spur of premium prices, some clippers now waited until much later in the season to sail. In 1870 the fastest passages were all made by ships sailing in October, which could run down the China Sea with favourable north-easterly monsoon winds. For several years the clipper owners were able to maintain their premiums by claiming that tea transported in steamers didn't taste as good, but the end was in sight and soon even the best clippers failed to find a cargo at any price.

The only year in which *Thermopylae* and *Cutty Sark* raced head-to-head from China was in 1872. *Thermopylae* under Captain Kemball and *Cutty* Sark under Captain Moodie left Shanghai on the same tide on 17 June, trimmed to race by

carrying lighter loads of tea than usual. They played cat-and-mouse through a series of gales down the China Sea, first *Thermopylae* and then *Cutty Sark* leading. Both ships were being driven very hard, and suffered split sails. Each took twenty-eight days to the Sunda Strait, passing Anjer with *Thermopylae* narrowly in the lead, but they emerged into the heavy winds that *Cutty Sark* loved and she soon opened up a big lead in the Indian Ocean. However, during a heavy gale in mid-ocean, a huge sea carried away her rudder. She had two stowaways aboard, by strange fortune a blacksmith and a carpenter. *Cutty Sark* was hove to for six days with heavy seas washing the length of her deck while a jury rudder was fashioned from planks laboriously cut from a 21.5m spar. The blacksmith fashioned new iron fittings over a makeshift brazier on deck then the carpenter, tied to a rope and close to drowning, after several attempts managed to fit it in place, and *Cutty Sark* was back in the race though now some thirteen days behind. By then *Thermopylae* had rounded the Cape of Good Hope and was tearing up the Atlantic, (Map, see p. 62) but *Cutty Sark* clawed her way back, arriving in the Thames as the moral victor only seven days after the Aberdeen ship.

It was increasingly difficult to find paying cargoes from China and 1872 was the last real tea race, but *Thermopylae* and *Cutty Sark* continued their great rivalry for another twenty years in the Australian wool trade. *Thermopylae* won the first battle in 1873, reaching Melbourne in seventy-one days, four days faster than *Cutty Sark*, and she was fourteen days faster from Shanghai back to London. She generally had the best of it during the 1870s, but the Dumbarton ship came back strongly in the 1880s with the great Richard Woodget in command. Both made many great passages, with many daily runs of over 550km, and both often reached 16 to 17 knots. *Thermopylae* had the edge in light winds, but with a driver like Woodget, *Cutty Sark* was faster on the stormy run through the Roaring Forties to Australia:

A tremendous sea was running and needs must we carry on or be pooped … the ship took a green sea over the stern and it appeared as though there were just three sticks set in the ocean as it swept the length of the deck.

(*Cutty Sark* crewman quoted by Basil Lubbock, 1924)

In testimony to their Scottish builders, both *Thermopylae* and *Cutty Sark* lasted many years longer than their competitors. *Thermopylae* was sold and re-rigged as a barque in Canada in 1890, but she still made some very fast voyages carrying rice and timber across the Pacific. In 1895 she became the training ship *Pedro Nunes* for the Portuguese navy. Eventually time caught up with her, but she was saved from the indignity of rotting as an abandoned hulk; on 15 October 1907 she was towed out of the Tagus and sunk with full naval honours at sea. Her arch-rival *Cutty Sark* also spent time under the Portuguese flag as the *Ferreira* then the *Mario do Amparo*, and was dismasted off the Cape of Good Hope, before being sold back to Britain in 1922, and eventually ending up thirty years later in a permanent dry dock at Greenwich on the Thames as a museum ship. Almost completely destroyed by a major fire in 2007, she has been the subject of a controversial restoration, which unfortunately gives little idea of her grace and beauty in the heyday of her rivalry with the equally fast and graceful *Thermopylae.*

References

Campbell, G.F., 1974, *China Tea Clippers*, David McKay Co., Inc., New York.

Chapelle, H.I., 1958, *The Search for Speed Under Sail, 1700–1855*, Bonanza Books, New York.

Crosse, J., 1974, *Thermopylae versus Cutty Sark, the 1872 Official Logs*, The Mariner's Mirror, 60, 63–72.

Crosse, J., 1968, *Thermopylae and the Age of Clippers*, Historian Publishers, Vancouver.

Hume, C.L., and Armstrong, M.C., 1987, *The Cutty Sark and the Thermopylae Era of Sail*, Brown, Son & Ferguson, Glasgow.

Lubbock, B., 1921, *The Colonial Clippers*, James Brown and Son, Glasgow.

Lubbock, B., 1922, *The China Clippers*, James Brown and Son, Glasgow.

Lubbock, B., 1924, *The Log of the Cutty Sark*, James Brown and Son, Glasgow.

MacGregor, D., 1983, *The Tea Clippers: Their History and Development,1833–1875*, Conway Maritime Press, London.

Villiers, A., 1953, *The Cutty Sark: Last of a Glorious Era*, Hodder and Stoughton, London.

St Brendan and fellow *peregrini pro Christo* landing on an Atlantic island from their leather naomhóg.

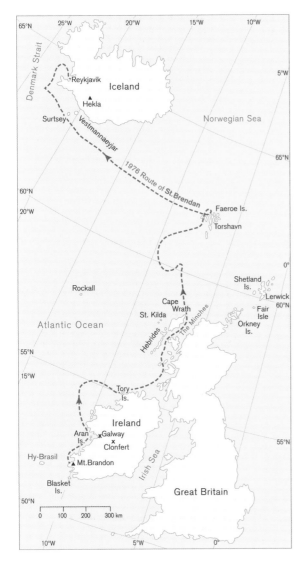

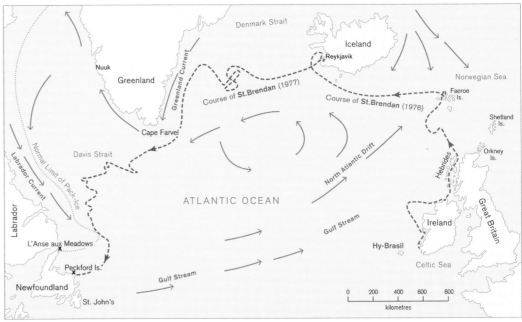

View from the sixth-century monastic settlement on Skellig Michael off the coast of Kerry, Ireland. (Rorke Bryan)

Longboat from HMS *Guerriére* rows towards USS *Constitution* to surrender, 19 August 1812.

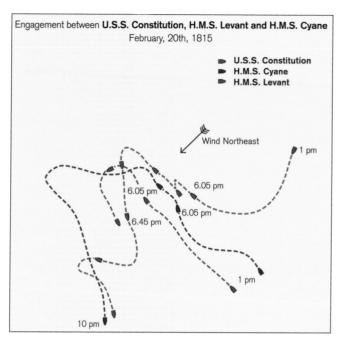

Engagement between U.S.S. Constitution, H.M.S. Levant and H.M.S. Cyane
February, 20th, 1815

■▶ U.S.S. Constitution
■▶ H.M.S. Cyane
■▶ H.M.S. Levant

Wind Northeast

1 pm
6.05 pm
6.05 pm
6.05 pm
6.45 pm
1 pm
10 pm

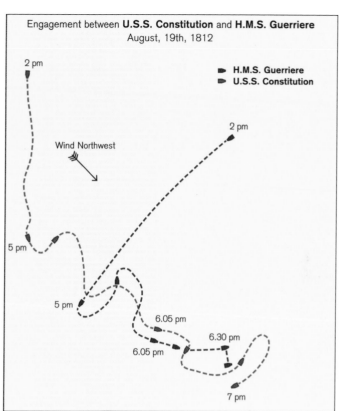

Engagement between U.S.S. Constitution and H.M.S. Guerriere
August, 19th, 1812

■▶ H.M.S. Guerriere
■▶ U.S.S. Constitution

2 pm
2 pm
Wind Northwest
5 pm
5 pm
6.05 pm
6.05 pm
6.30 pm
7 pm

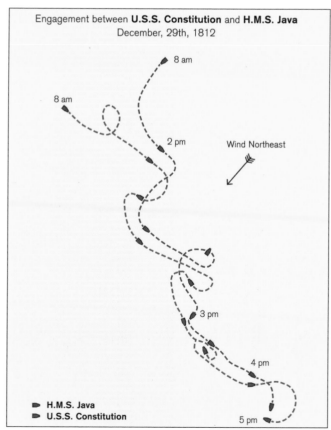

Engagement between U.S.S. Constitution and H.M.S. Java
December, 29th, 1812

8 am
8 am
2 pm
Wind Northeast
3 pm
4 pm
5 pm

■▶ H.M.S. Java
■▶ U.S.S. Constitution

Admiral Horatio Nelson's flagship, HMS *Elephant* attacking the Danish line at the Battle of Copenhagen, 2 April 1801.

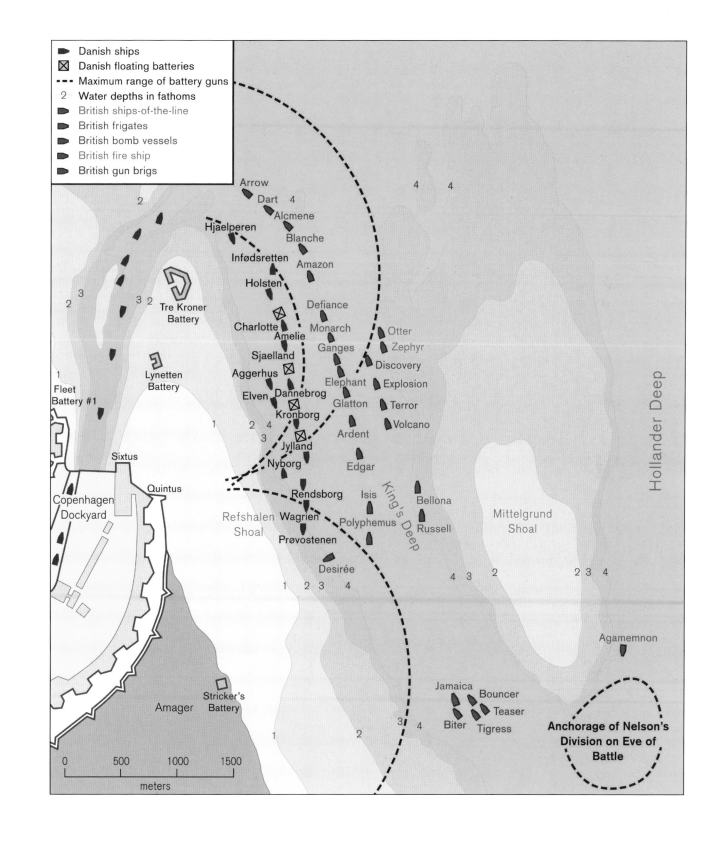

Danish ships

Danish floating batteries

Maximum range of battery guns

2 Water depths in fathoms

British ships-of-the-line

British frigates

British bomb vessels

British fire ship

British gun brigs

Arrow
Dart 4
Alcmene
Hjaelperen
Blanche
Infødsretten
Amazon
Holsten
Defiance
Tre Kroner
Battery
Charlotte
Monarch
Otter
Amelie
Ganges
Zephyr
Sjaelland
Discovery
Lynetten
Aggerhus
Elephant
Explosion
Battery
Elven Dannebrog
Glatton
Terror
1
Kronborg
Volcano
Fleet
Ardent
Battery #1
Jylland
Nyborg
Edgar
Sixtus
Rendsborg
Isis
Bellona
Quintus
Refshalen Wagrien
Polyphemus
Mittelgrund
Copenhagen
Shoal
Russell
Shoal
Dockyard
Prøvostenen

Desirée

4 3 2   2 3 4

1   2 3   4

Agamemnon

Stricker's
Battery
Jamaica
Bouncer
Amager
Teaser
Biter Tigress

Anchorage of Nelson's
Division on Eve of
Battle

3 4

1   2

Hollander Deep

King's Deep

0   500   1000   1500

meters

HMS *Beagle* passing through the Straits of Magellan en route to the Pacific, January 1834.

Charles Darwin sketching and taking notes about frigate birds, Galápagos Islands, September 1835.

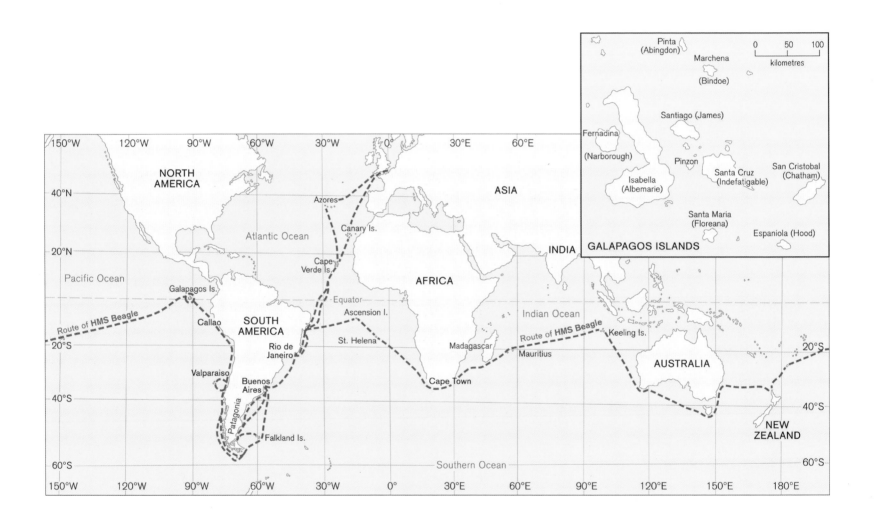

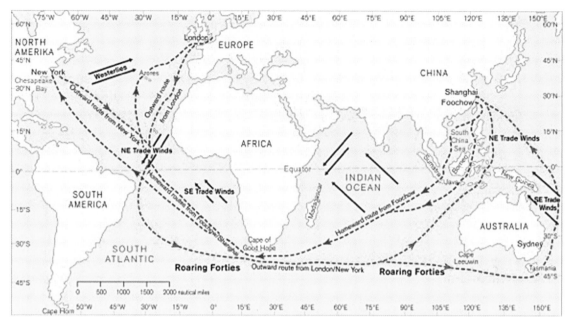

La Peruvian's steamer *Yavarí* departing for a voyage on Lake Titicaca, Peru.

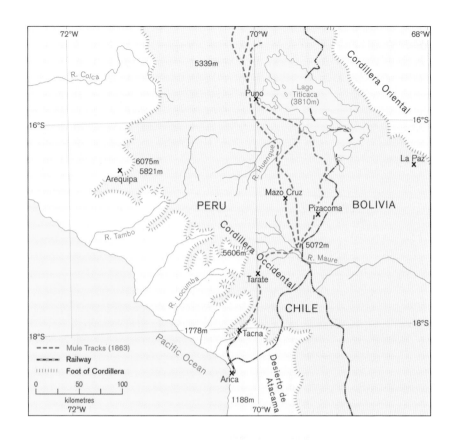

Bolsa constructed of totara reeds by the
Uros people on Lake Titicaca at Puno, Peru.
(Rorke Bryan)

8 YAVARÍ: THE FIRST STEAMER AT THE ROOF OF THE WORLD

Yavarí:	one of two pin-built gunboats built by James Watt & Co., Birmingham, for the Peruvian government in 1861.
Tonnage:	140t
Length:	30.5m
Beam:	5.18m
Draught:	3.18m
Engine:	two-cylinder non-condensing, 60hp with 15t tubular boiler
Rig:	two masts and bowsprit
Armament:	two 7.62cm naval Armstrong pivot guns
Construction:	built in 1,388 pieces of maximum weight 203.6kg then disassembled and shipped to Arica, Peru, in 1862.
Career:	1863–1869: transported by rail and mule teams to Puno at 3,811m above sea level on Lake Titicaca; 1870: launched on Lake Titicaca; 1871: maiden voyage serving communities around Lake Titicaca; 1876: hijacked by Enrique Bustamente, aground in Bolivia: 1890 turned over to La Peruvian; 1895: major refit – hull lengthened to 45.73m, engine replaced by 320hp, two-stroke Bolinder engine; 1874: retired from passenger service; 1987: purchased by Ms Larken, restored by The Yavarí Project; 2001: re-launched on Lake Titicaca. Moored at Puno, Peru.

There is nothing commonplace about Lake Titicaca – the Sacred Lake of the Incas – that straddles the border between Peru and Bolivia, 3,811m above sea level. It is not the highest lake in the world, but, with a surface area of 8,372km² and reaching 281m in depth, it is much larger and more important than the handful of lakes that are slightly higher. With the surrounding 6,000m-high snow-capped peaks reflected in its calm azure waters, it is one of the most beautiful lakes in the world and is the cultural heart of the Quechuan and Aymaran peoples who settled here more than 2,000 years ago. Vital for agriculture in the area, the lake offers easier travel than the steep peaks and deep canyons of the surrounding cordillera, but there are few boat-building materials to be found above the tree line on the 'altiplano', the surrounding high, dry plateau. The Uros people overcame this obstacle by building unique boats, or *bolsas*, out of the *totara* reeds, which grow at the shallow edges of the lake. Most bolsas were small, but some reached up to 8m in length and included woven reed sails. Two thousand years later, bolsas are still used by the Uros and they also use totara reeds to construct the large woven rafts on which many of them still live.

Bolsas were sufficient for earlier agrarian societies but quite inadequate to meet the nineteenth-century commercial and industrial aspirations of Peru and Bolivia as they freed themselves from Spanish colonial rule and struggled to build viable independent economies. This was a turbulent period as the emerging ex-colonies, riven by internal political rivalries, vied with one another for territory and resources while Spain vainly tried to cling onto its waning power. Peruvian independence was declared in 1821, but it would be another fifty-five years before Spain formally renounced its claims. In between, Peru had to fight to preserve its territory, first in 1836–39 in confederacy with Bolivia against Chile and Argentina, then against Spain in 1866 over ownership of the coastal Chincha Islands, and finally, again with Bolivia, against Chile in the War of the Pacific between 1879 and 1884. The main foci of hostilities were the valuable guano resources of the coastal islands and vital trading ports, but Peru's wealth also included rich metallic mineral deposits in the cordillera and many tropical forest products from beyond the mountains in the Amazon basin. These had to be vigilantly protected against neighbouring Ecuador, Brazil and Columbia, but it was incipient hostilities with Peru's erstwhile ally, Bolivia, that persuaded President Ramon Castilla to invest in gunboats for Lake Titicaca in 1860.

Establishing a naval force on a lake at an altitude of nearly 4,000m above sea level, separated from the sea by 6,000m-high mountains, posed serious challenges. No navigable rivers link Lake Titicaca with the Pacific Ocean so the gunboats would either have to be built at the lake or transported overland from the coast. In 1860 no shipbuilding capability existed at Lake Titicaca and transport of an intact vessel of any size along mule tracks across the rugged terrain of the cordillera was not possible. The only solution was a pre-fabricated vessel that could be carried across the mountains in pieces and assembled at the lake. By the mid-nineteenth century shipbuilding technology was evolving extremely rapidly; steam power was well established, propellers were replacing paddle wheels, presaging the end of commercial sailing ships, and riveted iron hulls were rapidly replacing wood as the industry standard. Large iron ships were still uncommon, but the huge *Great Eastern* designed by Isambard Kingdom Brunel had been launched on the Thames in 1854 and even the notoriously conservative Royal Navy had commissioned construction of the ironclad frigate HMS *Warrior* in response to the French ironclad *Gloire* launched at Toulon in 1859. Led by inspired engineers like Brunel, Britain led the world in shipbuilding technology and with a far-flung empire that stretched from the turbulent canyons of British Columbia to the shoals of the Murray-Darling river in Australia to administer, and had become expert in constructing 'knock-down' and 'pin-built' kit assembly ships. In 1861, Admiral Ignacio Mariategui was dispatched to Britain to order a 300t pin-built iron gunboat constructed in pieces weighing no more than 3½cwt (178.2 kg.), equal to 14 'arrobas', the maximum weight that could be carried on a mule.

Even British shipyards balked at building a 300t pin-built vessel in such small pieces, but eventually James Watt & Co. of Birmingham undertook to construct two 140t propeller-driven steam gunboats in four months for a cost of £8,000 each. These would deliver a speed of 9 knots using a half-ton of coal per hour, but would also be rigged for sail with two masts and a bowsprit. Each gunboat would be fitted with two pivot guns mounted fore and aft, the 7.62cm calibre naval version of the newly developed breech-loading Armstrong 12lb field gun with rifled wrought-iron barrels. The contract specified two-cylinder non-condensing 60hp engines with 16in diameter and 16in stroke, 15t tubular boilers of Low Moor and Staffordshire iron plate fitted with brass tubes, and a wrought-iron propeller shaft with a brass-lined stern tube, as well as numerous valves, gauges and fittings. The 1.85m-diameter brass propeller was designed to be hoisted to the deck through a tunnel when the vessel was under sail. The engines, boilers and running-gear pieces, of maximum 4cwt (203.6kg) weight, would be delivered to the Thames Ironworks and Shipbuilding Company in London, where HMS *Warrior* had been built, which was sub-contracted to build the 30.8m long, 5.24m wide and 3.08m deep wrought-iron

hull to draw 1.85m. Engines were assembled, tested and then knocked down in Birmingham, while the hull pieces, drilled for riveting, were bolted together in London. Everything was then disassembled into 2,766 pieces, 1,388 for the *Yavarí* and 1,378 for the *Yapurá*, which were carefully crated for stowage on the steamer *Mayola*.

The *Mayola* sailed from the Thames on 28 June 1862, accompanied by seven men led by William Partridge from the James Watt Foundry as 'engine erector' – the chief engineer who would supervise re-assembly at Puno on the shores of Lake Titicaca. Passing through the Straits of Magellan, *Mayola* arrived at the port of Arica, which then belonged to Peru, on 15 October. Progress then slowed dramatically; seven months elapsed before Lieutenant Amaro Tizon of the Peruvian Navy arrived to assess the weights to be transported; these were estimated at 463t, without the Armstrong guns and gunpowder, which would be stored in Arica until the ships were ready. Another three months passed before Comandante Dueñas arrived to organize transport from Arica to Puno. The first stage, in September 1863, was 59km by railway up from Arica to Tacna at 552m elevation in the interior desert. From Tacna everything had to be carried by mule; the pieces were unpacked and a contract signed with Colonel González Mugaburú whose chief muleteer, Lucas Quelopana, claimed he could complete the job with 100 mules in six months.

Tacna lies at the foot of the Cordillera Orientale, 300km from Puno. All trails climb from Tacna to Tarate at 2,000m elevation, and then drop to the Maure River, before rising to nearly 4,000m through Mazo Cruz or Pizacoma. (Map, see p. 64) In 1863, three main mule tracks crossed the mountains. All were rough and narrow, descending into deeply incised valleys and clambering up precipitous, unstable slopes across high passes, continually threatened by rock slides, earthquakes and avalanches. The high passes could be bitterly cold and altitude sickness posed another challenge for the muleteers. Within weeks the movement of loads slowed to a trickle as Quelopana griped about the heavy, awkward loads, some of which were abandoned by the River Maure. In Puno, the British group waited impatiently, and one engineer succumbed to tuberculosis in February 1864. By May, barely one-third of the loads had arrived, and not necessarily those needed for initial assembly. By July all transport halted despite impassioned correspondence between Dueñas and Quelopana, as the naval authorities were distracted by the Spanish occupation of the Chincha Islands. President Perez, Castilla's successor, reached an unpopular

Mules transporting bits of *Yavarí* over the Andes.

deal with Spain in return for four warships, provoking a revolution in southern Peru led by General Mariana Ignacio Prado. This dragged on well into 1865, as revolutionary troops occupied Puno.

In August 1865 Partridge wrote that only two-thirds of the parts had arrived and, unsurprisingly, he began to doubt if the ships would ever be completed. Meanwhile, Prado took over as president, but the unrest continued as he revived a tax on indigenous peoples, triggering a new rebellion around Lake Titicaca. This was eventually suppressed by Peruvian troops, but disruption of transport across the mountains continued. Most of the English workers left in 1866 when their contracts ended, but a new group arrived, and Partridge stayed on until 1868 when he was replaced by Richard Hopkin. Another major setback occurred later in the same year when Arica and its port were wiped out by a major earthquake and tsunami.

Despite the obstacles, enough bits had arrived by 1 January 1869 for the keel of the first gunboat, *Yavarí,* to be laid. By then the Armstrong guns stored at the coast had been seized; they would not be recovered, and henceforth the 'gunboats' became passenger and cargo steamers. Construction started but there were still major challenges as hull riveting began; the pieces available were a mixed bag of those for

Yavarí and *Yapurá* and did not all fit together. Some re-drilling was needed, and construction was complicated as all the original plans had disappeared along the way; inspired guesswork was necessary to fit the bits together. It did not help that barely a month after the keel was laid, three of the British team were drowned when *Yavarí*'s lifeboat capsized during a trip across the bay. Possibly this was intended to demonstrate the safety and stability of the iron lifeboats, in which case it was spectacularly unsuccessful, but Mardi Gras celebrations may also have been involved.

Yavarí's hull was finally finished and launched on Christmas Day 1870, more than nine years after the contract with the Watt Foundry was signed. *Yavarí* was still not complete; many materials for the decks and interior still had to be carried from Lima and another six months of fitting out were needed before her maiden voyage captained by Lieutenant Romulo Espinar in June 1871. The problem of fuel for her boilers was still unsolved so the first voyage took place under sail. Lake Titicaca lies above the tree line and though surrounding mountains are rich in minerals, there is no coal. The eventual solution turned out to be *taquia* – dried llama dung. It seemed a daunting task to collect enough dung, as one circumnavigation of Lake Titicaca would require 1,400 sacks, but fortunately llamas are tidy creatures who defecate communally in a concentrated area.

With *Yavarí*'s career at last under way, the construction team could concentrate on building *Yapurá*. Her keel was laid in April 1871 and she completed her maiden voyage just over two years later, on 7 August 1873 before joining *Yavari* to provide a regular service to communities around Lake Titicaca. The two ships travelled around the lake in opposite directions carrying passengers and cargo, primarily lumber and livestock. Up to twenty first-class passengers travelled in staterooms, while second-class passengers slept on benches in the saloon and forty more were carried on deck. The ships' commercial careers expanded rapidly after 1874 when the railway reached Puno, contributing significantly to development around the lake. However, there were still hiccups: in 1876 *Yavarí* was highjacked by Enrique Bustamente, on the run after a failed revolt against President Prado, and was run aground at the southern end of the lake, in Bolivia. When the War of the Pacific with Chile ended in 1884, Peru had lost Arica and Tacna and was virtually bankrupt. In 1890 the ships were turned over to the private Peruvian Corporation – La Peruvian – funded by British investors led by Irish businessman, Michael Grace.

By 1892 another steamer was needed to meet the growing demand and *Yavarí* and *Yapurá* were joined on Lake Titicaca by the 51.82m-long, 546t SS *Coya*, built by Denny's in Dumbarton, Scotland. Three years later *Yavarí* was significantly modified; at new machine shops in Puno, she was cut in half and a 15.4m section was added, increasing her length to 45.73m. In 1905 another new 'knock-down' steamer arrived, the 1809t, 67m-long SS *Inca*, built by Earle's of Hull. *Yavarí*'s old two-cylinder engine originally powered by *taquia* wasn't really up to the demands of the larger hull and in 1914 it was replaced by a large four-cylinder Bolinder Type E 320bhp two-stroke hot-bulb engine manufactured in Sweden. Hot-bulb engines, patented by Harold Ackroyd Stuart in England in 1890, are often referred to as semi-diesels as they can run on similar fuels, but fuel is injected into the cylinders at low pressure and is ignited by hot-bulb vaporisers, which on the Bolinder Type E are heated by blowlamps. Hot-bulb engines typically run at 100–300rpm, and are less efficient than true diesels, but are much simpler, require little attention and, unlike older diesels, start easily in cold weather.

Reinvigorated by the more powerful Bolinder engine, *Yavarí* continued regular service to the communities around Lake Titicaca for decades. Business continued to grow and in 1930 La Peruvian purchased another knock-down steamer from Earles of Hull, the much larger 79.25m-long, 2,200t SS *Ollanta*, with accommodation for eighty-six passengers. In 1957 a major change occurred when *Yavarí* was reconfigured as an oil tanker; four large tanks were installed in her hold, providing capacity for approximately 220 barrels of oil. By the early 1970s faster diesel and ro-ro ferries began to appear on Lake Titicaca and in 1974, after a century of service, *Yavarí* and *Yapurá* were retired. A year later La Peruvian was nationalised and management passed to the state railway company, ENAFER. *Yapurá* was returned to the Peruvian navy in 1976 as a hospital ship and coastguard, and was renamed BAP *Puno* (ABH-306), but *Yavarí* was left to decay quietly beside a wharf in Puno.

In the ordinary run of events, this would probably have ended the *Yavarí* story, but good luck and a determined fairy godmother changed the narrative. In 1983, while exploring the possibility that a steamship on Lake Titicaca had been built by her great-grandfather, Sir Alfred Yarrow, Meriel Larken saw *Yavarí* in Puno. In her book *The Ship, The Lady and the Lake*, Ms Larken evocatively describes her first visit to the rather derelict old ship, and the visual impact of the immense Bolinder engine. She was unable to confirm that *Yavarí* was a Yarrow ship, but this visit kindled the idea of purchasing and restoring her to running order. An epic of persistent detective work followed as she tracked down information and surviving pieces of the old ship in Peru and Britain.

Back in Britain, Ms Larken doggedly ferreted out information about the gunboats, progressively eliminating Yarrow and then Lairds in Liverpool as possible builders. It was several years before the original contract was traced to the Watts Foundry in Birmingham. In the process she came to realise the importance of *Yavarí* as an example of a critically important transitional period in shipbuilding technology. In Peru agreement was eventually secured from the Ministry of the Navy to purchase *Yavarí* for her scrap value of US$5,000, but bureaucratic wheels turned slowly and despite support from President Garcia, she had to leave Peru before the purchase was finalised. In Britain Ms Larken continued to search for information about the gunboats and also started to raise funds and support. She could not then forecast that what became 'The Yavari Project' would stretch out for more than twenty years. The full story of the twists and turns on the way to final success, handicapped by political and financial instability and the activities of the 'Sendero Luminoso' in Peru, is a cautionary tale for anyone contemplating restoration of an old ship.

After a professional survey of *Yavarí*, the tortuous barriers preventing a foreigner purchasing a Peruvian naval vessel were overcome in 1987 by establishing La Asociación Yavarí dominated by Peruvian members, while The Yavarí Project was also registered as a charitable trust in Britain. *Yavarí* was pretty dilapidated and many pieces had drifted off, but her iron hull, preserved in Lake Titicaca's cold waters, was in remarkably good condition. Plans were drawn up for modifications so that *Yavarí* could meet modern marine safety standards, and a crew was assembled in Puno to start the restoration, while Swedish support was received to rebuild the massive Bolinder engine. By 2001 *Yavarí* was back in the water, tied up to a new pontoon and opened as a museum for visitors. Later the same year, red-funnelled and resplendent in La Peruvian's black, white and green livery, *Yavarí* made a new maiden voyage around Taquile Island, 32km from Puno.

Over the next few years, the ship's cabins were refurbished to provide bed and breakfast tourist accommodation and generate sustainable revenue. While promising, this does not yet cover the costs of crew and maintenance and the dream of running cruises on the lake is not yet fulfilled. Meanwhile complete responsibility has been turned over from The Yavari Project in Britain to La Asociación Yavarí in Peru. *Yavari*'s future is still not completely secure, but she has been more fortunate that several of La Peruvian's fleet. SS *Coya* was left high and dry by floods in 1984 but, saved at the last minute from the scrapyard, is now a restaurant, while SS *Inca* was scrapped in 1994. *Yapurá* (as BAP *Puno*) is still afloat as a hospital ship, and SS *Ollanta* has been refurbished for tourist cruises by Peru Rail. Even if not yet fully active, *Yavarí* survives as an impressive testament to the ingenuity of Victorian shipbuilding and the determination needed to set her afloat at 3,811m above sea level on Lake Titicaca. In 2012 her unique place in maritime history was recognised by a Heritage Award from the Institute of Mechanical Engineers in Britain.

Acknowledgement: The story of the Yavarí was laboriously pieced together by Meriel Larken; this account depends almost entirely on her fascinating book.

References

Larken, M., 2012, *The Ship, the Lady and the Lake,* Bene Factum Publishing Ltd, London.

Ruffell, W.L., *The RBL Armstrong 12-pr Field Gun,* www.riv.co.nz/hist/arm/arm5.htm

9 YUKON STERNWHEELERS AND THE LURE OF GOLD

SS *Klondike*:	representative of many sternwheel riverboats on Yukon River, Canada, during the 1898 Klondike Gold Rush, launched in 1929 for the British Yukon Navigation Co.
Tonnage:	1,362t
Length:	64m
Beam:	12.5m
Draught:	0.6m light, 1m loaded
Engines:	two 525hp jet-condenser steam engines
Cargo Capacity:	270t
Crew:	23
Career:	1929–36 carried freight and passengers on the Yukon River. 1936: ran aground and destroyed at junction with the Teslin River; engines salvaged and used for near identical riverboat launched in 1937. 1937–50: carried freight and passengers on the Yukon. 1950: laid up and brought ashore at Whitehorse, Yukon Territory. 1955: donated to Parks Canada. 1966: restored and designated a National Historic Site at Whitehorse, Canada.

It started in California with the 'Forty Niners' who rushed to pan placer gold from the creeks feeding the Sacramento River. When these gold deposits dwindled, hardened veteran prospectors packed their mules and moved into the Sierra Nevada, then north to the Fraser and the Cariboo in British Columbia, chasing each rumour of a strike and searching for the 'colour' in the river sands that could make them rich. A handful became fabulously wealthy, but most remained poor, lucky to eke out a grubstake to allow them to press on into the mountainous wilderness of the north-west. None of the goldfields were easy to reach, but as western lands were staked, fenced and tamed, their options narrowed to the frozen wastelands of Alaska and the Yukon. The remote north-west corner of the North American continent was truly inaccessible, hidden beyond a hazardous sea journey, or some of the highest mountains in the world. The only 'easy' way in is along the Yukon River; one of the longest rivers on the continent, it actually rises only 24km from the Pacific, but flows first north across the Arctic Circle, then west, meandering its way over 3,000km, to finally reach the Bering Sea through a massive delta, a labyrinth of shifting sandbanks and shallow twisting channels, many only a few centimetres deep.

The Yukon valley has been inhabited by aboriginal communities for thousands of years, but for a long time the only 'outsiders' who found their way in were fur trappers from Russia or the Hudson's Bay Company. Several trading posts were built along the river and rumours about gold started to trickle out, but the fur traders did not welcome anyone who might disturb the fur industry. This changed in 1867 when Canadian Confederation ended the Company's 200-year monopoly of Rupert's Land, and Russia sold Alaska to the United States. The first hard-bitten prospectors soon began to work their way into the valley. Most threaded their way through the delta in canoes, but a few crossed the mountains from the mighty Mackenzie River, then down the Porcupine River to the Yukon, or clawed their way over the coastal mountains through the daunting Chilkoot Pass. Travel was always difficult; in winter prospectors struggled through snow-laden, bitterly cold birch and spruce forests, and during the short summer had to slog through mosquito-ridden swamps. Though easier, the river journey was more dangerous. Melting snow and ice from the mountains feed the Yukon; in spring giant ice floes race down river like battering rams, building massive ice jams, which collapse violently without warning. In summer powerful currents rush through many rapids and canyons, while in between the river spreads and splits into a maze of shallow channels between ever-shifting gravel and sand bars.

Navigating up the Yukon from the delta was always a challenge though the canoes of the fur traders and prospectors could at least be portaged around the worst obstacles. However, progress was slow as the handful of tough prospectors worked their way up the Yukon, probing its small tributaries. Panning gravel bars for gold is tedious, back-breaking work with meagre rewards. There were occasional patches of 'colour' to tease, but most barely provided grubstakes and excited no interest in the outside world. Occasionally, enough gold turned up for clusters of prospectors to gather in small communities. Most consisted of little more than a few tents, log shacks and bars, but with the remaining fur trading posts, they created a demand for more substantial river transport than the prospectors' canoes. The only larger type of vessel that could operate safely on the treacherous, dangerous Yukon was the sternwheeler riverboat, which reached its final flowering there.

Paddlewheel riverboats appeared in North America almost as soon as steam power was invented. Travel along rivers was a bit easier than through roadless forests, and riverboats had been vital to commerce for decades, but they were slow and inefficient. Downstream journeys were relatively easy, but it was brutally slow and laborious to drag clumsy, heavy keel boats and flat boats upstream, particularly against the powerful, fast-flowing currents of the giant Mississippi River. The first steam engines, though crude, still gave a great boost to the American heartlands, but alone they were not sufficient. Many rivers, though fast flowing, were narrow and very shallow with shifting mudbanks, sandbars and rapids and required specially designed vessels.

It took time for satisfactory riverboats to emerge; Fulton's steamboat *New Orleans* was launched on the Allegheny River in 1811 and in the next nine years at least sixty steamboats appeared on western rivers, but it wasn't until the following decade that really effective steamboats emerged. To navigate most rivers, hulls had to be narrow and very shallow; all were shallow draughted and some could operate in only 15cm deep water. To provide reasonable cargo capacity, they had to be very long, typically some 35–40m long and 9–10m wide. Hulls varied considerably, but most had two or three decks, were built of oak and white pine, and usually lacked keels. Typically the hull contained watertight compartments (snag rooms), with the engines, firebox, boilers, cargo space and sometimes a kitchen on the main deck. Passenger cabins, dining rooms and observation lounges were on the upper decks. Mostly these were fairly basic, but some sternwheelers like the *Susie, Sarah* and *Hannah* of the Alaska Commercial Co. were luxuriously furnished with mahogany-panelled dining rooms and two and three-berth staterooms for first-class passengers. Officers' quarters were above the top cabin deck, behind the pilot house, which was sometimes mounted even higher up to provide a good view of sandbanks, snags, rocks and floating logs. To minimise the power needed to drive boats upstream against powerful currents, the long, shallow, narrow hulls were very lightly built

and, with powerful paddle wheels mounted right at the stern, were very prone to 'hogging'. This was countered by iron 'hog chains' or 'hog rods' attached to massive central 'kingposts' adjusted by turnbuckles. These were attached to the keelson and rose well above the top deck, sometimes backed up by smaller 'hog posts'.

Despite light, shallow hulls, a lot of power was needed to drive riverboats upstream. There were usually two big single-cylinder high-pressure engines, with massive riveted iron plate boilers, up to 1.2m diameter and 4.9–9.2m length. Boilers were mounted on firebricks as far forward as possible to provide good draft for the firebox from very tall funnels which rose at least 13.7m, and sometimes as much as 24.3m. There were gauge cocks for boiler water level and several safety valves, but explosions and fires were not uncommon. Though powerful, the engines were inefficient and very fuel-hungry, but along most rivers trees or driftwood piles were abundant. Most seagoing paddle steamers were sidewheelers, but these were too liable to damage in narrow channels lined by overhanging trees, so stern-mounted paddle wheels soon became standard. Unlike sidewheelers, sternwheelers did not require wharves for loading and unloading; the snub-nosed bow could be simply run up against the bank while the big stern paddle wheel remained in deeper water.

Sternwheeler design, honed by years of operation on western rivers, was fairly standardised by the time the Yukon valley started to open up. The first to enter the Yukon River was a small boat belonging to the Alaska Commercial Co., appropriately named the *Yukon*, which left the Bering Sea port of St Michael on 4 July 1869. She drew only 38cm but was soon aground on a sandbank in the delta, and it took five years to complete her mission to establish a trading post at Fort Reliance, 2,560km upstream. This was near a flat gravel patch where a small river called the Thron-duick by local Tagish people entered the Yukon. This was known by the Tagish as the finest salmon river in the valley, but the veteran prospectors aboard dismissed the site as a useless 'moose pasture'. The *Yukon* lasted another six years before she was trapped by winter ice and became the first casualty of the fearsome spring break up. Two more small sternwheelers soon followed, the *St Michael* and the *New Racket*, but it was 1889 before the first large, powerful steamer appeared on the Yukon. The 38m-long *Arctic*, launched for the Alaska Commercial Co. in 1889, transformed transport on the river and in 1895 covered 22,400km in two months. By then quite a few prospectors had reached the valley; in 1886, 200 prospectors struggled over the dreaded Chilkoot Pass and panned $100,000 worth of gold dust in one year at Sixty Mile where the Stewart River enters the Yukon. A string of small communities like Fort Yukon, Circle City, Fort Reliance and Forty Mile were scattered after modest strikes along the river, but none was rich enough to catch the attention of the outside world like the Californian or Cariboo strikes. This would soon change.

A veteran prospector, Robert Henderson, scouting round the Thron-duick in spring of 1896 found good 'colour' in gravels along one tributary, which he called Gold Bottom Creek. Heading downstream for supplies from Fort Reliance he bumped into George Carmack on the 'moose pasture' where the Thron-duick joined the Yukon. Carmack,

the son of a Californian 'Forty Niner', was fishing for salmon with his Tagish wife Kate and her brothers, Skookum Jim and Tagish Charley. In response to Henderson's excitement, Carmack and his partners set off to Gold Bottom Creek and then wandered along other small tributaries. While resting beside Rabbit Creek on 16 August, one member of the party who was washing out a pan found a large gold nugget in the creek. One quick rinse with the pan produced 7 grams of gold, forty times the threshold amount for a good prospect. The partners immediately staked four claims, each running 152.4m along the creek (later called Bonanza Creek), then Carmack set off for Forty Mile to register the claims. The first reaction was general disbelief, but overnight Forty Mile

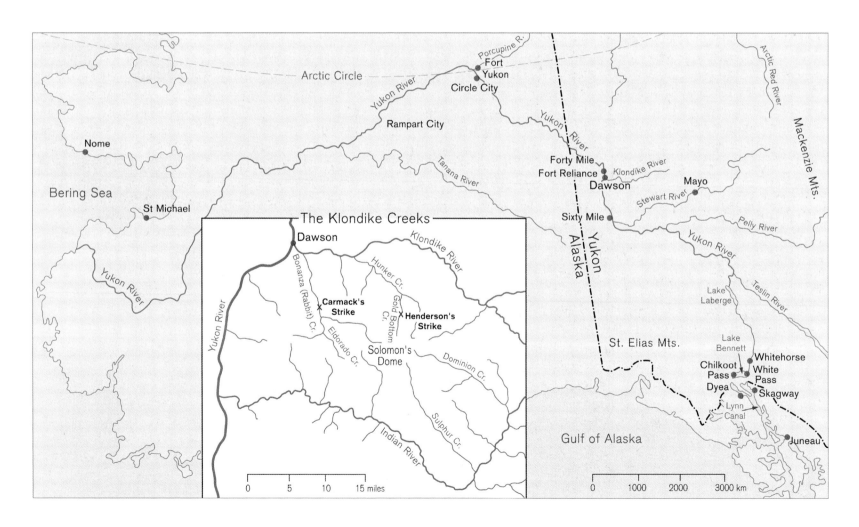

emptied as men slipped away quickly towards the Thron-duick (almost immediately changed to the more easily pronounced Klondike). Word spread like wildfire along the Yukon, camp after camp emptied and, as prospectors converged on the Klondike, the next great gold rush was born. Spurred by the reports, the *Arctic* made a dangerously late trip to Dawson, becoming the first riverboat to reach the site on 17 October 1896. She was frozen in and the following spring was wrecked at Circle City during the spring break-up.

Most of the prospectors headed directly for the creeks and by September many were completely staked, including the fabled Eldorado, which joined Bonanza just below Carmack's claim. This would eventually produce more than $30 million in gold. Claim No.16 alone yielded $1.53 million (in 1896 dollars). One of the shrewdest of the veterans didn't go to the creeks at all; Joe Ladue staked 80ha on the 'moose pasture' to set up the first saloon in what would become Dawson City. By the following summer there were ten saloons and Ladue's building lots were selling for $16,233 a metre. By the time Eldorado and Bonanza were staked, it was too late for the word to filter down the frozen Yukon to the outside world, but the following summer Dawson's population rose to 600. That summer eighty-five

Gold diggers in the Klondike.

miners left Dawson on the *Alice* and *Portus B. Weare*, with their decks reinforced to bear the weight of $1.5 million of gold carried in anything that could hold gold dust. The gold reached San Francisco on the steamer *Excelsior* on 16 July and Seattle on the *Portland* the next day. Gold mania was instantaneous and within days the Klondike was a household word around the world.

It is impossible to exaggerate the impact of the Klondike on a generation ground down by economic depression, starved of opportunities to escape tedious class-ridden societies and stifled by Victorian rectitude. Soon every prospector in North America was on his way north, but so were clerks, farm hands, teachers, remittance men, card sharps and prostitutes. In days every ship that could be found set off, including the veteran old paddlewheeler *Eliza Anderson*, built in 1858, and reclaimed from its role as gambling hall on a mudbank near Seattle. The *Anderson* lacked even a compass and managed to ram another ship on the way, then ran out of coal in a storm before being abandoned by frustrated passengers on Kodiak Island, Alaska. Every ship was overloaded and could have had ten passengers for each one carried. Some headed for the Bering Sea, but this 6,400km route to Dawson was long, slow and expensive; most headed up the narrow Lynn Canal to Skagway or Dyea at the foot of the towering coastal mountains to dump tons of sacks, boxes and barrels on the tidal mudflats. By the time most got there winter had arrived. Everything had to be carried over the terrible rocky, icy 35° steep Chilkoot Pass, overhung by glaciers and swept by avalanches (one killed sixty men in a day), or over the lower but much longer White Pass, infamous as 'Dead Horse Pass', where hundreds of overworked pack horses expired. Each prospector had to pack a ton of supplies to the summit, necessitating at least twenty return trips, followed by as many descents on the far side to the shores of Lake Bennett. At the lake the surrounding forests were hewn down to build an armada of crude boats while prospectors waited for the lake to thaw and allow them to reach the Yukon headwaters, 56km away. Amongst the armada were several full-sized sternwheelers, equipped with machinery laboriously carried over the Chilkoot Pass.

Some prospectors got through in 1897, but most of the 7,000 boats built had to wait until the 1898 spring. Once they reached the Yukon, it was still nearly 900km to Dawson City, with the most dangerous part still to come; 150km below Lake Bennett, the Yukon thunders through the vertical-sided Miles Canyon, a 30m-wide slot carved through lava, for 5km, then jumps the Squaw and Whitehorse Rapids in a series of 3m high standing waves. Even in a big sternwheeler Miles Canyon was daunting; the *Bellingham* made it through in June 1897, but *Joseph Clossett* hit the canyon wall which crushed her thin planks like an eggshell, and sank in the rapids. Meanwhile, the ragtag armada clustered at the entry as prospectors mustered up courage to face the canyon. At least thirty-five drowned trying to run the rapids, and many chose the tedious but less hazardous portage around the canyon and rapids instead.

Miles Canyon and the Rapids were not the only obstacles. In 1897 the flow of the Yukon was unusually low. Sternwheelers on the lower Yukon had great difficulty amongst the shallow shoals and sandbanks and several were stranded near Circle City for the winter, while some miners trying to leave Dawson had to turn back. In the interval many sternwheelers were being built in Seattle, Victoria, St Michael and at Lake Bennett. Shallow-draughted sternwheelers with almost no freeboard were not suitable for the 4,000km sea journey across the Gulf of Alaska and the Bering Sea to the mouth of the Yukon, but some like the *Monarch*, built in Seattle, did it anyway. By summer, 1898, a tidal wave of prospectors had reached Dawson, the Alaska Commercial Co. was operating sixty sternwheelers and dozens were often tied up along the riverfront at the same time. Many new riverboats, like John Irving's *Yukoner* with a great gold eagle decorating its pilot house, were luxurious palaces that equalled anything along the Mississippi. The vacant 'moose pasture' of 1896 had become a rowdy, wide open, freewheeling city of 40,000 people, thrown up over the patchy permafrost, complete with numerous bars, dance halls, gambling halls and brothels, where the universal currency was gold dust. Dawson was peopled by colourful characters: 'Arizona Charlie' Meadows, 'Lucky Swede' Anderson, 'Big Alex' MacDonald, 'Swiftwater' Bill Gates and the 'soiled doves', Snakehips Lulu and Diamond-tooth Gertie, but the fabled Dan McGrew and Sam McGee, were creations of Robert Service's imagination. There were also several churches, a hospital, seventy doctors, electricity, phones, movie and live theatres and a Northwest Mounted Police post, but there was no sewage treatment and the 'street'" became sloughs of malodorous mud as the river flooded and the permafrost melted.

Many predicted a thriving future for Dawson but its tide had already crested. By the time most prospectors arrived, the best claims around the Klondike had been staked and the hills stripped of their trees for

Sternwheel riverboat *Clifford Sefton* negotiating Miles Canyon on the Yukon River, Canada, 24 July 1900, en route downriver to the Klondike goldfields. (H.C. Barclay photo, Yukon Archives, Pinneo Collection, University of Alaska Archives)

cabins, sluice boxes and firewood. Many late arrivals never even went out to the diggings. The pioneers had taken some $300 million in gold out of the Klondike, but of the thousands who set out for Dawson, fewer than 4,000 became rich. When word of a new gold strike at Nome on the Bering Sea reached Dawson in the spring of 1899, many prospectors set out for the coast. By 1902, Dawson's population had declined to 2000, and it continued to drop, to 500 in the 1960s. There was still gold in the Klondike gravels, but most of it was beyond the reach of men with shovels and simple sluice boxes. As the veterans moved out, mining companies with the capital to set up hydraulic mining and build big dredges to churn up the deep gravels moved in.

As the furor of the gold rush subsided a railway over the White Pass to Whitehorse was completed in 1900, shortening the journey from Dawson to Vancouver to eight days, but there was still work for sternwheelers along the Yukon River. Over the next sixty years another $300 million in gold would leave the valley. However, the wear and tear of navigation on the difficult river and the ever-present hazards of snags, shoals and ice dams took their toll and the fleet shrank swiftly.

Some were driven ashore by ice floes, or drawn up on the river banks to rot slowly; at least one, the *Columbian*, expired dramatically in 1906 when a passenger accidentally fired a shot into its cargo of gunpowder. The shores of the river and the harbour at St Michael were soon littered with rotting hulks, but there was still enough business to support a handful of boats and every so often a new sternwheeler was launched. British Yukon Navigation launched the 1,079t *Casca* in 1911, the *Nasutlin* in 1912 and a new *Yukon* in 1913, and for a while operated eleven boats on the river, but the decline continued and only two new boats were launched after 1920, the 39.6m-long *Reno* in 1922 and the biggest of all the sternwheelers to work on the Yukon, the 64m-long, 1,362t *Klondike* launched in 1929. Her career was curtailed in 1936 when the captain missed a turn and ran her aground at the junction with the Teslin. Her high-pressure engines were salvaged and were installed with the boiler from Irving's *Yukoner* in a new identical *Klondike II* launched the same year along with a new 30.5m-long, 1,300t *Casca*.

The fate of the Yukon sternwheelers was finally sealed by the construction of the Alaska Highway during the Second World War. This not only provided faster, more efficient transport for ore but also introduced low road bridges across the river, which obstructed the riverboats. The *Klondike* was refurbished as a tourist boat with a dance floor and lounge in 1953, but this was not successful and in 1955 she was hauled out to join the *Casca* and *Whitehorse*, built in 1901, on the banks of the river just below Miles Canyon and the rapids.

The *Reno*, launched in 1922, had a longer career carrying silver, lead and zinc ore down river from Mayo to Stewart, but in 1960 was the last sternwheeler to navigate the river before being hauled ashore at Dawson City. *Casca* and *Whitehorse* were destroyed by fire in 1973, but *Klondike,* which had been moved to another site, and *Reno* survive as museums and the last of the more than 200 sternwheelers that opened up the Yukon.

References

Berton, P., 1972, *Klondike, 1896–1899: The Last Great Gold Rush,* McClelland and Stewart, Toronto.

Downs, A., 1972, *Paddlewheels on the Frontier: The Story of British Columbia and Yukon Sternwheel Steamers,* Gray's Publishing, Sidney, B.C.

Downs, A., 1995, *British Columbia – Yukon: Sternwheel Days,* Heritage House Publishing, Surrey, B.C.

Ferrell, N.W., 2008, *White Water Skippers of the North: The Barringtons,* Hancock House Publishers, Surrey, B.C.

Kane, A.L., 2004, *The Western River Steamboat,* Texas A & M University Press, College Station.

Newall, G.R. (ed.), 1966, *The H.W. McCurdy Marine History of the Northwest,* The Superior Publishing Co., Seattle.

Yardley, J., 1996, *Yukon Riverboat Days,* Hancock House Publishers, Surrey, B.C.

10 THE *CHARLES W. MORGAN*: LAST OF THE SAILING WHALERS

Charles W. Morgan:	three-masted sailing whaling barque double topsail, 351.3-ton (Old Tons) whaling barque built by Jethro Hillman, New Bedford, for C.W. Morgan consortium in 1841.
Tonnage:	313.8 (New Tons)
Length:	34m
Beam:	8.38m
Draught:	5.33m
Sail:	1,200m^2 on three masts; ship-rigged when launched but later re-rigged as a barque; 1881: twin topsails
Crew:	33
Career:	1841–45: maiden voyage under Captain Norton to Azores, Galapagos, Kodiak, fifty-nine whales worth $56,068. 1845–1913: thirty-seven voyages to whaling grounds in most parts of the world. 1863: most valuable voyage under Capt. T. Landers with cargo worth more than $165,405. 1913: laid up. 1916: sold to Capt. B. Cleveland; appeared in several films and whaled in the West Indies. 1921: whaling career ended. 1924: refitted and open to public in Dartmouth. 1941: moved to Mystic, Connecticut, as core of Mystic Seaport. 1967: listed as a National Historic Landmark. 2010–13 restored and re-launched. 2014: sailed on tour to New Bedford and New England ports.

She is no ocean greyhound like *Thermopylae* but a solid, chunky, immensely strong maritime equivalent of a heavyweight prizefighter, ready to go fifteen rounds with Moby Dick. The *Charles W. Morgan* was built to withstand the worst of ice and storms during voyages to the ends of the Earth, which could last five years. Launched at New Bedford, Massachusetts, in 1841, she was one of hundreds of whale ships crowding the great North Atlantic whaling ports like Dundee, Aberdeen, Sandefjord, Nantucket, New Bedford and Boston. The American whaling fleet alone numbered 735 vessels, with a total capacity of 235,000t. Whalers were robust ships, built to last, and some had extraordinarily long careers like *Truelove*, built as a privateer in Philadelphia in 1764 and captured by British forces during the

War of Independence, which served as a whaler out of Hull for over 100 years before retiring to the Norwegian timber trade. However, none has outlasted the *Charles W. Morgan*, still in seagoing condition 175 years after she was launched.

Whaling probably started amongst Basques along the Bay of Biscay during the twelfth century, carried out in small, swift rowing and sailing boats, which set out when watchmen in towers or 'vigias' alerted whalers that whale spouts had been seen. The industry got a major boost when the Catholic church, believing that 'hot' red-blooded meat encouraged licentious lust, forbade its consumption on holy days. As there were 166 holy days per year, this greatly increased the demand for authorised 'cold' meats, those species usually immersed in water such as fish, whales and beaver. The initial demand was for whale meat, but thriving markets soon developed for bone for furniture and fences, blubber to make oil for paint, soap, ship caulking and high-quality lighting, whale tongue delicacies for the aristocracy, and long flexible strips of baleen used for skirt hoops, corsets, whips and decoration for knights' helmets. Whaling was so profitable that whalers from France, Norway and the Azores soon joined in. It was initially confined to coastal waters, but as merchants became aware of the huge potential profits, they started to send large ships off on long-distance whaling voyages. In 1610 the English Muscovy Company was started in an attempt to monopolise the rich whaling off Spitzbergen in the Barents Sea, but the Dutch Noordsche Compagne challenged vigorously and after several armed encounters, they agreed to share the spoils.

Whaling persisted to the twentieth century in the eastern Arctic, but its greatest expansion was in North America and in the western Arctic, exploiting the abundant whales where the Gulf Stream meets the cold, nutrient-rich Labrador Current. By the mid-sixteenth century Basque fishermen set up the Terranova whaling station in Newfoundland, and in the following century east-coast settlers in America began to use beached, 'drift' whales as aboriginal populations had done for years. These putrefied rapidly, so nobody wanted the meat, but baleen and oil from blubber soon became jealously guarded commodities. Demand for whale oil grew quickly, swiftly exceeding the supply of beached whales, so enterprising boatmen started to hunt whales in coastal waters. Although shore-based in protected shallow bays, this was dangerous work. Harpooners had to get dangerously close to the whale's massive tail flukes, which whalemen referred to as 'the hand of God'; these could easily capsize or reduce the whaleboat to splinters, leaving the crew to flounder in frigid waters. If immediate destruction was avoided, the crew's troubles were only starting; an enraged whale would either 'sound', threatening to drag the whaleboat down unless the harpoon line was quickly cut, or would take off quickly for the horizon, towing the whaleboat behind like a child's bathtub toy in the infamous, adrenalin-pumping 'Nantucket sleigh ride'. This death dash could last for hours while the whaleboat was towed far out to sea, sometimes to disappear forever. Even if it survived, the huge carcass had to be laboriously towed back to the beaches where the blubber was stripped off (flensed) and rendered to oil over fires.

Starting on Long Island, shore-based whaling quickly spread to Nantucket Island. Nantucket had few resources but in the late seventeenth century organised communal whaling with teams of watchmen in tall towers to watch for whales around the clock. They were so successful that Nantucket became dominant in American whaling for the next fifty years. Shore-based whaling in Nantucket reached its peak in 1726 when eighty-eight whales were killed, but the industry was changing as ship owners began to fit out ships for much longer deep-sea voyages. The incentive was the great profit to be made from sperm whales, the largest toothed species. Found only in deep waters, these were particularly valuable because of the curious spermaceti, which fill a large cavity or 'case' in the whale's head, as well as the excellent, clean-burning oil from their blubber. Spermaceti were highly valued for medicines and candles, which burned with a particularly bright light. Even more valuable were waxy ambergris concretions found in whales' stomachs. Renowned for incense, aphrodisiacs, confectionery and for perfumes, these were literally worth more than their weight in gold.

Sperm whale hunting is very ancient in some cultures, but it's not certain when it started in North America. The brigantine *Happy Return* of New York may have hunted sperm whales as early as 1688, but it is usually attributed to Christopher Hussey of Nantucket in 1712. It led to expansion of the Nantucket whaling fleet to sixty ships by the

mid-eighteenth century, yielding half the annual North American oil production at over 11,000 barrels, mostly from sperm whales. The first deep sea voyages to Bermuda, the Bahamas or the West Indies with small schooners, brigs or brigantines of less than 100t were quite short, but soon voyages extended throughout the Atlantic, Pacific, Indian and Southern Oceans, and bigger vessels were needed. These had to be self-contained, with room for supplies for very long voyages, wood for carpenters to make barrels and replace whaleboats destroyed by wounded whales, and space to store barrels of whale oil and stacks of whalebone. As whales were now being captured far from land, arrangements to render down blubber on board also had to be made.

Nantucket whalers pioneered long deep-sea whaling voyages (on 'ye deep') and whaling soon dominated the complete community: wharves were extended and carpenters, caulkers, rope makers and blacksmiths flooded into the island. Successful ship owners and captains became very wealthy 'captains of industry' and few men were regarded as good marriage prospects until they had completed at least one whaling voyage. The entire community was linked to whaling and even the architecture was affected; houses were built with 'widows' walks' for wives to scan the horizon anxiously for the return of their husbands. Voyages might last three–five years so women became unusually prominent in business and community affairs. The island community triggered rapid expansion of the complete North American whaling industry, and export of whale oil (mainly to Britain) became vitally important to the New England economy. This halted abruptly with the War of Independence in 1775.

By 1775, Nantucket had 150 whale ships, nearly half the American fleet, but the war wreaked havoc with the industry. Britain stopped American ships whaling in the rich Labrador and Newfoundland waters, and closed the vital British market to American oil, while Royal Navy ships seized whale ships and pressed their crews into naval service. All New England ports suffered, but none more than Nantucket, almost totally dependent on whaling, and viewed with grave suspicion by both sides. The islanders tried to stay neutral and one prominent ship owner, Francis Rotch, attempted to relocate his eleven whale ships first to the Falkland Islands, then to Britain and finally to France. When the war ended Nantucket had only thirty ships and further setbacks occurred during the 'quasi-war' with France and the 1812–15 war with Britain. However, Nantucket gradually recovered as a key producer throughout the nineteenth-century heyday of American whaling.

However, as voyages became longer and ships larger, it lost ground to New Bedford, founded specifically as a whaling centre, which had better access to timber and agricultural supplies. Even more important, it had a deep harbour, while Nantucket's harbour had a major sandbar, which restricted it to ships of 2–3.3m draught. Heavy-laden ships could anchor off and unload into lighters, but this greatly increased costs and was easily disrupted by bad weather. In 1842 a solution was found by using 'camels', pontoons which could be flooded with seawater, then pumped out to form a dry dock to float laden ships across the bar, but by then New Bedford was the industry leader.

Many types of vessels were employed in the early whaling industry but, by the early nineteenth century, specialised whale ships had evolved, which didn't change greatly by the time *Charles W. Morgan* was launched in 1841. Rather simple, extremely strong ships, they could be built quickly and cheaply in small shipyards by artisan shipwrights, usually without plans. Varying in size from around 150 to 500t, they could be 'cut off by the yard' to different dimensions, depending on the owners' wealth. They were most commonly owned by consortia whose members had specific shares in profits; the *Charles W. Morgan* was built for an eight-man consortium led by Charles Morgan with an 8/16 share. Built at the Hillman yard in New Bedford, she was a typical contemporary whale ship, three-masted and slab-sided with a bluff bow and transom stern registering 351 tons (builder's old measure) and 32.8m long. She was flush decked with the captain, officers, boat steerers, cook and carpenter housed around a mess aft and twenty-four crew in the lower deck fo'c'sle, above a large hold for storage of oil barrels. She was modified several times during her career, and a stern 'hurricane house' was added to protect the helmsman, house the toilet and galley and for storage. She had a deck capstan and a windlass just aft of the foremast, later moved to the foredeck. She was ship-rigged when launched, with undivided topsails, topgallants and royals on each mast, stu'nsails on the fore and main masts, a spanker on the mizzen and four headsails, but was later re-rigged as a barque.

The *Morgan* had massive wooden davits along each side for the four 8m-long clinker-built whaleboats, carried three to port and one to starboard. Whaleboat designs varied, but most were lightly built, double-ended boats that could be rapidly manoeuvred when close to whales. The *Morgan*'s whaleboats were manned by three starboard oarsmen and two to port, with 4.9–5.5m oars, and a 7.1m steering oar in the stern. A mast and sail could be rigged, and lots of specialised

The whaler *Charles W. Morgan*.

equipment was carried: harpoons, killing lances, tubs for hundreds of fathoms of manila line, a water barrel to douse the harpoon line as it ran around a loggerhead, and knives and axes to cut it in emergencies. Several additional boats were carried on raised skids between the fore and mainmasts, together with spare timbers for the carpenter to build replacement boats. A section of the starboard bulwark could be removed for a cutting stage, padded iron rings above double topgallant cross trees were manned by lookouts, and there was a 1.5m-high brick 'tryworks' for rendering blubber.

Whale carcasses towed back to the ship were chained below the cutting stage, heads separated, and cutting tackles with huge 51cm-diameter blocks attached to the masthead were hooked into 'blankets' of blubber, flensed by men with large 'spades'. These were hoisted up, then lowered through a hatch to the blubber room, and cut into 'horse pieces', which were rendered down in the tryworks'

Whalers in a longboat.

whaling grounds, from Desolation Island in the Southern Ocean to the Bering Sea in the north. During her career she earned more than $1.4 million but her best voyage was the sixth, from October to May 1863, under Captain Thomas Landers, when she brought back a cargo worth $165,405.

As a lucky ship, it was relatively easy to attract crews, but even on successful ships, whaling was a hard, dangerous, dirty life where few crew made much money. Instead of wages, after the owners took their share (usually around 70 per cent) each crew member received a share of the voyage's profits depending on their status. The captain typically got 1/8 to 1/16, the officers and the harpooner, 1/20 to 1/40, but a novice crew member might get only 1/200. This was usually greatly reduced by deduction of expenses, such as loans advanced in port, purchase of clothes from the captain's 'slop chest', fees paid in port to recruiting 'crimps', or the cost of stocking a medicine chest. Even after a successful voyage, a crew member often received only a few hundred dollars after three–four years of brutally hard, dangerous work; there were even cases of crew returning with a net income of 10 cents, or in debt to the owners or the captain.

Life on a deep-sea whaler was seriously hazardous; even successful, well-run ships like the *Morgan* suffered frequent accidents and deaths. Most routine tasks were dangerous, even on board ship, but the most common accidents were to whaleboat crews, capsized or crushed by a whale's flukes, or bitten to splinters by enraged sperm whales.

cauldrons. Flensed carcasses were cut loose, and spermaceti was scooped out of the separated head in buckets. Meanwhile, the tryworks was kept 'boiling' day and night until the blubber was rendered. This could take three days, with relays of men in stinking, oil-soaked clothes feeding the cauldrons, while clouds of smoke and flames and the stench of blubber conjured up a vision of Hades. The iron-reinforced brick tryworks had two stove pipes and blubber was rendered in two 136-gallon iron cauldrons before being transferred to cooling tanks. Beneath the tryworks was a water tank (the 'goose pen') to protect the deck, but even so, ships sometimes caught fire. The tryworks was broken down when whaling was finished to allow the deck to dry out and avoid rot.

The *Morgan* sailed from New Bedford on 6 September 1841 for Fayal in the Azores to complete her thirty-five-man crew, then south to Cape Horn. It took her almost a month more to fight her way westward into the Pacific and capture her first whale. After this she headed north to Callao, Peru, for provisions, then cruised between Peru and the Galápagos where they had good luck finding sperm whales, taking six in one day in November. There were then several long dry spells before they headed back to New Bedford, reached on 1 January 1845. The voyage proved very successful, returning with oil and bone worth $56,068, $4,068 more than the *Morgan* cost to build. She was known as a lucky ship throughout her career; almost all her voyages were 'greasy' (oil-rich) and, unlike many later whalers, she never came back 'clean'. Over eighty years she explored all the world's

The jaw of the whale shot up one side of the boat and his head on the other, not three feet from me I pushed off with my feet from the boat, and heard the crash of splinters and the cries of the men as I swam clear. I looked round just in time to see the whale as he spouted after cutting off the head of the boat … when we had gone 40 or 50 feet we looked back and saw the whale snapping at everything he could get hold of and whenever he felt anything against his flukes he knocked it sky high.

(Benjamin Doane, deck hand on the whaler *Athol* of St John, New Brunswick, off Callao, 1846, cited in Doane, 1987)

Very few voyages passed without at least one death. Whaleboats were sometimes towed out of sight by harpooned whales, never to be seen again. On the *Morgan*'s sixteenth voyage in 1890 a boat was towed out of contact by a 100-barrel bull whale; short of provisions, the men cut the whale loose and set sail for Saghalin Island in Russia, 160km distant. Initially imprisoned as suspected spies, they eventually made their way to Hong Kong, and finally back to San Francisco, only one month after the *Morgan* had reported them missing. There were also cases of enraged sperm whales ramming and sinking whale ships, as in Herman Melville's apocryphal tale of Moby Dick's attack on Captain Ahab's *Pequod*. The most notorious incident was when the 240t *Essex* from Nantucket was attacked and sunk by a sperm whale in the Pacific in November 1820. After sailing for three months and many thousands of kilometres, some of the crew survived only by resorting to cannibalism.

The danger, dreadful working conditions, strict discipline, miserable wages and long, uncertain duration of voyages often led to discontent, desertions and even mutiny. This depended to some extent on the quality of the crew – the waterfront crimps in most whaling ports were seldom picky about the men recruited; many were short of money,

Sometimes the whale wins.

often drunk and sometimes on the run from the law. It also depended greatly on the captain and the mates; as a generally successful, well-run ship, the *Morgan* fared better than many but was not immune to trouble. Her thirtieth voyage, from San Francisco in November 1904, with a new captain quickly ran into problems. Several men were placed in irons for refusing orders and four seamen deserted off Norfolk Island but were soon recaptured and placed in irons until they agreed to obey orders. The carpenter, Adolf Koch, then attacked the mate with an axe and was jailed in Tahiti. Morale was usually better on 'hen frigates' where the captain was accompanied by his wife and sometimes children. This first such voyage on the *Morgan* was in 1864 when Lydia Landers joined her husband in San Francisco. A special gimballed bed was installed in the after cabin, which turned into a nursery when a son was born at Guam. Despite her calming influence, the remaining two years of the voyage were fractious, including trouble with the mate, desertion and a steward who arrived at Barbados in irons. The most successful of the '*Morgan*'s wives' was Charlotte Church, who acted as assistant navigator and log keeper on two voyages between 1908 and 1913.

The *Morgan*'s career started just before the peak year for the American industry in 1846, when 736 whale ships totalled 233,000t capacity. After the Civil War, decline started as petroleum products began to replace whale oil for lighting and lubrication. The *Morgan* still fared better than many during the industry's long twilight, and was regularly maintained and modified. Re-rigged as a barque in 1867, she was periodically re-rigged, re-caulked and re-coppered and, in 1881, a twin topsail was fitted, many yards were replaced and some new wire stays fitted, and her windlass was moved to the foredeck. As whaling progressively shifted to the northern Pacific and the Bering Sea, she was moved to San Francisco in 1886 where she was refastened and strengthened for work in ice and a boiler and steam deck engine were added. Frequent, careful maintenance enabled the *Morgan* to continue to make money, but as the price for whale oil continued to decline even short voyages in the Pacific ceased to be profitable. In 1904, she returned to New Bedford and made several successful voyages, but by 1913 the price of sperm oil had dropped 24 per cent to 43 cents per gallon, and she was laid up. She deteriorated quickly and the Wing brothers, her owners for fifty-three years, sold her to Captain Benjamin Cleveland for $6,000 in 1916. Restoration was expensive, but some costs were covered when she was hired for a film called 'Miss

Petticoats'. She then made several reasonably successful whaling trips to the West Indies and South America, but by 1921, when the oil price dropped to 30 cents per gallon, her whaling career ended.

However, the *Morgan*'s luck continued to hold and her career was prolonged by roles in two more films, *Down to the Sea in Ships*, and *Java Head*. She was then laid up again, but a marine artist, Harry Nyland, launched an initiative to turn her into a museum ship. In 1924 she was nearly destroyed as a burning steamer drifted up against her. Rescued by Edward Green, grandson of her 1849–59 owner, she was refitted and opened to the public in Dartmouth. A hurricane in 1938 nearly finished her, but she was saved again by Carl Cutler, curator of Mystic Seaport, Connecticut, and towed to Mystic in 1941. After the war momentum grew to restore her to heyday condition and she was fortunate to be in a traditional shipyard familiar with old wooden ships. Meticulously restored, she became an icon for Mystic Seaport and in 1967, was listed as a National Historic Landmark. In 2013 after further restoration, she was re-launched in Mystic, ready again to feel the waves as a living museum, 172 years after she first slid into New Bedford harbour.

References

Ashley, C., 1926, *The Yankee Whaler,* Houghton Mifflin Company, Boston and New York.

Doane, B., 1987, *Following the Sea: A Young Sailor's Account of the Seafaring Life in the Mid-1800s,* Nimbus Publishing Ltd, and The Nova Scotia Museum, Halifax.

Dolin, E.J., 2007, *Leviathan: The History of Whaling in America,* W.W. Norton, New York.

Hoare, P., 2010, *The Whale: In Search of the Giants of the Sea,* Harper Collins, New York.

Leavitt, J.F., 1973, *The Charles W. Morgan,* Mystic Seaport, The Marine Historical Association, Inc., Mystic, Connecticut.

Shapiro, I., and Stackpole, E., 1959, *The Story of Yankee Whaling,* Harper and Row, New York.

Stackpole, E., 1967, *The Charles W. Morgan: The Last Wooden Whaleship,* Meredith Press, New York.

Stackpole, E., 1972, *Whales and Destiny: The Rivalry Between America, France and Britain for Control of the Southern Whale Fishery, 1785–1821,* University of Massachusetts Press, Amherst.

11 NIMROD: A VETERAN SEALER'S MOMENT IN THE SUN

Nimrod:	three-masted auxiliary sealing barquentine (originally schooner) built by Alexander Stephens, Dundee, for Job Bros., St John's, Newfoundland, in 1866.
Tonnage:	458t
Length:	41.5m
Beam:	9.3m
Draught:	5.34m
Hull:	elm on oak frames with greenheart ice sheath
Engine:	60hp, coal-fired boiler
Speed:	6 knots
Career:	1867: maiden voyage in Newfoundland seal hunt, 2,600 seal. 1907: purchased by Shackleton for British Antarctic Expedition; refitted at Blackwall as barquentine. 1908: towed by SS *Koonya* from New Zealand to ice front; established Cape Royds base on Ross Island, Antarctica. 1909: three-man sledge party reached South Magnetic Pole. 1909: Shackleton with three others sledged to 155km from the South Pole. After expedition, *Nimrod* became merchant ship. January 1919: wrecked in gale on Barber Sands off Norfolk coast with loss of eleven lives.

She looked impossibly small, scruffy, old and unprepossessing, tied up in the Victoria Dock in London. *Nimrod* was dirty and stank of seal oil and old blubber, her masts were rotten, her cap rail was scarred with grooves from hawsers and her black hull, scored by years of hard use, seemed to show every one of the fifty-one years she had spent in annual wars with pack ice off the unforgiving Newfoundland coast. By 1907 she was obsolete and in bad condition. Her engine and boiler, though replaced in 1889, weren't very powerful and she was too small to compete with larger, newer wooden barques and steel-hulled steamers. *Nimrod* wasn't Ernest Shackleton's first choice to carry his British Antarctic Expedition to the Ross Sea. He would have liked to buy the new 598t barque *Bjørn*, which Belgian Antarctic explorer, de Gerlache, found for him in Sandefjord harbour, Norway, but the £11,000 asking price was too much for the meagre funds he had

collected. *Nimrod* had many deficiencies, but at £5,000 she was less than half the price of *Bjørn*. In the end, she far exceeded expectations and shared the glory won by pioneering the way to the South Pole, but there were many difficult kilometres to sail before she returned to cheering crowds along the Thames.

By the 1890s nationalism was rampant all over Europe, and Antarctica provided a tailor-made showcase for national prowess. Beneath a veneer of international scientific cooperation, competition was intense and within a decade expeditions from Belgium, Sweden, France, Germany and Britain all wintered in Antarctica. However, the continent was still almost unknown and the prize for the first expedition to reach the South Pole was still elusive. Even within Britain rivalry was fierce; the first expedition to winter on the continent was nominally British though led by Norwegian Carsten Borchgrevink, but the real rivalry started during the 1901–03 *Discovery* expedition led by Captain Scott. The brainchild of Sir Clements Markham, formerly of the Royal Navy, this was modelled on naval Arctic expeditions over the previous fifty years, and most personnel came from the Royal Navy. Amongst the exceptions was an experienced young Irish Merchant Navy officer, Ernest Shackleton, who had served with distinction with the Shire and Union Castle Lines.

Shackleton and Scott were both young professional sailors, but their personalities differed dramatically. Shackleton, gregarious and charismatic, was a born romantic adventurer, bored and stifled by the Victorian society in which the somewhat shy, studious and introspective Scott seemed at home. They respected each other's professional competence, but their personalities clashed in the closely confined isolation of the Antarctic winter. Expedition members had virtually no experience of polar regions, were woefully unprepared for the realities of Antarctic travel and encountered many difficulties with dog-team sledge travel in the exceptionally cold, harsh, dangerous conditions. These were gradually overcome, but the expedition wasn't very successful, the major tangible result being a long sledge journey by Scott, Shackleton and Wilson across the vast Ross Ice Shelf to reach 82°16'S. With a vitamin C-deficient diet, all three nearly died of scurvy and they had no idea how to drive sledge dogs. These suffered badly on a dried stockfish diet and eventually failed, leaving the weakening men to man-haul their sledge hundreds of kilometres back to base. Stress and isolation exacerbated the personality clash and back at base, Scott ordered Shackleton home aboard the relief ship *Morning* on dubious medical grounds.

Humiliated and furious, Shackleton loyally supported the expedition back in England, but was determined to return to Antarctica with his own expedition to strike for the South Pole. Funding and organising an expedition was not helped by stubborn opposition from the influential Sir Clements Markham who saw a threat to his own ambitions for Scott. One of Shackleton's biggest obstacles was to find a ship. Already there was controversy about the best ship design for polar expeditions, typified by Colin Archer's revolutionary *Fram* built for Fridtjof Nansen and the more orthodox, but very expensive, *Discovery*. However, a specially built ship was out of question; the only options were old, wooden whaling or sealing vessels used in Norway for Arctic whaling or in the Newfoundland seal hunt. Even these were quite expensive and only the help of the wealthy industrialist, William Beardmore, allowed Shackleton to buy *Nimrod,* one of the oldest vessels still afloat.

Nimrod was built in 1866 at the famous Dundee shipyard of Alexander Stephen on the lines of the ships that had dominated polar whaling and sealing for over 100 years. She was a small ship, only 41.5m long and 458t gross, but she had a massively strong elm hull over oak frames and an outer greenheart sheath to withstand the grinding of ice floes. Most of Stephen's ice ships were barques, but *Nimrod* was a schooner, probably for easier handling in the treacherous Newfoundland coastal waters. She was built without plans, but her construction was closely supervised by the experienced Captain Edward White of Bonavista, Newfoundland, who became her first master.

Nimrod joined the 1867 seal hunt at St John's and her crew of 140 brought back 2,600 seal for the season. The sealing industry was in transition; *Nimrod* was one of the earliest ships with auxiliary engines, introduced in 1863. The engines were usually less than 75hp, not sufficient for ice breaking, but they made manoeuvring in small pack ice leads easier, allowing ships to reach the seal herds. The full benefit of engines was only realised with more powerful engines and larger ships towards the end of the century, but even then, the seal hunt remained a hazardous, precarious occupation, though one of immense social importance. Most ships belonged to prosperous St John's owners like Job Brothers or Bowring Brothers, but the very large crews came mostly from small outports scattered around the Newfoundland coast. Outport life was harsh, difficult and dangerous, depending almost entirely on cod fishing. Cod were abundant, but most profits wound up with merchants in St John's who controlled the availability of essential supplies. For many outport families, the extra income earned in the seal hunt was often the only margin against real hardship and poverty.

Harp and hood seals gather to whelp on coastal pack ice in late February and sealing fleets would start to leave ports like St John's and Harbour Grace in early March. Most ships were about the same size as *Nimrod* but some carried 200–300 sealers. Life on board was miserable, crowded into the hold on makeshift bunks, with a single toilet suspended over the bow and dreadful food. The bunks would be removed later to make space for seal pelts, forcing the sealers to share bunks or sleep on the blubbery seal pelts. Once they reached the ice front, sealers would fan out across shifting floes to kill and skin as many seals as possible, then drag the pelts back to be iced down in the holds. Normally men would return to their ships each night, but the early spring weather is notoriously treacherous and it was not uncommon for sealers to be caught out on the ice and freeze or starve to death in gales lasting for days, or to drown in the frigid water as unstable floes split apart or were driven far out to sea. In 1898, twenty-four sealers from the *Greenland* were lost during a single night. Even on board they were not safe as pressure ice driven before hurricane winds could squeeze, hole and sink vessels, and large floes rafting onto their decks could cause them to capsize.

Rewards for the precarious, dangerous work were paltry and uncertain; in some years successful 'high liner' captains like Abram Kean would bring back over 30,000 seal (*Florizel* caught 48,918 in 1912), but many ships would come back with only a few hundred. *Nimrod* was never particularly successful; her record in fifty-four voyages was 19,087 in 1871 and her worst was in 1897 when she returned with no seal at all. Her average was 6,147 per voyage. Sealers received no fixed salary, but shared one-third of the voyage's profits, so income depended on the number of seal taken and variations in the price obtained (the value of seal taken on a Sunday was often subtracted).

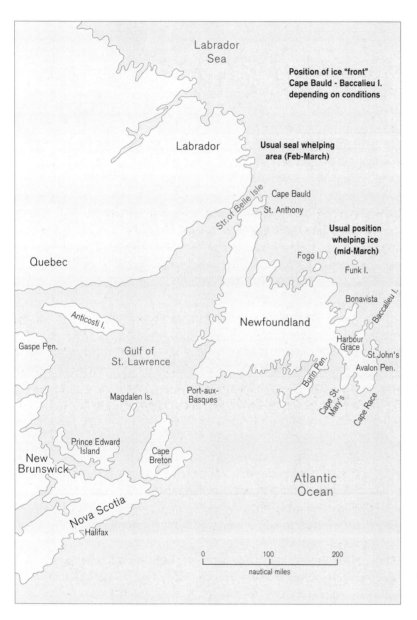

Labrador
Sea

Position of ice "front"
Cape Bauld - Baccalieu I.
depending on conditions

Labrador

Usual seal whelping
area (Feb-March)

Str. of Belle Isle

Cape Bauld
St. Anthony

Usual position
whelping ice
(mid-March)

Fogo I.

Funk I.

Quebec

Bonavista

Baccalieu I.

Anticosti I.

Newfoundland

Gaspe Pen.

Harbour
Grace

Gulf of
St. Lawrence

St. John's

Burin Pen.

Avalon Pen.

Magdalen Is.

Port-aux-
Basques

Cape St. Mary's

Cape Race

Prince Edward
Island

Cape
Breton

New
Brunswick

Atlantic
Ocean

Nova Scotia

Halifax

0   100   200

nautical miles

Nimrod didn't return to St John's until 7 May 1907, and it was mid-June before Shackleton got a chance to examine her in London. He was not impressed:

> She was much dilapidated and smelt strongly of seal-oil, and an inspection in dock showed that she required caulking and her masts would have to be renewed. She was rigged only as a schooner and her masts were decayed, and I wanted to be able to sail her in the event of the engine breaking down or the supply of coal running short.
>
> (Shackleton, 1910)

There was a great deal of work to be done by the Green shipyard at Blackwall, but miraculously by 7 August she was ready. Completely stripped and cleansed, with new crew accommodation in the fo'c'sle and officers' cabins in a deckhouse on the poop, below which a hold was converted to accommodate the wintering party scientists, the infamous 11.26m^2 'Oyster Alley'. *Nimrod* was re-rigged as a barquentine, her rotten masts were replaced and a more efficient 60hp engine was installed, claimed to give a speed of 6 knots.

On the voyage south, *Nimrod* stopped at the Cape Verde Islands and Cape Town for coal and she didn't reach Lyttelton, New Zealand, until the end of November. Here they had to pack in all the stores, building materials and equipment needed for the next eighteen months. There wasn't nearly enough room; the crate with the 15hp Arrol-Johnson car donated by Beardmore had to be carried on deck, along with ten Manchurian ponies, while nine huskies were tethered on the bridge, but the biggest problem was coal. Steaming at full speed, *Nimrod* would use 6t per day. There wasn't space in the holds for enough coal to steam to the Ross Sea and back and leave heating coal for the wintering party. The crisis showed Shackleton at his persuasive best; he managed to get the chairman of the Union Steamship Company to lend the steamer *Koonya* to tow *Nimrod* as far as the ice, and to share the complete cost with the New Zealand government.

On New Year's Day 1908, bedecked with flags, with only a metre of freeboard and her Plimsoll line well below the waterline, *Nimrod* steamed out of Lyttelton harbour to pick up *Koonya's* tow. The first attempt didn't work well as *Koonya's* windlass pulled out, but they were soon underway joined by 350m of steel hawser and chain. Initial progress was good, over 150km per day, but then they were hit by a full Southern Ocean gale with mountainous seas. Conditions on

This could be as high as $5/seal, but usually ranged $1.50–2.00 so a sealer might receive $20 for a voyage lasting five or six weeks. On her last voyage in 1907, *Nimrod* caught only 2,500 seal, which provided a mere $10.50 per man.

Nimrod were awful with 'water teeming over both port and starboard bulwarks and spray reaching halfway up the mast', and the ship rolling through more than 100°. Time after time solid green water swept her from stem to stern, smashing in bulwarks, washing away a deck house and a whaleboat, and injuring one of the ponies, which eventually had to be put down. Geologist Raymond Priestley described Oyster Alley, without ventilation and crammed with fifteen wet scientists, as 'more my idea of Hell than anything I have ever imagined'. But *Koonya* ploughed on, setting a staysail to keep her course, and despite the storm, reached the ice edge south of the Antarctic Circle having towed *Nimrod* 2,111km in two weeks. At 66°31'S, she slipped her tow and headed for New Zealand as *Nimrod* steamed through light pack ice to reach the Ross Ice Barrier on 23 January.

The Ross Ice Barrier is one of the most awe-inspiring sights on earth: an 800km long, 60m high wall of ice barring the way towards the South Pole. It is dangerously unstable as massive blocks of ice fall away into the sea, giving birth to the icebergs of the Ross Sea. For weeks Shackleton searched for a safe base site, but with summer running out, *Nimrod* eventually had to retreat to Ross Island, near the old *Discovery* hut, to set up a new base at Cape Royds, under the shadow of the 3,795m-high active volcano, Mt Erebus. (Map, see p. 100) The anchorage was far from secure in recurrent gales sweeping down off the ice shelf and to Shackleton's chagrin, Captain England refused to bring *Nimrod* close to shore to ease the unloading. All 180t of stores and equipment, including the 2t car, had to be manhandled onto whaleboats, rowed through the ice floes and dragged up the rocky shore, while some of the men started immediately to build a hut. It was a massive, back-breaking task, even for the tough volunteers, interrupted by violent blizzards that pushed *Nimrod* far out to sea, but in two weeks they finished and *Nimrod* could escape to the north from the already-forming sea ice. Shackleton and England had one last battle about coal; nervous about returning to New Zealand with little ballast, England would only leave 18t to see the shore party through the Antarctic winter. Shackleton lost the argument but didn't forget; the following season England was replaced by the stalwart Frederick Evans, erstwhile master of *Koonya*.

The fifteen men of the wintering party, abruptly cut off from the outside world, had much to do before they were pinned down by constant winter blizzards as temperatures dropped to –50°C. The roof was on, but the hut was far from complete, and the stores, encased in ice after a four-day hurricane, had to be laboriously chipped out. Dogs and ponies had to be looked after and as soon as the sea ice formed, depots had to be laid for the following spring. Meanwhile scientific research started and one party managed a gruelling first ascent of Mt Erebus. There was plenty of work for the small group throughout the winter to prepare for the major exploration journeys in the spring. Spring comes late to Antarctica, and it was the end of September before depot laying could start. On 5 October a three-man party left for the South Magnetic Pole and at the end of the month, a four-man party led by Shackleton started for the South Pole.

The polar route lay across the Ross Ice Shelf, which Shackleton had explored with Scott six years before, but once beyond the fairly level surface of the Ice Shelf travel became much more difficult. They had to find a way through the many crevasses at its inland edge, and then climb 3,000m through the enormous Transantarctic Mountains to the bleak Polar Plateau. At the foot of the mountains the last pony and some supplies were lost down a huge crevasse. The already short rations had to be cut further as the four men hauled their heavy sledge up the steep, heavily crevassed Beardmore Glacier, the largest in the world, to reach the Plateau on 7 December, still 350km from the South Pole. All suffered headaches from the altitude and though it wasn't bitterly cold, the short rations with less than half the necessary calories were telling and they struggled to pull the sledge uphill against the wind. They struggled on until 9 January but then, only 155km from the Pole, Shackleton courageously decided to turn; they could have reached the Pole but would certainly have died on the way back. As Shackleton later told his wife, better 'a live donkey than a dead lion'.

They were still faced with a desperate 1,200km race against starvation back to Cape Royds. With temperatures dropping quickly and depots hard to find, the journey was brutally difficult. By 20 February they were 'down to half a pannikin of half-cooked horsemeat and four thin biscuits a day' and had to pull the sledge 30km through a blizzard and –35°C to reach the next depot. This saved them from starvation, but they now faced the possibility of missing *Nimrod*, due to start back to New Zealand on 26 February. This would leave them marooned on the shore, unable to reach Cape Royds for additional supplies until new sea ice formed. Adams and Marshall were ill with dysentery so Shackleton and Frank Wild raced on the last 53km to reach the shore on 28 February. There was no sign of *Nimrod*, but in a desperate attempt, they set Scott's old magnetic hut alight in the hope of attracting attention. Luckily someone up in the rigging saw the flames and *Nimrod* was brought back in. They had reached safety, but, characteristically, Shackleton immediately set off back to rescue the sick men left on the Ice Shelf. By 4 March, all, including the South Magnetic Pole party, were aboard and *Nimrod* set off for New Zealand.

The old sealer pulled into Lyttelton harbour to a tumultuous reception and Shackleton was the hero of the hour. After he had reached the South Pole, the great Norwegian explorer, Roald Amundsen, wrote that 'Shackleton's exploit is the most brilliant incident in the history of Antarctic exploration'. The reception in New Zealand was nothing compared with that when *Nimrod* finally returned to England in late August; in London cheering crowds pulled Shackleton through the streets in a horse carriage. A long way from the smelly old ship of two years previously, *Nimrod*, moored at Temple Pier, was a centre of attention. While Shackleton was knighted and lectured to packed halls, the old ship toured the British coast, but eventually excitement died down and she had to be sold to pay the expedition's debts. She quietly reverted to a career as an ordinary merchant ship, which was abruptly cut short on a wild night in January 1919. En route from Blyth to Calais she was blown by a severe gale onto the Barber Sands off the Norfolk coast. Her distress signals were seen, but Yarmouth tugs and the Caister lifeboat couldn't save the old ship; she broke her back and sank quickly with the loss of all but two of her thirteen-man crew.

References

Bryan, R., 2011, *Ordeal by Ice: Ships of the Antarctic,* The Collins Press, Cork.

Feltham, J., 1995, *Sealing Steamers,* Harry Cuff Publications, St John's, Newfoundland.

Riffenburgh, B., 2004, *Nimrod: The Extraordinary Story of the 1907–1909 British Antarctic Expedition,* Bloomsbury, London.

Ryan, S., 1987, *Seals and Sealers: A Pictorial History of the Newfoundland Seal Fishery,* Breakwater Books, St John's.

Ryan, S., 1995, *The Ice Hunters: A History of Newfoundland Sealing to 1914,* Breakwater Books, St John's.

Shackleton, E.H., 1910, *The Heart of the Antarctic,* Heineman, London.

Shackleton, J., and MacKenna, J., 2002, *Shackleton: An Irishman in Antarctica,* The Lilliput Press, Dublin.

Wilson, D.M., 2009, *Nimrod Illustrated: Pictures From Lieutenant Shackleton's British Antarctic Expedition,* Reardon Publishing, Cheltenham.

12 A TALE OF TWO BOATS

HMS *Bounty's* launch:	double diagonally planked carvel-built naval launch. Rowed by three oars per side and lug sails could be set on a midships mainmast and small foremast.
Length:	7.01m
Beam:	2.06m
Draught:	0.84m
Career:	Lieutenant Bligh and eighteen men cast away in launch after mutiny in the South Pacific. Sailed 5,781km to Dutch East India Co. station at Coupang in West Timor in forty-one days with loss of one life.

HMS *Bounty*

The evening of 27 April 1789 was idyllically peaceful in the South Pacific Tongan Islands. HMS *Bounty* moved gently through the calm waters, 50km south of Tofua Island, while fascinated crew on deck watched the fireworks from its active volcano. Despite a difficult and unsuccessful attempt to round Cape Horn in winter, *Bounty's* commander, Lieutenant William Bligh, was pleased with their voyage to collect breadfruit plants for the West Indies. More than five months spent in Otaheite (Tahiti) had restored crew morale and the *Bounty's* decks were now crammed with potted plants. Bligh chatted briefly with the officer of the watch, John Fryer, then went below to sleep in his small windowless cabin. No sentry guarded his door, kept unlocked so that he could be easily reached in an emergency. Five hours later, just before dawn, Bligh was wrenched from sleep by the master's mate, Fletcher Christian, holding a bayonet to his throat. Despite threats of instant death, Bligh shouted for help as he was hustled on deck by five mutineers, dressed only in a nightshirt and with hands tied behind his back.

Accounts of the confusion of the next two hours vary, but eventually Bligh was forced into the *Bounty's* launch with eighteen crew members and set adrift. Some men remaining on board *Bounty* were forcibly held, but most enthusiastically supported the mutiny, which turned the small, insignificant *Bounty* into one of the best-known ships in Royal Navy history. Every detail of *Bounty's* rather obscure voyage was publicly analysed by conflicting enquiries which spawned numerous books, plays, poems and films over the next 200 years. Charles Laughton's Hollywood depiction of Bligh as a raving, despotic tyrant proved particularly indelible, but in fact Bligh and Fletcher Christian both appeared at times as both heroes and villains. The mutiny generated several centuries of controversy but also produced one of the most extraordinary survival tales in all of maritime history.

Though slightly larger than the leaky, worm-eaten cutter in which Christian originally intended to cast Bligh adrift, *Bounty's* launch was tiny. Only 7.01m long, she was, however, quite robust and, with double diagonal planking, almost leak-proof. She had a mounted windlass amidships and a stern derrick fitted for transporting anchor cables out to ships. Easily rowed with three oars per side, she could also set small dipping lugsails on a small foremast and a mainmast amidships, but without decking she was very exposed and, with nineteen men on board, was dangerously overloaded with only 18cm of freeboard.

As the *Bounty* sailed slowly away with the mutineers' shouts of 'Huzza for Otaheite' (Tahiti) echoing across the calm sea, the castaways' future looked very dark indeed. In the confusion only a haphazard collection of equipment and scant provisions found their way onto the launch. Bligh's clerk, John Samuel, had secured 68kg of bread, 14.5kg of pork, 3.4 litres of rum, six bottles of wine and 143 litres of water, barely five days rations for nineteen men. The men had an assortment of clothing, grabbed in the confusion, but, critically important, they did have a sextant, a quadrant, a compass, a log line and two books of mathematical and astronomical tables. Four cutlasses were thrown into the launch at the last minute, but there were no firearms or charts.

Although thousands of kilometres from safe haven with grim odds against survival, Bligh was remarkably confident: 'I felt an inward satisfaction which prevented any depression of my spirits.' An expert navigator, schooled by Captain James Cook during his last voyage, Bligh had the essential instruments, but without charts, he had to rely on memories from his previous South Pacific visit on HMS *Resolution* and *Discovery*. The food supply was clearly inadequate: '[T]he quantity

HMS *Bounty* – Bligh being forced into the launch.

of provisions I found in the boat was 150lb of bread, 16 pieces of pork, each piece weighing 2lb. 6 quarts of rum, 6 bottles of wine, with 28 gallons of water.' So he decided first to collect breadfruit and water at Tofua before setting course for the largest Tongan island, and eventually heading for a Dutch settlement in the East Indies, 5,760km away. (Map, see p. 102)

Next morning they managed to land through heavy surf on a rocky beach at Tofua to collect a few coconuts from the surrounding cliffs. After a night in a sea cave, they met several Tofuans and received a few breadfruit and plantains. Next day many more islanders appeared with food to trade, but, discovering that the ship had been lost, they quickly become hostile, something they demonstrated by knocking stones together. Bligh recognised this from his experience with Cook

at Hawaii, and realised that they had to escape quickly. They tried to retreat unobtrusively to the launch, but while casting off the stern rope, quartermaster John Norton was set on by some 200 islanders and stoned to death.

As they rowed away from Tofua, a violent storm arose and waves breaking over the stern threatened to sink the heavily laden launch. Bligh ordered all surplus clothing and equipment to be thrown overboard to increase freeboard and provide space to bail. Even without Norton, the launch was very crowded, so the men were divided into three watches so that off-watch men could lie on the bottom boards. Without firearms, it was not safe to visit any island for food and, begged by the men to get them safely home, Bligh decided that the food supply would have to last for at least eight weeks. He introduced strict rationing using a scales made from coconut shells with musket balls as weights. Even soaked and rotten bread had to be used; initially each man received about 50g of bread, breadfruit or coconut, initially three times per day, with a little pork and coconut milk, and a teaspoon of rum, but later this had to be reduced.

For days they could only run before the storm, struggling to keep the launch from broaching. The balmy South Pacific weather disappeared and, continually soaked by breaking waves, the men were numbed by cold at night. Nine days passed before Bligh could stream a logline, then steering and navigating as best he could, he set course for New Holland (Australia). By then the launch was amongst many reefs and islands but they didn't dare to land and sometimes had to row hard to escape hostile native canoes. Suffering badly from thirst, they managed to collect some rainwater, increasing their supply to 155 litres, but the only fish caught was lost as they tried to get it into the launch. A brief calm spell allowed them to rig a canvas spray cloth, but the storms soon returned with thunder and lightning and for another week conditions were miserable and dangerous:

Our limbs so cramped … we could scarce feel the use of them … our situation extremely dangerous, the sea frequently running over our stern … baling with all our strength.

(Bligh, 1790)

Frequent rainfall provided drinking water but threatened to swamp the launch. Continually soaked, the men got some relief by stripping and wringing out their clothes in sea water but:

some of my people looked half dead ... our little sleep was in the midst of water and we constantly awoke with severe cramps and pains in our bones.

(Bligh, 1790)

After a month at sea they saw fleeting sunlight and many birds, including boobies and noddies, never found far from land. Several were caught to be swiftly consumed, complete with entrails. On 28 May they reached 13° 26'S, 39° 04'W, close to the Great Barrier Reef, and soon passed through a gap to land on an island, which Bligh named Restoration Island. There they found good supplies of fresh water and oysters and, using a magnifying glass to light a fire, Bligh 'made a stew that might be relished by people of more delicate appetites'. Despite warnings, some men ate berries and suffered severe stomach cramps as well as sunstroke as the launch continued northwards along the coast to Torres Strait. Discipline was starting to break down and both the master John Fryer and the carpenter William Purcell began to question Bligh's leadership. Despite a slight increase in the food supply, health was deteriorating quickly: 'an extreme weakness, swelled legs, hollow and ghastly countenances' convinced Bligh that time was running out. On 2 June he navigated successfully through the dangerous Torres Strait reefs and after another ten days and 1,920km, at last sighted the island of Timor:

It appeared scarce credible, that in an open boat, and so poorly provided, we had been able to reach the coast of Timor in forty-one days ... a distance of 3,618 miles, and that no one should have perished.

(Bligh, 1790)

Fryer and Purcell wanted to land immediately, but Bligh was still wary of hostile islanders, and continued round the western end of Timor to reach the Dutch East Indian Company station at Coupang on 14 June, to complete the greatest open boat voyage then known. The men were received with great hospitality and most recovered fairly quickly, though the gardener, David Nelson, died of fever five weeks later. In August, Bligh purchased and refitted a small schooner, then sailed via Java to Batavia, transhipped for the Cape of Good Hope and eventually landed from an English ship at Portsmouth on 14 March 1790. Initially celebrated as a hero, his reputation was gradually destroyed by powerful friends of Fletcher Christian. He received a personal commendation from Nelson for his bravery at the Battle of Copenhagen, but his career declined, though he did achieve the rank of Vice-Admiral before his death in 1817.

References

Alexander, C., *The Bounty: The True Story of the Mutiny on the Bounty*, Viking, New York.

Bach, J. (ed.), 1987, *The Bligh Notebook*, Allen and Unwin, London.

Bligh, W., 1790, *A Narrative of the Mutiny, on Board His Majesty's Ship Bounty; and the Subsequent Voyage of part of the Crew, in the Ship's Boat, from Tofua, one of the Friendly Islands, to Timor, a Dutch Settlement in the East Indies*, George Nicol, London.

Kennedy, G., 1989, *Captain Bligh: The Man and His Mutinies*, Duckworth, London.

Mackenzie, G., 1936, *The Life of Vice-Admiral Bligh*, Faerar and Rhinehart, New York.

Madison, R.D. (intro), 2001, *William Bligh and Fletcher Christian: The Bounty Mutiny*, Penguin Books, New York.

Weate, P., and Graham, C., 1972, *William Bligh: An Illustrated History*, Paul Hamlyn, New York, 1972.

Sir Ernest Shackleton and the *James Caird*

James Caird:	double-ended, carvel-built launch built in London for Sir Ernest Shackleton's 1914–16 Imperial TransAntarctic Expedition on *Endurance*.
Tonnage:	3.75t capacity
Length:	6.86m
Beam:	1.83m
Career:	October 1915: rescued when *Endurance* was crushed by ice in Weddell Sea. April 1916: with launches *Dudley Docker* and *Stancomb Wills* sailed from ice edge to Elephant Island. Rebuilt by carpenter McNish then sailed by Shackleton and five companions 1,280km to reach South Georgia on 10 May. Shackleton, Crean and Worsley then crossed unexplored mountains to reach Stromness whaling station on 19 May, then organise rescue of the twenty-two men marooned on Elephant Island. *James Caird* is preserved at Dulwich College, London.

Circumstances for a second great open boat voyage could hardly have been more different. Just as the First World War started, Sir Ernest's Shackleton sailed from England on *Endurance* to attempt the last great Antarctic journey, the crossing from the Weddell Sea to the Ross Sea. It was a bad ice year in the Weddell Sea and he had to wait at South Georgia until mid-December before heading south into heavy pack ice. By 19 January 1915, she had fought her way to 96km from Vahsel Bay at the southern end of the Weddell Sea, where the trek should start, but there *Endurance* was beset by heavy ice.

For ten months *Endurance* remained stuck, with ice floes jammed against the ship by powerful currents and winds. The explorers settled down to endure the long Antarctic winter as the ship was carried by currents away to the north-west. By force of personality Shackleton kept morale high in the cramped, cold conditions and everything was under control until October when ice pressure suddenly increased, pushing the ship over and 'ripping off the rudder as though it had been made of matchwood' (Shackleton, 1919).

Stressed and twisted by massive ice floes, *Endurance*'s strong timbers cracked and leaked and she had to be abandoned, marooning the twenty-eight men and sixty-nine dogs on the ice, 2,000km from the nearest settlement.

Apart from sledges, tents and assorted equipment, enough supplies were rescued to last for fifty-six days. They also had three boats, the clinker-built cutters, the 6.7m, 1.5t capacity *Dudley Docker,* the 1.25t capacity 6.32m *Stancomb Wills* and the 6.86m long, 3.75t capacity double-ended *James Caird.* Shackleton initially planned to drag the boats over the shifting, broken pack to Paulet Island to a Swedish cache of stores laid ten years earlier. In four days of intense labour, sinking deep into the soft, wet ice, they moved only 5.6km and had to give up. By Christmas the drifting ice had brought them closer and they tried again, but could manage only 1.5km per day; at this rate it would take ten months to reach Paulet Island.

The only alternative was to settle down on the largest ice floe, in 'Patience Camp', and wait until it carried them to the ice edge; this took three-and-a-half months. Though supplemented by seal and penguin, food rations had to be cut further and eventually the dogs had to be shot to eke out supplies. It was 7 April before the ice floes cracked open near the open sea and, moving into the boats, they set out for the closest land, Elephant Island. Conditions were terrible, exposed to wind and spray with temperatures dropping to –24°C for a week before they could land through heavy surf onto the bleak rocky shore of Elephant Island: 'We were a pitiful sight … terribly frost-bitten and half delirious (Hurley, 1925).

Temporarily safe, their ordeal was just beginning. Elephant Island is a barren place of rocks and ice, and by the late Antarctic autumn, few penguins or seal remained for food and fuel. Shackleton knew that the chances of the men surviving until the next summer and possible rescue by a passing whaler were virtually non-existent. His only hope was to seek help by attempting a voyage across the one of the stormiest seas in the world, the desperately dangerous Southern Ocean where giant 20–30m-high waves – the fearsome Cape Horn 'greybeards' – sweep unimpeded around the globe driven by winds that can reach 250km/h. The only realistic objective was South Georgia, 1,280km to the north-east; Tierra del Fuego and the Falkland Islands were closer, but would be impossible to reach against strong winds and currents. (Map, see p. 104)

Only the *James Caird* was big enough to have any chance of surviving. Carpenter 'Chippy' McNish used bits from the other boats, strengthened her, increased her freeboard and decked her over with canvas thawed out over a blubber fire. Two small masts were fitted and her planks caulked with a mixture of seal blood and artist's paint. She was nearly swamped being launched through surf before a ton of sand and shingle ballast was loaded. In the cramped space between the ballast and the canvas deck Shackleton, Crean, Worsley, Vincent, McLeish and McCarthy, would cook and try to sleep. On 24 April they set out, leaving Frank Wild, on his fourth Antarctic expedition, to look after twenty-one marooned men, living under the upturned boats and trying to survive on penguin and seal meat. Everyone knew the odds against *James Caird* reaching South Georgia were huge and it would need pinpoint navigation to avoid being driven past into the Atlantic.

As *James Caird* cleared the ice floes near Elephant Island, the wind increased and soon every wave washed over them, slopping through the small hatch and saturating everything inside. Even sleeping bags, right up in the bow became soaked as the wind strengthened to a full gale. There was nothing to stop waves continually drenching the helmsman, while below they had to crawl over the sharp ballast. They had to pump non-stop while Tom Crean, bent double over a Primus, which blocked continually with hair from the reindeer sleeping bags, strove to cook 'hoosh'. Navigator Frank Worsley had to kneel on the after-thwart washed by waves, attempting to read the sextant while Shackleton crouched below with the one chronometer left from twenty-four on *Endurance* trying to note figures in the soaked logbook.

On the sixth day, 381km out, the wind veered east and strengthened towards hurricane. To stay afloat, sails had to be furled and a sea-anchor streamed. All night *James Caird* pitched wildly to the sea anchor; by morning, the complete boat was encased in ice. Each man in turn had to crawl out on the canvas deck continually washed by waves and try to break off the ice with an axe without tearing the canvas. This took at least an hour and had to be repeated regularly. Eventually the sea anchor line broke, so a sail had to be hoisted to keep the boat's head to the wind. The gale blew for three days before it eased, allowing Worsley to take a sextant sight; they were half way to South Georgia.

Two days with light winds allowed good progress, but twelve days out it started to blow up again. Shortly after midnight on 5 May, Shackleton, at the helm, thought that the clouds were clearing, then, suddenly realised that he was looking at the foaming crest of an enormous wave. Caught in a blinding, suffocating maelstrom of water, the tiny boat was completely swamped. Miraculously she stayed afloat, but it took two hours of bailing with anything that would hold water to make her safe. Conditions were still bad by morning and with salt-contaminated drinking water, they were suffered badly from thirst. However, with a glimpse of the sun Worsley calculated that they were only 145km from South Georgia.

Fog then enveloped them, but on 8 May fragments of kelp and two cormorants showed that land was close and they soon glimpsed the sheer black cliffs of South Georgia (later identified as Cape Demidov) although landing through heavy surf at the cliff foot was impossible. They stood off overnight to seek a better site, but with dawn the wind increased to the worst hurricane they had ever seen (which sank a 500t steamer on the way from Buenos Aires to South Georgia). Continually driven towards cliffs and glaciers on the lee shore, they were in extreme danger, and had no idea what reefs were in

their way. *James Caird* was labouring heavily and immense seas drove squirts of water through the bow planking seams. All day they fought off Annenkov Island looking straight up at the snow-capped peak, 'foot by foot we staggered and lurched drunkenly past the ravening black fangs of the rocky point' (Shackleton, 1919), but by nightfall they had clawed their way clear, and with the wind dropping by morning they were approaching King Haakon Bay. They tacked again and again against the northerly wind, but as dusk approached, they sighted a gap in the reefs. This was so narrow that they had to draw in the oars but in minutes they surfed through, driven by the swell onto a narrow, gravel beach and 'a moment later we were down on our knees drinking the pure ice-cold water' (Shackleton, 1919).

The boat journey was over, but the rescue was by no means achieved. First they had to regain some strength, resting for four days in a cave, feasting on young albatrosses and penguins. Then, unable to climb the cliffs, they re-launched *James Caird* and sailed to the end of the bay where they camped again. They had to reach one of the whaling stations to fetch help, but these all lay on the north side of the island. The closest, Stromness, was only 32km away as the crow flies (though 250km by sea), but in between lay massive, unexplored and heavily-glaciated mountains rising over 1,800m.

The *James Caird* setting off from Elephant Island.

Only Shackleton, Crean and Worsley were fit enough to try the crossing. Although magnificent sailors, they were not mountaineers and their equipment was pathetic: odds and ends of rope joined to give 15m length, McNish's adze as an ice axe and brass screws from *James Caird* driven into their boots as crampons. In clear moonlight at 2 a.m. on 19 May they set out. Three times they struggled up 1,500m to impassable cols and had to backtrack. As darkness fell they reached another col above a steep snow slope. They couldn't see the bottom but a night's exposure at this height would be fatal, so, sitting on the rope, they tobogganed into the void, dropping 460m in a few minutes, then headed down to what they thought was Fortuna Bay; it wasn't! As they climbed uphill again they began to recognise landmarks around the real Fortuna Bay, but Stromness was still 20km away. They had now been climbing for twenty-seven hours but had to continue. Two hours later, with great relief, they heard the steam-whistle at the whaling station. Shackleton said: 'Never had any of us heard sweeter music. It was the first sound created by outside human agency that had come to our ears since we left Stromness Bay in December 1914.' After another six hours they struggled in to the station, where two children took the fright of their lives at the filthy, ragged, weather-beaten apparitions.

Though safe at the hospitable whaling station, they couldn't rest. First, McLeish, Vincent and McCarthy (and *James Caird*) had to be rescued, then immediately they had to mount an attempt to reach the men marooned on Elephant Island. It was difficult to borrow a ship in the middle of a war, and it took four attempts with different ships before Shackleton was able to land at Elephant Island from the Chilean tug *Yelcho* on 30 August. Almost a month later they all entered Valparaiso triumphantly on the tiny *Yelcho*. Almost 100 years later, *James Caird* is still intact at Shackleton's old school, Dulwich College in London.

References

Alexander, C., 1998, *The Endurance: Shackleton's Legendary Antarctic Expedition,* Bloomsbury, London.

Bryan, R., 2011, *Ordeal by Ice: Ships of the Antarctic,* The Collins Press, Cork.

Dunnett, H.M., 1996, *Shackleton's Boat: The Story of the James Caird,* Neville & Harding, Cranbrook.

Hurley, F., 1925, *Argonauts of the South,* G.P. Putnam's Sons, New York and London.

Lansing, A., 1959, *Endurance: Shackleton's Incredible Voyage,* McGrawHill, New York.

Shackleton, Sir Ernest, 1919, *South: The Story of Shackleton's 1914–1917 Expedition,* William Heineman, London.

Shackleton, J., and McKenna, J., 2002, *Shackleton: An Irishman in Antarctica,* The Lilliput Press, Dublin.

Worsley, F.A., 1974, *Shackleton's Boat Journey,* The Folio Society, London.

13 SMS *EMDEN*: THE SWAN OF THE EAST AND THE TWILIGHT OF CHIVALRY

SMS *Emden*:	light cruiser launched by KaiserlicheWerft, Danzig (Gdansk), in May 1908 for the German Reichsmarine.
Tonnage:	3,664t
Length:	118.3m
Beam:	13.5m
Draught:	5.53m
Engine:	coal-fired, twelve water tube boilers, two triple-expansion engines, 13,500hp.
Maximum Speed:	24.01 knots
Range:	6,843km at 12 knots
Armament:	ten 10.5cm guns, eight 5.2 cm guns, eight Maxim machine guns and two 50cm torpedo tubes.
Crew:	18 officers, 343 men
Career:	under Commander von Müller sank or captured twenty-five Allied ships including two warships, totalling 104,683t during three-month, 48,000km mission in Pacific and Indian Oceans. Destroyed by HMAS *Sydney* at North Keeling Is., Cocos Islands, November 1914 with 133 German deaths. Detached party of forty-six escaped on schooner *Ayesha* to Red Sea then through Arabia to Constantinople and eventually to Berlin.

In warfare, the victors write the history. Opponents may respect one another, but the vanquished don't usually receive eloquent praise in the victors' newspapers, particularly while the war is in progress. Nevertheless, *The Times* of London, reporting the destruction of the German light cruiser *Emden* in November 1914, praised:

her daring and enterprising actions … Commander von Müller … a valiant and chivalrous adversary … few events in the new history of sea warfare … are more remarkable than the bright career of the little *Emden*.

(*The Times*, 1914)

Such generous accolades soon ended with the bloody squalor of the Western Front and the horrors of unrestricted U-boat warfare, but 100 years later, von Müller is still remembered with the greatest respect.

The *Emden* was a product of the newly unified Germany and Kaiser Wilhelm II's attempt to match the Royal Navy and challenge Britain's global hegemony. When she was launched at the Kaiserliche Werft in Danzig (now Gdansk) in 1908, the arms race was in full flight and both Britain and Germany were pouring money into turbine-driven battleships and battle cruisers as Europe slid towards war. Most German naval resources went to capital ships, but Admiral von Tirpitz realised that fast, light cruisers, built more quickly and cheaply, were vital to protect German colonies and commercial interests in Africa, the South Seas and the Far East. In 1897, following the murder of two Lutheran missionaries, three German cruisers occupied Tsingtao on the Yellow Sea as a precursor to the 1900 Boxer Rebellion, and imposed a ninety-nine-year lease for a naval base at Kiachow Bay. By 1914 Germany had invested more than $2 million, German shipping lines were running regular services, and a heavily defended base had been established for the German Far Eastern Cruiser Squadron.

The *Emden* and sister ship *Dresden* were built as part of the acceleration of light cruiser construction started in 1904, which brought Germany's light cruiser fleet to forty-nine by 1914. Both ships were 3,664t and 118m in length with ram bows and carrying crews of 360. *Dresden* was fitted with a turbine driving four propellers giving 25.2 knots but could reach 27 knots in an emergency, while *Emden* had two triple-expansion engines and two propellers giving 24.01 knots. Both ships had high steel masts, three tall funnels braced by wire stays, and carried the same armament but very little armour.

Dresden was visiting San Francisco when the war started, while *Emden* was posted directly to Asia, reaching Tsingtao in September 1910. The weak Far Eastern Squadron was strengthened in 1911 by the powerful 12,985t armoured cruisers SMS *Scharnhorst* and SMS *Gneisenau*, which could steam at 22.7 knots. Heavily armed with eight

21cm guns, eighteen 8.8cm guns and four submerged torpedo tubes, they had much heavier armour than *Emden*. *Scharnhorst* became Admiral von Spee's flagship when he took command of the Squadron in March 1913. Meanwhile *Emden*, nicknamed the 'Swan of the East' because of her graceful lines, had several captains before von Müller, soon to be the most famous commander in Germany, was appointed in spring 1913. Almost immediately he won the Order of the Royal Crown for action against rebels along the Yangtze in March 1914.

First World War naval strategy was dominated by fuel and communications. Steam-driven cruisers consumed an immense amount of coal, particularly at close to top speed. At 12 knots *Emden* burned 2t per hour with range of 6,843km, but at top speed, this rose to 15.7t per hour while range dropped to 2,106km. Coal capacity could be pushed to about 1,000t, but operational efficiency was reduced. Cruisers had to be supported by strategically placed coaling stations or accompanied by colliers, reducing their operational speed. Coal quality was critically important; hard steam coal was essential otherwise hearths rapidly clogged, boilers lost efficiency and speed declined. With a network of colonies Britain had a clear strategic advantage, but Germany countered with the 'Etappe' system; the oceans were divided into zones controlled by naval communications offices, usually located in capital cities. In war, the complete German merchant marine could be organised through the 'Etappe' system to resupply naval ships, success depending on rapid, effective communication.

Britain, pioneers of undersea telegraph cables, still depended on an extensive cable network (475,000km by 1907) to communicate with her colonies when war broke out. Very few British ships had wireless equipment, but Germany, with a much more limited overseas empire, swiftly adopted telegraphy and, by 1906, virtually all Kaiserliche Marine ships were equipped with radios and by 1914 most German merchant shipping lines followed suit. By linking them to arms sales, Germany had also successfully set up a network of transmitting and relay stations. Transmission was somewhat erratic, but communications over very long distances were possible and were extremely valuable for the Etappe system and tracking fleet movements.

Given freedom of action by Berlin, von Spee's strategy, with Tsingtao as a base, was to raid widely throughout the Pacific with *Scharnhorst*, *Gneisenau*, *Emden*, *Nürnburg* (3,396t) and *Leipzig* (3,200t), before returning to Germany round Cape Horn. Von Müller, with *Emden*, was left in command of Tsingtao, with two gunboats, the old cruiser,

Cormoran, and the obsolete Austrian cruiser *Kaiserein Elizabeth* with two powerful 22.6cm guns. During July it became clear that Germany would be opposed by France, Russia, Britain and Japan, undermining von Spee's strategy. Tsingtao was strongly defended with 10,000 men, three powerful modern forts and *Kaiserein Elizabeth*'s guns but was entered through a narrow strait that could be easily blockaded by Japanese battleships. It was decided that von Müller would have to put to sea immediately war was declared.

Through Etappe von Müller ordered 5,000t of coal to Pagan in the Marianas, 5,000t to 'Assembly A' (35°51′N, 120°20′E) and food, ammunition, oil and coal to 'Assembly B' (25°N, 135′E). *Emden*'s wooden panelling was stripped and on 31 July, together with the collier SS *Elsbeth*, she headed for the Straits of Tsushima. At dawn on 4 August in a gathering gale she intercepted the new 3,500t Russian passenger ship *Rjäsan* and after a short chase and a few warning shots, landed a boarding party and took her first prize. *Rjäsan* was ideal for conversion to an armoured cruiser so, evading both French and British patrols, *Emden* brought her back through newly laid minefields to Tsingtao for refitting. On 6 August *Emden* left again to join von Spee at Pagan with the 4,505t freighter *Markomannia* as a collier.

Emden reached Pagan on 8 August, and von Müller persuaded von Spee to release her as an independent raider. (Map, see p. 106) On 14 August, together with *Markomannia*, *Emden* departed on her career as a corsair, heading south-west for Timor where the neutral Dutch refused to allow them to coal from collier *Tannenburg*, but her bunkers were topped up from *Markomannia*. The first officer, Lieutenant von Mücke, constructed a dummy fourth funnel to camouflage *Emden* as British cruiser HMS *Yarmouth*, then they passed through Lombok Straits into the Indian Ocean. Informed by the Dutch that a German warship was on the loose, British naval HQ in Singapore detached the slow, heavy cruiser HMS *Hampshire* to give chase. On 9 September off Sumatra, *Emden* captured the 7,480t Greek steamer *Pontoporos*, carrying 6,600t of coal for the Allies. Next day the 3,413t British steamer *Indus*, outfitted as a troop carrier was intercepted. She was in ballast, but yielded 150 cases of soap and other luxuries. After transferring sixty crew members to *Markomannia*, *Indus* was sunk by gunfire. On 11 September another empty troop carrier, the 6,102t British *Lovat*, met the same fate, then *Emden* headed for the Calcutta–Colombo shipping lanes and late on 12 August stopped the 4,657t Ellerman and Bucknall steamer *Kabinga* en route to New York. To avoid offending neutral America, von Müller didn't sink her, but used her to house prisoners. Three hours later the 3,544t British collier *Killin* with 6,000t of Indian coal was captured and scuttled at daybreak. Near Calcutta, the 7,615t British freighter *Diplomat* carrying tea to London was sighted and soon joined the casualty list.

While *Diplomat* was being scuttled *Emden* chased another ship, the neutral Italian 4,149t *Loredano*, which was released when her captain promised not to reveal *Emden*'s presence. The promise was not kept and the news that a German raider was loose in the Bay of Bengal set the cat amongst the pigeons. Britain desperately needed colonial forces to reinforce the British Expeditionary Force in France and *Emden* threatened vital supply lines. With von Spee raiding in the south Pacific and the *Königsberg* causing havoc off Zanzibar, the Admiralty was bitterly criticised in Australia and New Zealand. Reluctant ship owners refused to send ships to sea and a critically important convoy of 30,000 troops for Europe was postponed indefinitely. Meanwhile *Emden* intercepted and released another Italian neutral before stopping the empty 4,028t British collier *Trabboch* en route to Calcutta. Her crew was moved to *Kabinga*, which was released to bring the prisoners to shore, while *Trabboch* was scuttled spectacularly with a violent explosion of coal dust in her holds. Thirty minutes later *Emden* chased the 4,775t British *Clan Matheson* carrying a valuable cargo, including several Rolls-Royces, to Calcutta. Aware that *Emden*'s presence was known, von Müller now headed south-east, pausing at sea to take on 450t of poor Indian coal from *Pontoporos*. This coal reduced her performance and also produced thick black clouds of smoke, revealing her position at long distance.

On 17 September *Emden* intercepted the neutral Norwegian *Dovre* off Rangoon, whose captain agreed to take off the crew of the *Clan Matheson*. HMS *Hampshire* came within 18km, nearly catching her while she coaled at the Andaman Islands, but she slipped away towards Madras to set the Burmah Oil Company's storage tanks alight on 22 September. Damage was limited, but civilian morale plummeted and many fled Madras and trade at Calcutta ceased completely. As *Emden* headed south to the Colombo–Singapore shipping lanes, von Müller knew about the chaos caused from the intense coded Allied wireless traffic and read about the bitter criticism of the Admiralty in captured newspapers.

Off Ceylon the 3,650t British *King Lod* was sunk, a neutral Norwegian tanker, *Oceanus*, was intercepted and released, then the 3,314t British freighter *Tymeric* carrying 4,000t of sugar was sunk just off the Colombo light. The captain of *Tymeric*, assured by the Royal Navy that the shipping lanes were safe, was furious! Next the 4,437t British *Gryfevale* was captured and retained to house prisoners, and on 27 September the brand-new 4,337t British *Buresk* was captured with an invaluable 6,600t of first-class Cardiff steam coal. The little convoy of *Emden*, *Markomannia*, *Gryfevale* and *Buresk* was barely under way when another chase started, which ended in sinking the 3,500t British freighter *Ribero*, in ballast, then the 4,147t British *Foyle*, also in ballast. Next day *Gryfevale* was released to land the prisoners, who surprised von Müller and his crew by cheering them as they departed!

The First Lord of the Admiralty, Winston Churchill, was almost apoplectic about HMS *Hampshire* and HMS *Yarmouth*'s failure to track down the elusive *Emden*, and proposed that the Japanese cruiser *Chikuma*, the Russian cruisers *Zemchug* and *Askold*, and the powerful new Australian cruiser HMAS *Sydney* should join the hunt. *Emden* now badly needed maintenance and headed for the secluded Chagos Archipelago. After coaling on 30 September *Markomannia* left to meet *Pontoporos* at Simalur to collect more coal and supplies, where her luck ran out; on 12 October as coal was being transferred, HMS *Yarmouth* appeared, recapturing *Pontoporos* and sinking *Markomannia*.

Emden steamed slowly southwards with each engine in turn closed down for maintenance as worn tubes were replaced in her four boilers. After three active months, her railings were bent from repeated coaling, her smart grey paint was replaced by bare metal and rust, and her bottom was thickly encrusted with barnacles. On 9 October, in a tranquil lagoon at Diego Garcia, in the Chagos Archipelago, barnacles were scraped off and the hull repainted. No one on Diego Garcia had heard about the war, so they could buy supplies and loads of fruit, though creative explanations were needed for *Emden*'s disreputable appearance. With maintenance complete, 1,000t of coal were loaded from *Buresk*, and *Emden* steamed off to the north-west, turning north-east as soon as they were over the horizon. This deception saved her; two days later, HMS *Hampshire* with her auxiliary armed cruiser *Empress of Russia*, arrived, after fruitlessly searching the Maldive Islands.

As *Emden* left Diego Garcia, von Müller intercepted a wireless message proclaiming the Aden–Colombo shipping lane to be now completely safe, so he immediately ordered *Emden* back to her happy hunting ground off the Minicoy light. This quickly paid off; on 16 October the 3,948t *Clan Grant* was captured with a cargo of beer,

250,000 cigarettes and live cattle. The next interception initially caused consternation as her strange superstructure looked like a warship; the seagoing dredger *Ponrabbel* was en route to Tasmania and her crew were delighted to be saved from what they viewed as a 'rolling coffin'. Scarcely had her crew been transferred to the crowded *Buresk* than *Emden* claimed her next victim, the 4,806t *Ben Mohr*. These ships were all heading east; with nothing coming from the west, von Müller realised that *Emden*'s activities in the Bay of Bengal had triggered emergency measures. With unerring instinct he headed north of the normal shipping lanes and the fox really entered the hen coop; almost immediately the brand-new 7,562t Holt Line steamer *Troilus* carrying copper, tin and rubber on her maiden voyage from Yokohama to London was captured, followed by the 5,596t *St Egbert*, laden with sugar. Three hours later, the 4,542t *Exford* with 5,500t of the best Cardiff steam coal was taken, then the new 5,146t *Chilkana*, delivered to her owners barely a month previously.

Emden now had to pause; providing prize crews had depleted her officer ranks, and 500–600 prisoners spread over various ships had to be off-loaded. All these were moved aboard *St Egbert* to be dropped off in India, *Emden*'s officer ranks were replenished, and the crew rested from interceptions. With lights out, they let one ship pass in the night; she turned out to be the hunter *Empress of Russia*. One can scarcely imagine the frustration in the Admiralty as their cruiser forces criss-crossed the Indian Ocean chasing the will-o'-the-wisp *Emden*, while few merchantmen were prepared to run the gauntlet from Indian ports. As *Emden* headed east, well south of the shipping lanes, to meet *Buresk* for coaling in the Nicobar Islands, the crew rested and practiced gunnery. This time no coal was stored on deck; she was heading for a raid on Penang and needed unrestricted access to her guns. As 28 October dawned, *Emden* tore round Pulo Island into the narrow, crowded Penang harbour to put a torpedo into the Russian cruiser *Zhemchug*, which, after a second torpedo, disintegrated in yellow smoke. Five minutes later, *Emden* intercepted the 4,696t *Glenturret*, carrying explosives, at the harbour entry but had to leave her as the French destroyer *Mousquet* took this inopportune moment to appear. She soon turned to flee, but *Emden*'s guns bracketed her; she managed to launch a torpedo at her attacker, but sank after twenty-two salvoes from *Emden*, which rescued thirty-seven survivors.

Leaving Penang, *Emden* headed north at high speed to the Singapore–Rangoon shipping lanes, easily outdistancing the French

destroyer *Pistolet*. On 30 October they stopped the 3,000t freighter *Newburn*, off-loading the French survivors for transport to the nearby island of Sumatra, then continued to meet *Buresk* near Padang to coal, before steaming towards Sunda Strait. Her hunters were now at fever pitch, gradually closing the net. On 5 November, she turned west to meet the *Exford* for coal, then with supplies replenished, headed for Direction Island in the Cocos group to destroy an important British wireless station. At sunrise on 9 November fifty men led by Lieutenant von Mücke landed and made their way towards the station. Three charges destroyed the wireless mast but not before the message 'Strange ship off entrance' had been transmitted, followed by 'SOS *Emden* here' as the fake fourth funnel was recognised.

Minutes later, *Emden* intercepted a message from an unknown ship. The signal strength indicated that this was about 400km distant, so the funnel stays were removed for coaling and *Buresk* was called in. In two hours the unknown ship appeared – the new, heavily armoured 5,700t Australian turbine cruiser HMAS *Sydney* with eight 15.2cm and four 4.7cm guns, and a top speed of 27 knots. She had transmitted her message at half power and actually had been only 83km away. *Emden* was in trouble and her lookouts soon made a crucial mistake. At first the approaching smoke was thought to be the *Buresk*, but then, recognising a warship's twin tall masts, they mistook her for the light cruiser HMS *Newcastle*, which *Emden* could easily handle.

Immediately the mistake was realised, *Emden* left the landing party ashore and, with battle flags flying, raced to the north-west. As she struggled to get steam up and reach top speed, *Sydney* rapidly closed the range; at 5,500m *Emden* opened fire, bracketing the Australian cruiser. She knocked out *Sydney*'s fire-control with her fourth salvo, but this was the only serious punch she landed. The Australian ship drew back a bit, but her big guns were still in range and quickly destroyed *Emden*'s bridge and wireless room. From outside *Emden*'s range she soon sliced the lightly armoured cruiser to pieces with lyddite shells, knocking out the after guns and aiming system, and causing an explosion and serious fire near the stern. With most guns disabled and many crew dead or wounded, *Emden*'s only chance was to get close enough to the *Sydney* to hit her with a torpedo. At high speed the cruisers circled, seeking a tactical advantage, but after an hour *Emden*'s foremast toppled, her torpedo flat was flooded and the electrical system was down. The explosions at the stern had damaged the rudder and she could now be steered only by the

British Yukon Navigation Company's sternwheel paddleboat SS *Klondike* loading
cargo at a community on the Yukon River, Canada.

Whaler *Charles W. Morgan* at New Bedford, Massachusetts, on the eve of departure for her maiden whaling voyage in the Atlantic and Pacific, 5 September 1841.

Whaler *Charles W. Morgan* unloading barrels of whale oil after her successful maiden voyage, New Bedford, Massachusetts, 2 January 1845.

Tryworks on the whaler *Charles W. Morgan* at Mystic Seaport, Connecticut. (Rorke Bryan)

Lieutenant Ernest Shackleton's ship *Nimrod* unloading stores at Cape Royds, Ross Island, Antarctica, 11 February 1908.

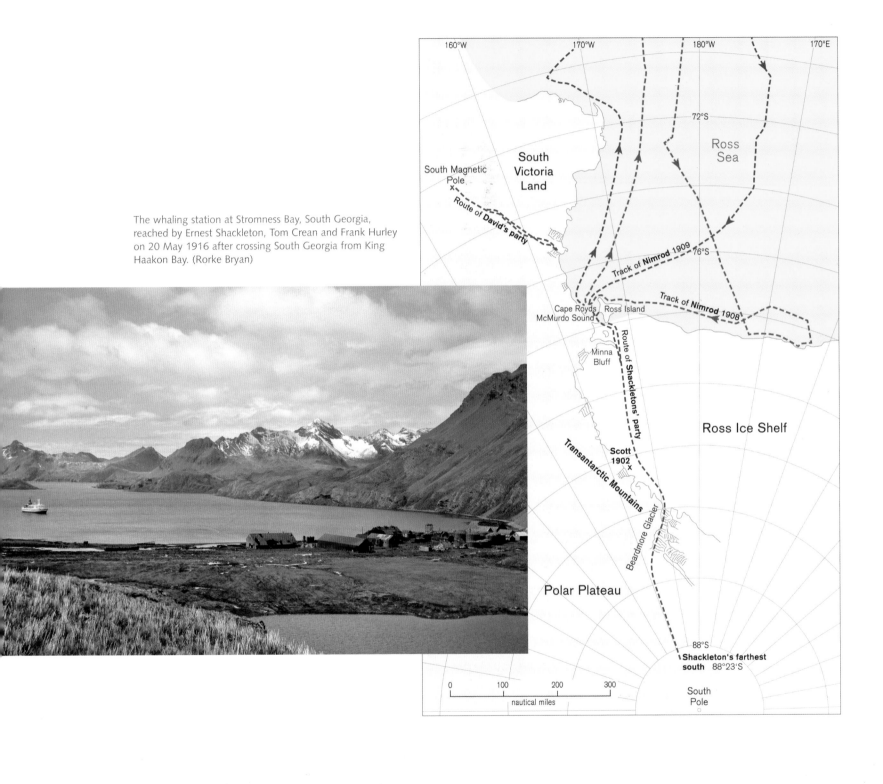

The whaling station at Stromness Bay, South Georgia,
reached by Ernest Shackleton, Tom Crean and Frank Hurley
on 20 May 1916 after crossing South Georgia from King
Haakon Bay. (Rorke Bryan)

160°W 170°W 180°W 170°E

72°S

South
Victoria
Land

Ross
Sea

South Magnetic
Pole
×

Route of **David's party**

76°S

Track of **Nimrod** 1909

Track of **Nimrod** 1908

Cape Royds Ross Island
McMurdo Sound

Route of **Shackletons' party**

Minna
Bluff

Ross Ice Shelf

Transantarctic Mountains

Scott
1902 ×

Beardmore Glacier

Polar Plateau

88°S

**Shackleton's farthest
south** 88°23'S

0   100   200   300

nautical miles

South
Pole

Lieutenant Bligh with his fellow victims of the mutiny on HMS *Bounty* sets course for the Dutch settlement of Coupang on the island of Timor, May 1789.

HMS *Bounty* under command of Lieutenant William Bligh attempts a westerly rounding of Cape Horn, January 1788.

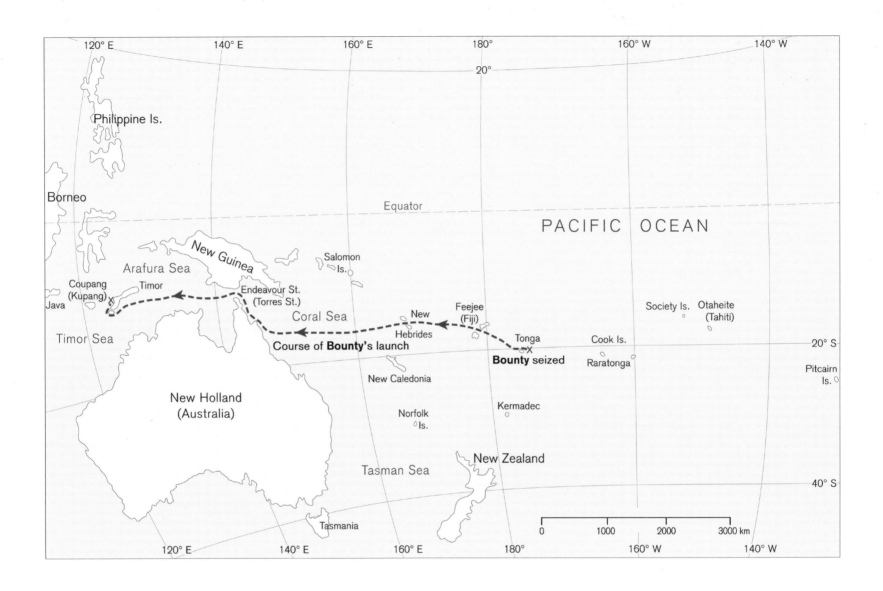

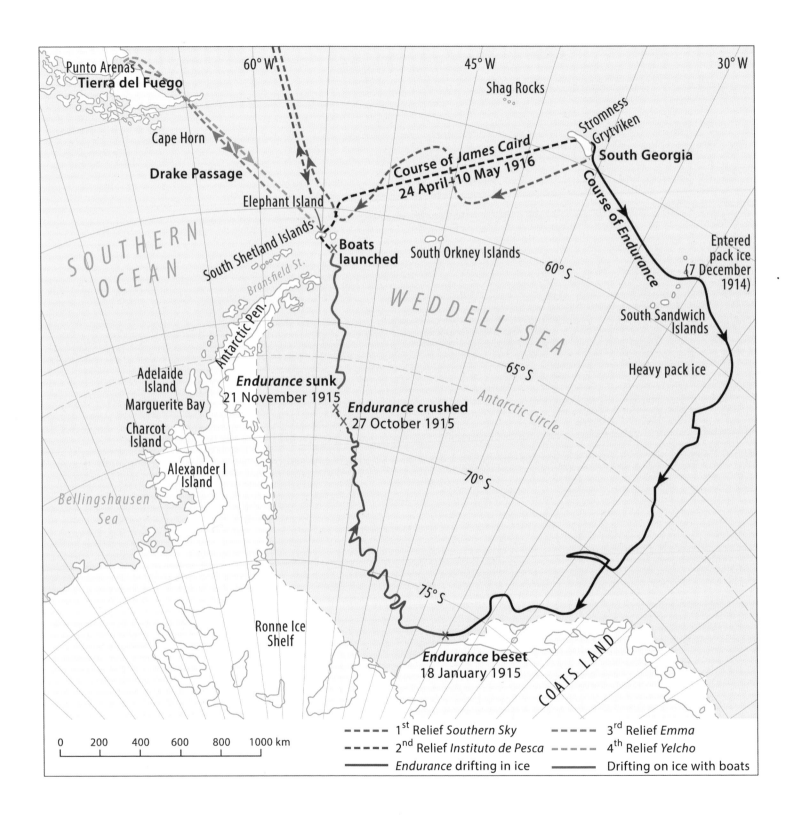

Punto Arenas
Tierra del Fuego

Cape Horn

Drake Passage

60° W

45° W

30° W

Shag Rocks

Stromness
Grytviken

Course of James Caird
24 April–10 May 1916

South Georgia

Course of Endurance

Elephant Island

SOUTHERN

OCEAN

South Shetland Islands

Bransfield St.

**Boats
launched**

South Orkney Islands

Entered
pack ice
(7 December
1914)

60° S

WEDDELL SEA

South Sandwich
Islands

Antarctic Pen.

Heavy pack ice

Adelaide
Island

Marguerite Bay

Endurance sunk
21 November 1915

Endurance crushed
27 October 1915

65° S

Antarctic Circle

Charcot
Island

Alexander I
Island

70° S

Bellingshausen
Sea

75° S

Ronne Ice
Shelf

COATS LAND

Endurance beset
18 January 1915

0   200   400   600   800   1000 km

1st Relief *Southern Sky*

2nd Relief *Instituto de Pesca*

Endurance drifting in ice

3rd Relief *Emma*

4th Relief *Yelcho*

Drifting on ice with boats

The beach at Point Wild, Elephant Island, Antarctica, where twenty-two of Shackleton's men were marooned for nearly five months in 1916. (Rorke Bryan)

German merchant raider, light cruiser SMS *Emden* commanded by Fregattenkapitän Karl von Müller, opens fire on a merchant ship in the Indian Ocean, November 1915.

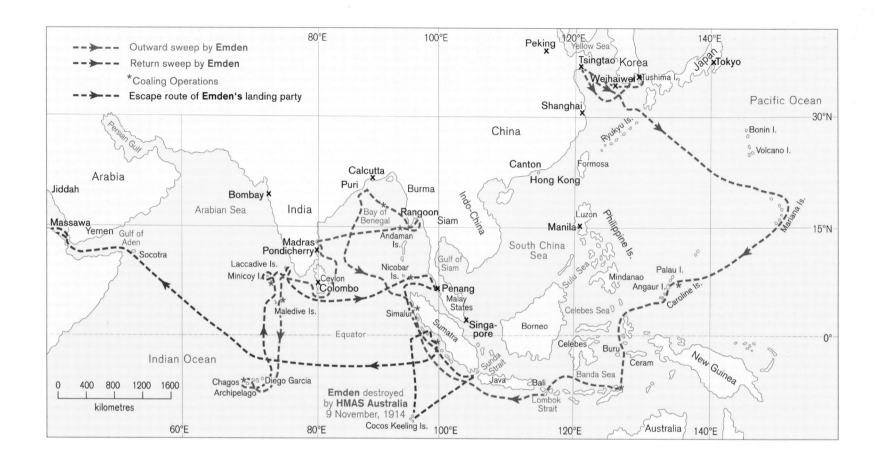

Outward sweep by **Emden**
Return sweep by **Emden**
*Coaling Operations
Escape route of **Emden's** landing party

Peking
Yellow Sea
Tsingtao Korea
Weihaiwei Tushima I.
Japan Tokyo
Pacific Ocean
Shanghai
30°N
China
Bonin I.
Canton
Formosa
Volcano I.
Hong Kong
Ryukyu Is.
Mariana Is.
Arabia
Jiddah
Calcutta
Puri
Bombay
Burma
Indo-China
15°N
Massawa
Arabian Sea
India
Rangoon
Luzon
Yemen
Bay of
Benegal
Siam
Manila
Gulf of
Aden
Socotra
Madras
Andaman
Is.
Philippine Is.
Pondicherry
South China
Sea
Palau I.
Laccadive Is.
Nicobar
Is.
Gulf of
Siam
Mindanao
Angaur I.
Minicoy I.
Ceylon
Colombo
Sulu Sea
Caroline Is.
Maldive Is.
Penang
Simalur
Malay
States
Celebes Sea
Equator
Singa-
pore
0°
Sumatra
Borneo
Celebes
Buru
Indian Ocean
Java
Banda Sea
New Guinea
Ceram
0 400 800 1200 1600
Sunda
Strait
Bali
kilometres
Chagos
Diego Garcia
Emden destroyed
Archipelago
by **HMAS Australia**
9 November, 1914
Lombok
Strait
Australia
Cocos Keeling Is.
60°E 80°E 100°E 120°E 140°E

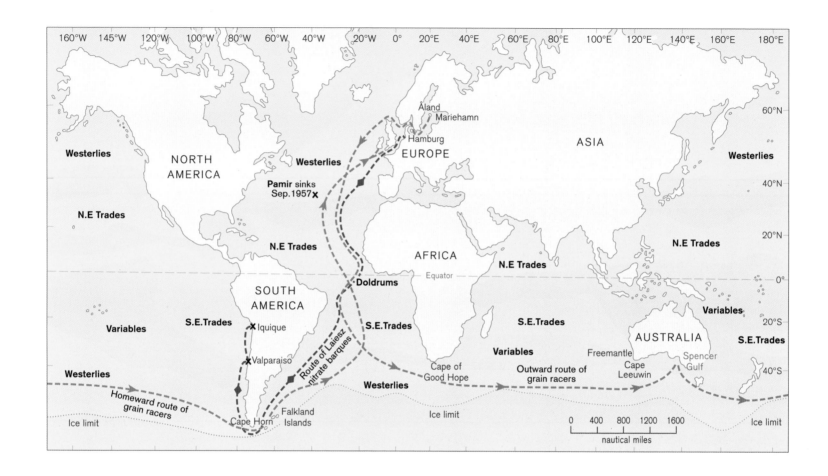

160°W 145°W 120°W 100°W 80°W 60°W 40°W 20°W 0° 20°E 40°E 60°E 80°E 100°E 120°E 140°E 160°E 180°E

Westerlies

NORTH
AMERICA

N.E Trades

Westerlies

Pamir sinks
Sep.1957 **X**

N.E Trades

Åland
Mariehamn

Hamburg

EUROPE

ASIA

Westerlies

60°N

40°N

20°N

AFRICA

Equator

Doldrums

N.E Trades

N.E Trades

0°

SOUTH
AMERICA

X Iquique

S.E.Trades

Variables

S.E.Trades

Route of Laiesz
nitrate barques

S.E.Trades

AUSTRALIA

Variables

20°S

X Valparaiso

Spencer
Gulf

S.E.Trades

Variables

Freemantle

Westerlies

Homeward route of
grain racers

Cape Horn

Falkland
Islands

Westerlies

Cape of
Good Hope

Outward route of
grain racers

Cape
Leeuwin

40°S

Ice limit

Ice limit

Ice limit

0   400   800   1200 1600

nautical miles

Ice limit

Cunard liner RMS *Lusitania*, torpedoed by *U-20*, sinking off the Old Head of Kinsale, Ireland, 7 May 1915.

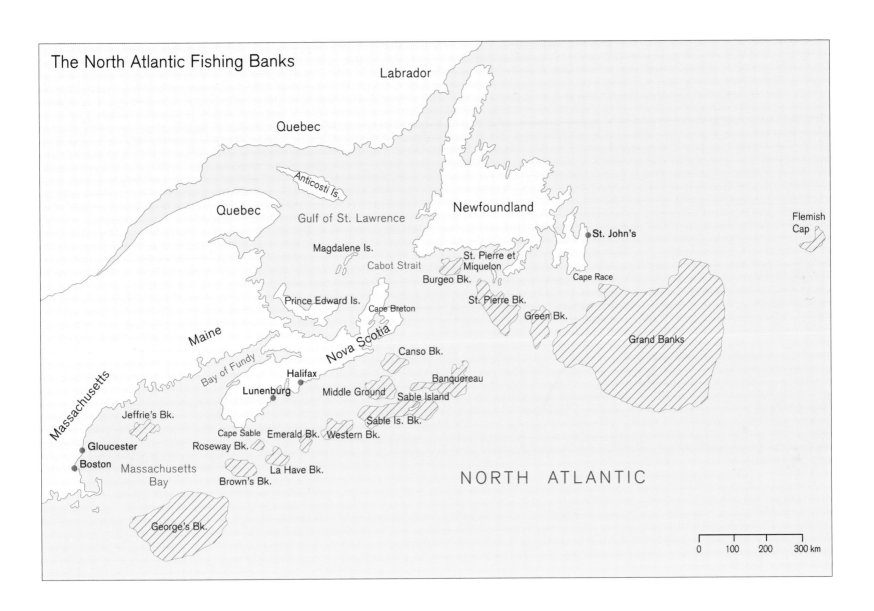

The North Atlantic Fishing Banks

Labrador

Quebec

Anticosti Is.

Quebec

Newfoundland

Flemish Cap

Gulf of St. Lawrence

St. John's

Magdalene Is.

St. Pierre et Miquelon

Cabot Strait

Burgeo Bk.

Cape Race

Prince Edward Is.

St. Pierre Bk.

Cape Breton

Green Bk.

Maine

Nova Scotia

Grand Banks

Canso Bk.

Bay of Fundy

Halifax

Banquereau

Massachusetts

Lunenburg

Middle Ground

Sable Island

Sable Is. Bk.

Jeffrie's Bk.

Cape Sable

Emerald Bk.

Western Bk.

Gloucester

Roseway Bk.

Boston

La Have Bk.

Massachusetts
Bay

Brown's Bk.

NORTH ATLANTIC

George's Bk.

0   100   200   300 km

Royal Canadian Mounted Police cutter *St Roch* frozen in for the winter at Pasley Bay, Boothia Peninsula, Nunavut, Canada, January 1942.

engines. With two funnels down, and the third badly damaged, the furnace draught dwindled, her speed dropped and, with the torpedo flat out of action, von Müller decided to run her aground on the North Keeling Island coral reefs, 29km from Direction Island, to save the remaining crew. At 11.15 a.m. she grounded on the reef, 100m from the shore.

Emden was reduced to a burning shambles of crushed metal, the red-hot stern could not be reached, the fo'c'sle was packed with dead and seriously injured, and the last boat had been destroyed. With *Sydney* still firing, von Müller gave permission to try to reach the shore, but many were lost in heavy surf. After *Sydney* stopped firing, she set off after the *Buresk*, which was scuttled by her crew as she was being captured. Returning to the *Emden*, *Sydney* resumed firing, killing or wounding another twenty-five before *Emden*'s crew managed to hoist a white sheet. She then set off south to Direction Island, but did not attempt to land in the dark. Meanwhile von Mücke moved quickly; realising that *Emden* could not return, he captured the little 97t copra schooner *Ayesha*, moored in the harbour. With half the island's supplies and 680 litres of water, they slipped off, evading the *Sydney* in the dark, to start an extraordinary odyssey, which ended months later in Constantinople. Foiled, *Sydney* returned to North Keeling Island to rescue the survivors of the *Emden*, but because of the heavy surf, it was difficult to retrieve the wounded before the next day. Von Müller, the last to leave, was received by Captain Glossop and an honour guard on *Sydney*. The lopsided nature of the battle was clear; *Emden* had fired some 1,500 shells, but only sixteen had struck *Sydney*, most of which bounced off her heavier armour. Her casualty toll was four dead and seventeen wounded, compared with 141 dead and sixty-five wounded on *Emden*. The wounded were transferred to hospital in Colombo on 16 November while the remaining crew became prisoners of war in Malta's Verdala barracks.

Designed for a crew of five, rotten, leaking and packed with fifty men, *Ayesha*, without detailed charts or a reliable chronometer, was at the mercy of winds and currents. She took a fortnight to wallow her way to Padang where she caused a flurry of diplomatic activity as Allied representatives tried to have the men interned. However, *Ayesha* slipped back out to sea and sailed and drifted until 15 December before meeting the German collier *Choising*, at a location arranged through a German consulate. Von Mücke took command of the freighter; after sinking the derelict *Ayesha*, and rejecting an attempt

Gunners on the *Emden*.

to return to Tsingtao or to reach von Lettau's forces in East Africa, he set off to reach Germany overland via the Arabian Peninsula. *Choising* was repainted and her name changed to *Shenir*, under an Italian flag, but they had to steer well clear of Allied warships. She could barely manage 7 knots, and it took three weeks to reach the Red Sea, find refuge with a Turkish garrison near Hodeida in Arabia and contact a German consulate. The following weeks were like a 'Boys Own' adventure, on camel back to Yemen, through deserts and mountains to the remote Red Sea port of Jebaua by mule, then by dhows until these were wrecked. On camels, they were led by a young Arab girl to Jedda, losing ten men in skirmishes with Bedouin bandits and several to drowning and typhoid. A further nineteen-day journey voyage by dhow got them to Wejh, then by camel train to Al'Ala on the Hejaz railway, which took them to Damascus, Aleppo, and on 23 May, to Constantinople from which they finally made their way back to Berlin.

There the *Emden* epic ended, five months after von Spee's cruisers were wiped out by Admiral Craddock's battle cruisers off the Falkland Islands. In a voyage lasting barely three months, *Emden* had steamed

48,000km, coaled at sea eleven times, captured or sunk twenty-five Allied ships, including two warships, totalling 104,682t of shipping, worth £2–12 million, not including the oil tanks in Madras or the disruption of Allied war plans as no less than seventy-eight Allied warships hunted her over thousands of hectares of ocean. Her exploits and von Müller's scrupulous humanity provided a priceless propaganda tool for the Germans. In praise of a gallant foe, the London *Daily Telegraph* wrote that:

> The war at sea will lose some of its piquancy, its humour and its interest, now that the *Emden* has gone.

(The *Daily Telegraph*, November 1914)

Over the next eighty years four German warships would bear *Emden's* name, and all were allowed to carry an Iron Cross decoration. Every officer and fifty crew were awarded Iron Crosses and all survivors were permitted to add 'Emden' to their names. In 1917, von Müller, seriously ill from malaria, was transferred from Malta to Britain and was awarded the 'Blue Max', *Pour la Merité*, the highest German decoration.

References

Gröner, E., 1990, *German Warships, 1815–1945*, Naval Institute Press, Annapolis, Maryland.

Hoyt, E.P., 1966, *The Last Cruise of the Emden*, The Macmillan Co., New York.

Lochner, R.K. (trans. T. and H. Lindauer), 1988, *The Last Gentleman-of-War: The Raider Exploits of the Cruiser Emden*, Naval Institute Press, Annapolis, Maryland.

McClement, F., 1968, *Guns in Paradise: The Saga of the Cruiser Emden*, McClelland and Stewart Ltd, Toronto.

Van der Vat, D., 1983, *The Last Corsair: The Story of the Emden*, Hodder and Stoughton, London.

Von Hohenzollern-Emden, Prinz F.J., 1989, *Emden: The Last Cruise of the Chivalrous Raider, 1914*, Lyon Publishing International, Brighton.

Von Mücke, H. (trans. White, H.S.), 1917, *The Ayesha, Being The Adventures of the Emden Landing Party*, Ritter and Company, Boston, Mass.

Walter, J., 1994, *The Kaiser's Pirates*, Arms and Armour Press, London.

14 PAMIR AND THE CAPE HORNERS' FAREWELL

Pamir:	four-masted steel barque launched by Blohm & Voss, Hamburg, for F. Laeisz Line, July 1905.
Tonnage:	2,796t
Length:	96.3m
Beam:	14m
Draught:	7.25m
Sail:	3,490m^2
Speed	**(maximum):** 16 knots
Career:	1905–14 Chilean nitrate trade average 64–70 days from Hamburg to Valparaiso. 1914–20: at Canary Isles. 1920–24: Italian war reparations, Naples. 1924: sold to F. Laeisz for nitrate trade. 1931: sold to G. Erikson, Mariehamn, Åland, for Australian grain trade. 1941: New Zealand war prize, ten voyages to San Francisco and Vancouver. 1948: returned to Erikson Lines. 1949: last cargo-carrying windjammer to round Cape Horn. 1951: modernised with auxiliary engine, refrigeration. September 1957: capsized and sank 1,100km south-west of the Azores in Hurricane Carrie with loss of eighty lives.

Looking up from the deck was like gazing at a range of snow-capped peaks, a cloud of white canvas that seemed to scrape the clouds. In harbour, it dwarfed surrounding sheds and wharves, but from the mainmast cap, 51.2m above the deck, *Pamir* looked like a toy boat in a bathtub. The heavy steel royal yard, 30cm in diameter and 14.3m long, did not feel secure, even on a still, calm day. It is hard to imagine clinging there in a hurricane, and looking down at the great Cape Horn 'greybeards' sweeping across the deck in a welter of foam or, worse, abandoning the mast's illusory security to struggle out along a footrope to the yard's end to thump heavy wet or frozen canvas into a semblance of a furl that could be safely secured. Then, clumsy in stiff oilskins and heavy boots, hands half frozen and senses numbed by the screeching wind in the rigging, to edge gingerly back, with the masts swinging to and fro across the sky like a berserk metronome, and climb down wet, slippery ratlines, to hurriedly grab a lifeline as another giant wave thunders across the deck. It's no wonder that the men and boys who drove the giant windjammers round Cape Horn in the dying days of sail felt that they were a breed apart, tested by experiences unknown to ordinary men.

The British P&O steamer *Delta* passing through the newly opened Suez Canal in November 1869 sounded the knell for commercial sailing ships, though their death throes would last for nearly 100 years. Thousands of sailing ships still carried much of the world's trade, but it became more and more difficult to find cargoes as steamers became increasingly efficient. Sailing ships first disappeared from high-value markets like the China tea trade and the transatlantic passenger service, and soon they could attract only bulk cargoes at the lowest freight rates. As profits declined, ship owners scrambled to cut costs; ships were made bigger in hope of realising scale economies, while crews became smaller and younger as wages were reduced. Crack tea clippers like *Thermopylae* carried crews of thirty or more seamen who, in an emergency, could whip the sails off three masts simultaneously, but the huge steel barques like *Pamir* that prolonged the age of sail into the twentieth century often carried fewer than twenty teenagers and only a couple of able seamen. These boys would have to handle twice as many sails spread on four or five masts while driving through the most dangerous seas in the world. The ships were magnificent, but there could only be one conclusion; it was only due to the vision and determination of two men that the huge steel barques, the pinnacle of sailing-ship evolution, survived into the second half of the twentieth century, Carl Laiesz of Hamburg and Gustaf Erikson of Mariehamn in Åland

Ferdinand Laiesz, born in 1801, was one of the first to appreciate the trading potential of South America as it emerged from colonial domination. In 1839 he founded Reederei Laiesz and took the 220t brig *Carl* on a pioneer voyage to Pernambuco with a cargo of silk hats. Reederei Laiesz would become one of the most important shipping companies in Germany, trading all over the world, and becoming the first European firm to trade with Japan, but it was the Chilean trade that made its fortune. Laiesz gradually expanded, purchasing or building new ships and in 1867 started a regular liner trade to Chile with monthly departures from Hamburg. Shortly after Reederei Laiesz was founded, the chemist von Liebig transformed global agriculture by demonstrating the extraordinary capacity of added inorganic nutrients to increase crop yields. The full impact of his discovery took some time to materialise as large inorganic sources of nitrogen are rare. One very large source is sodium nitrate, found in caliche deposits 2,500m up in Chile's Atacama Desert, but it took the astute Laiesz to develop the means to bring it to the tired fields of Europe. The rich caliche and the equally valuable nitrogen in guano deposits on coastal islands off Peru was contested and soon sparked a three-sided war between Chile, Peru and Bolivia. When the situation stabilised Carl Laiesz, Ferdinand's son, could develop the trade's full potential. Starting in 1887, he quickly expanded the Laiesz fleet, buying or building ships for the nitrate trade.

The nitrate trade required significant changes in shipping practices. To be profitable, ships had to be bigger and carry much larger cargoes. They therefore had to be built of iron; very large wood or composite ships couldn't survive the giant seas that sweep around Cape Horn. The rest of the ship had to match the hull in strength with iron masts, steel wire rigging and sails of the strongest canvas. The trade had to be predictable to make money; it was no good to build up a European farming clientele dependent on nitrate fertilisers if delivery could not be guaranteed. This was no easy challenge; the return voyage from Hamburg to Valparaiso is some 36,400km and in the best conditions would take at least five months. (Map, see p. 108) Ships would have to round Cape Horn in both directions; eastward rounding driven before the Roaring Forties, though dangerous, was fairly predictable but westward rounding against the wind was another matter. Like the *Bounty,* many ships spent months trying to beat against the westerlies before surrendering and running right around the globe before the wind. Others, forced far south in search of more favourable easterly winds, would meet pack ice and icebergs from Antarctica, sometimes disappearing without trace. For most captains, winds were a mystery of providence; almost none knew of the charts laboriously collected by Lieutenant Matthew Maury of the US Navy, fifty years earlier, but Carl Laiesz made sure that his captains used them.

There was no point in building powerful ships to successfully challenge Cape Horn hurricanes if they were not matched by skilful,

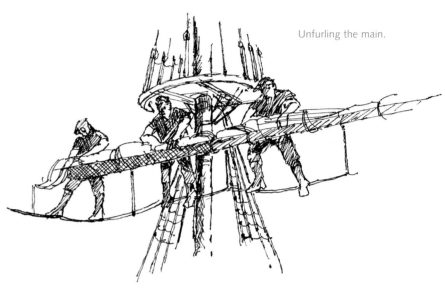

Unfurling the main.

experienced captains. At No. 1, Trostebrücke in Hamburg, Reederei Laiesz was at the heart of one of the world's greatest seaports and, with their reputation for sparing nothing to equip ships, could take their pick of the finest seamen. Over the next decades captains like Robert Miethe, Boye Petersen and the greatest, Robert Hilgendorf, the 'devil of Hamburg', would become revered amongst sailors. A careful student of Maury's charts, which took the guesswork out of wind forecasting, Hilgendorf rounded Cape Horn sixty-six times. He never took more than ten days between 50°S in the Atlantic and the same latitude in the Pacific, and he once completed an incredible two round voyages between Hamburg and Valparaiso within twelve months. Miethe's greatest exploit was to bring the great five-masted barque *Potosi* tearing up the Elbe during a hurricane on a filthy night when the helmsman could hardly see the bowsprit to anchor her safely at the only point on the river where she wouldn't collide with another ship.

Laiesz's first iron ships were bought from England, but starting with the 1,075t *Parsifal* in 1882 he had a ship built nearly every year by the Blohm and Voss shipyard in Hamburg. No expense was spared for equipment, but as a successful businessman, Laiesz fully understood the need to operate safely with the smallest possible crews. Virtually all ships in his fleet were barques rather than ship-rigged, and their names began with 'P', becoming the foundation of the famous 'Flying

P Line'. Ships' sizes increased steadily and after 1900 were all either four- or five-masted, culminating in the 4,026t five-masted barque *Potosi* in 1895 and the 5,081t *Preussen* in 1902. The fleet grew from seventeen ships totalling 8,641t in 1880 to fifteen ships of 35,064t in 1905. The unique *Preussen*, 124.4m long and carrying 5,587m^2 of sail, was the only five-masted ship-rigged vessel ever built, while the 111.6m-long *Potosi*, was only slightly smaller. They were magnificent, powerful ships, which could carry sail in the worst conditions, but they were somewhat impractical. It wasn't always possible to find enough cargo to fill their huge holds, and only the finest captains could handle them safely. *Preussen* was fast, once running 589km in twenty-four hours, and grabbing the record from the Lizard to Iquique in fifty-nine days, two days faster than *Potosi*, but she was a man killer, losing a crewman on almost every voyage during her eight-year career. Apart from Cape Horn, the English Channel was the most dangerous part of the journey; in November 1910 the cross-channel packet *Brighton* misjudged *Preussen*'s speed and carved across her bows, destroying her bowsprit and foremast. Several tugs got lines aboard but couldn't hold her against a rising gale and she was lost on the English coast.

After flirting with the huge *Potosi* and *Preussen,* Reederei Laeisz turned to slightly smaller but more practical ships: *Petschili* in 1903, *Pamir* in 1905 and *Peking* and *Passat* in 1911. All were four-masted barques of about the same size and all were very successful. The 2,796t *Pamir* was 96.3m long and normally carried thirty-one sails totalling 3,490m^2 on three 59.8m-high masts and a 50.6m jigger mast, and occasionally added stu'nsails. She had a full load capacity of 6,500t and sea-going ballast of 1,500t. Like all Laeisz P liners, she was a 'three-island' ship with a full bridge amidships where officers and crew were all housed in considerably greater comfort than on earlier ships. The raised poop, fo'c'sle and midships were all linked by gangways above the main deck, which made her much safer when the deck was awash with the great seas of the Southern Ocean, while the helmsman on the midships bridge also had greater protection than exposed on the poop.

Pamir was a fast ship, which on her second voyage ran from the English Channel to Valparaiso in sixty-four days. The next ten years were the Flying P Line's glory days at the peak of a global fleet of big square-riggers from fifteen countries numbering around 3,500 vessels. Many were employed in the Chilean nitrate or guano trade and thirty–forty big barques were often anchored off Valparaiso as crews vied to complete their loading in the shortest time. Amongst many fine passages, none surpassed *Potosi*'s outward voyage from Hamburg to Valparaiso around Cape Horn against the wind in fifty-five days (although the absolute record for rounding the cape was by a later Laeisz barque, *Priwall*, which raced from 50°S in the Atlantic to 50°S in the Pacific in five days and fourteen hours in 1938). It all stopped in August 1914 when German ships were forced back home or to neutral ports. Six Laeisz ships, *Pelikan, Potosi, Pommern, Peking, Pinnas* and *Petschili* were interned in Valparaiso along with another nineteen German ships. *Pamir* was off Cape Horn on her way home when war broke out on 4 August; unable to reach Hamburg, Captain Jürss put into the neutral Canary Islands where *Pamir* stayed for the next five and a half years.

Many windjammers were sunk or scrapped during the war, and the Treaty of Versailles delivered a body blow to Reederei Laeisz. By treaty terms the German commercial fleet, including all the famous P liners, was dispersed as war reparations amongst the victors. *Pamir* continued her long-interrupted voyage, unloading her nitrate cargo in Genoa before being turned over to Italy where she remained idle for four years. Reederei Laeisz didn't stay down for long; almost immediately it started to buy back ships at competitive prices; *Pamir* was re-purchased in 1924 for £7,000. A few new ships were also added, *Priwall* in 1920, and the last big iron square-rigger to be built, *Padua* in 1926. However, things had changed; with necessity, forced by the wartime blockade, Germany had invented synthetic nitrogen, undermining the demand for Chilean nitrate, so by 1933 Laeisz sold off all but newest ships. *Priwall* and *Padua* remained in the nitrate trade until the Second World War, but otherwise Laeisz turned to steamers and the tropical fruit trade

Pamir was sold by Laeisz in 1931 and in a rational economic world her story would probably have ended but for a canny Ålander with an eye for a bargain. Gustaf Erikson was born in 1872 into the vibrant seafaring tradition of the Åland Islands. His father was part farmer and part ship owner and almost inevitably he became a sailor, taking over his first command, the schooner *Adéle,* in 1893. By 1913 he was part owner of the Dutch-built *Tjerimai* and soon added his first big iron barque, the 3,300t *Renée Rickmers,* for the bargain price of £6,500. Over the next decade a bewildering sequence of acquisitions followed as the U-boat campaign, then poor freight rates throttled marine commerce. By the mid-1920s many good ships were being sold off for almost scrap value and Erikson expanded his fleet using credit from his London agents Clarkson & Co. He first bought the British barque *Lawhill* and by 1935 owned fourteen fine vessels, including *Penang, Pommern, Ponape, Passat* and *Pamir,* which he bought in November 1931 for £4,000.

With the decline of the nitrate trade, there weren't many opportunities for large sailing ships to make a living; coal and lumber provided some cargoes, but by far the most important was the wheat trade from Australia to Europe and most of Erikson's ships were soon involved. The 67,170km return voyage from Mariehamn to Spencer Gulf in southern Australia was an even longer grind than from Hamburg to Valparaiso. At least they missed the vicious westward rounding of Cape Horn but spent much longer in the big Southern Ocean seas, running their easting down to Australia. Erikson, known as 'Ploddy' or 'Pjutte Gustaf' to his employees, stayed in business only by the most rigorous cost control. His skippers were exhorted to avoid ships' chandlers and to use tugs only in the utmost peril. Fittings off scrapped or wrecked ships were religiously recycled amongst the surviving ships, but the most important saving was in crews' wages. To qualify for a second mate's certificate, apprentices in Finland had to serve three years in sailing ships, and Pjutte Gustaf was there to provide the opportunity – for a fee! While an experienced captain was paid up to 4,500 marks per month (about £45) and an able seaman, 550–650 marks, apprentices had to pay for the privilege of exceedingly hard work in dangerous conditions. Finnish apprentices paid 6,000 marks for two years; Germans 850 Reichsmarks, Swedes 1,800 kronor and Britons £100. Not surprisingly, few crew were able seamen; when Eric Newby sailed on Eriksson's barque *Moshulu* in 1938–39, only two of eighteen foremast hands were able seamen.

Few freights were available for the outward voyage to Australia and most ships arrived at Spencer's Gulf in ballast. There were often long delays at the little outports scattered around the Gulf as wheat slowly trickled down from up-country farms. Facilities were extremely limited and crews had to load and stow thousands of tons of wheat sacks by hand onto ships tied up at long wooden jetties or anchored offshore. Ships often anchored for several months in the Gulf before they could set out for home. Unlike the China tea trade, there was no formal race and ships seldom sailed on the same tide, but an eagerly contested informal annual 'Grain Race' soon developed. There were no premium

freight rates for the winners; in fact freight rates, which had reached 47 shillings per ton in 1928 when the races started, dropped as low as 16 shillings per ton two years later. The rewards were bragging rights and the race was judged by the shortest elapsed time from Spencer Gulf to the first port of call, usually Falmouth or Cobh. Despite the small, often inexperienced crews, there were many fine passages; *Moshulu*, which won the last race in 1939, reached Cobh in ninety-one days, averaging over 8 knots for the complete voyage. Many daily runs across the Southern Ocean compared well with the elite tea clippers. In 1932, *Pamir* went from Copenhagen to Port Victoria in seventy-seven days, compared with *Thermopylae*'s best passage in the wool trade of sixty-three days. In 1939, *Moshulu* was followed by *Padua* to the Fastnet in ninety-three days in second place and *Pamir* to Falmouth third in ninety-six days.

As in 1914, the war changed everything. When war broke out the windjammer fleet was spread out around the world. Some, like *Olivebank,* were soon sunk by mines. Others like *Pommern, Viking* and *Passat* were turned over for grain storage. *Priwall*, the last barque in the nitrate trade, was interned in Chile and was eventually accidentally burned off Peru in 1945. *Pamir* was in Göteborg when the war broke out and stayed there until the Finnish winter war with Russia ended in March 1940. She then sailed south as a neutral vessel and spent a year trading between the Seychelles and New Zealand before Britain declared Finland an enemy occupied territory in August 1941 whereupon she was seized in Wellington by the New Zealand government. The Union Steamship Co. was contracted to operate *Pamir* on behalf of the government, and she departed from Wellington in March 1942 for the first of five voyages between New Zealand and San Francisco. She was crewed primarily by young New Zealand apprentices who averaged 17½ years in age. The main cargoes carried were wool and tallow on the outward leg with timber, lubricating oil, asphalt, tin plate and bitumen on the return.

After the war *Pamir* made three voyages to Vancouver under the New Zealand flag, again with wool and tallow, returning with cargoes of wheat and coal, but each voyage lost money, and her future became increasingly uncertain. Many proposals were floated, including one from the Canadian government to operate her as a sail-training vessel, and one for use in a film by J. Arthur Rank. In the meantime, Gustaf Erikson vigorously tried to reclaim his property and after his death in 1948, she was handed back to Finnish authorities. In February 1949 she left Wellington under the command of her previous Finnish captain, Verner Björkfeldt, for Port Victoria on Spencer's Gulf where she loaded wheat for Britain. The recommissioned *Passat* under Captain Ivar Hägerstrand left Port Victoria two days later and with a cleaner bottom passed her on the way to Cape Horn; on 11 July, *Pamir* rounded Cape Horn, the last sailing ship to do so carrying a commercial cargo.

Gustaf Erikson's successors could see no way to operate *Pamir* profitably and, after a year as a grain hulk, in March 1951 she was sold to shipbreakers in Antwerp. However, before the magnificent old ship could suffer the indignity of being scrapped, she was brought back to Germany, together with *Passat*, by Heinz Schliewen of Lubeck. In Kiel she was radically modified with a lengthened poop, two 2.5t derricks, a large deep-water ballast tank, radar, an echo sounder, accommodation for eighty officer cadets and a 900bhp submarine diesel engine, which in calm weather gave her a speed of 8.5 knots. With a complement of ninety-one, including forty-six cadets, and a cargo of bagged cement she sailed for Rio de Janeiro. Her propeller dropped off in the English Channel, but the voyage and a return trip with 3,900t of iron ore were successfully completed. However, freight rates were dropping and after one more voyage, the operation went bankrupt. In 1954, she was bought by a German ship-owners' consortium (not including Reederei Laiesz), extensively refitted and, heavily subsidised as cargo-carrying sail trainer, completed several voyages to South America. In September 1957, homeward bound from Buenos Aires with a crew of eighty-six including fifty-two cadets, and a cargo of barley, *Pamir* was hit by a severe hurricane at 35°57′N, 40°20′W. All sails were soon lost and driven over to 45°, her cargo of loose barley (loaded by the cadets because of a longshoremen's strike) shifted, putting her onto her beam ends; with 10m waves washing over her, she quickly capsized and sank. Only six of the crew survived. By coincidence, a fortnight later *Passat*'s cargo of loose grain also shifted in heavy weather, but she managed to struggle into Lisbon. On returning to Germany, she was laid up and turned into a youth hostel. The catastrophe that destroyed *Pamir* marked the death of the Cape Horners; the experiment of combining cargo carrying with sail training would not be repeated. Some of the great steel barques survive as museum ships, like *Pommern* in Mariehamn, *Peking* in New York and *Viking* in Göteborg, but only *Padua* and *Kommodore Johnsen* still sail as the Russian sail trainers *Kruzenstern* and *Sedov*. They are, however, drastically changed and even they will never again 'drink delight of battle' with the great greybeards and screaming hurricanes off Cape Horn.

References

Boberg, L., 1990, *Pamir,* Wikens förlag, Höganäs.

Churchouse, J., 1978, *The Pamir Under the New Zealand Ensign*, Millwood Press, Wellington.

Greenhill, B., and Hackman, J., 1986, *The Grain Races*, Conway Maritime Press, London.

Kåhre, G., 1948, *The Last Tall Ships: Gustaf Eriksson and the Åland Sailing Fleets, 1872–1947*, Conway Maritime Press, Greenwich.

Knox-Johnston, R., 1994, *Cape Horn: a Maritime History*, Hodder and Stoughton, London.

Appolonio, S., 2000, *The Last of the Cape Horners: Firsthand Accounts from the Final Days of the Tall Ships*, Brassey's, Washington.

Newby, E., 1956, *The Last Grain Race*, Secker & Warburg, London.

Villiers, A., 1972, *Falmouth for Orders*, Charles Scribner's Sons, New York.

Wells. R.E., 1992, *The Vancouver Voyages of the Barque Pamir,* Sono Nis Press, Victoria, B.C.

15 RMS *LUSITANIA*, THE BLUE RIBAND AND THE FORTUNES OF WAR

RMS *Lusitania*:	luxury transatlantic Royal Mail liner launched by the John Brown shipyard, Glasgow for the Cunard Line, 7 June 1906.
Tonnage:	31,550t (gross register tonnage, grt)
Length:	239.9m
Beam:	26.5m
Draught:	33.6m
Engine:	six Parson's steam turbines forward propulsion driving all four propellers and two for going astern, which drove the inner two propellers 76,000shp.
Speed:	26.7 knots
Crew:	800
Passengers:	2,198 on six decks (552 First Class, 460 Second Class, 1,186 Third Class)
Career:	September 1907: maiden voyage to New York, set Blue Riband at 23.99 knots on second voyage. 1908: new propellers fitted, record raised to 25.1 knots. 1909: four-bladed 5.18m-diameter propellers fitted, record raised to 25.65 knots, but lost one month later to RMS *Mauretania*. 7 May 1915: torpedoed and sunk by German *U-20*, 18km off Old Head of Kinsale, with loss of 1,201 lives.

It was a banner day on 6 June 1906 at the John Brown shipyard in Glasgow. If all went well, just after midday the great new passenger liner *Lusitania* would slip gently into the murky waters of the River Clyde. Registering 31,550t (grt) and 239.9m long, *Lusitania* was the largest ship yet to be launched, 30m longer than the *Great Eastern*, Brunel's white elephant launched in 1858. She was also one of the first passenger vessels to be fitted with Parson's revolutionary steam turbines, introduced on the experimental *Turbinia* at the 1897 Spithead Naval Review. *Lusitania* and her sister ship *Mauretania*, launched shortly afterwards by Swan Hunter shipyard in Newcastle, were the cutting edge of modern ship design, but they were also the latest stage in several distinct competitions, one of which would soon end in war.

While clippers like *Thermopylae* were straining their rigging to the limit in the tea trade, James Baines' Black Ball Line clippers were blazing a fast, regular packet service across the Atlantic. The paddle steamers *Sirius* and Brunel's *Great Western* started regular passages to New York in 1838, but it would be decades before they could match the Black Ball clippers. However, one great maritime competition was initiated. The Blue Riband was awarded for the fastest westward Atlantic crossing, though it was 1910 before the name became widely known. The companies running *Sirius* and *Great Western* did not last long, put out of business by Canadian Samuel Cunard. He won a £60,000 Admiralty subsidy for a transatlantic mail service, which started with the paddle steamer *Britannia* in 1840 with a very seasick Charles Dickens amongst her passengers.

In 1850 the average crossing speed was raised above 12 knots by Cunard's 2,226t *Asia* and shortly afterwards to nearly 13 knots by the Collins Line's *Baltic*. Collins Line, handsomely subsidised by the United States government, was soon undermined by the sinking of two ships with considerable loss of life, while Cunard responded with several fine new ships equipped with watertight bulkheads. In 1863, the 3,871t *Scotia* carrying 323 passengers took the record at 14.46 knots, but the end was in sight for paddle steamers with inefficient coal-hungry boilers. Soon the ocean greyhounds were screw-driven and fitted with much more efficient double-expansion boilers, which significantly reduced coal consumption. Cunard's dominance was soon challenged and in 1872 their great competitor, Ismay's White Star Line, lifted the record with the long, narrow 3,868t screw steamer *Adriatic* built by Harland and Wolff in Belfast, initiating intense rivalry between the two shipping lines and between the Clyde and Belfast shipyards.

Competition for passengers on the transatlantic route placed immense demands on designers for bigger, faster ships but also to outdo one another by incorporating sumptuously luxurious first-class cabins and lounges. Other companies were soon drawn into the competition; the Inman Line held the record briefly in 1875 with the 5,491t *City of*

Berlin and again in 1889 with the 10,499t twin-screw *City of Paris*. The competition was very expensive as new ships became obsolete as Blue Riband contenders after a few voyages. White Star soon won the Blue Riband back at over 20 knots with *Majestic* and *Teutonic,* both built with Admiralty subsidies and designed to be easily converted into auxiliary cruisers, beginning to blur the distinction between civilian and naval vessels, which would ultimately have tragic results. Cunard also received Admiralty subsidies and soon regained the record with the magnificent new steel *Campania* and *Lucania,* while in Germany new liners were also designed with the needs of war in mind.

Newly unified and buoyed by victory in the Franco-Prussian War in 1871, Germany aspired to greater international prominence and was determined to challenge British maritime supremacy. In 1881 Norddeutscher Lloyd in Bremen entered the transatlantic competition, followed by the Hamburg Amerika (Hapag) Line in 1889. Their fast, luxurious ships attracted many passengers but failed to win the Blue Riband. Kaiser Wilhelm II, crowned in 1888, was determined to change this after examining the *Teutonic* at the Spithead Naval Review in 1889. The 9,988t, 177.4m-long liner participating in the Review as an auxiliary cruiser, was larger and faster than any existing battleship. With the Kaiser's support (but no government subsidy), German shipbuilding capabilities expanded quickly and in 1897, the four-funnel, 14,349t Hamburg Amerika Line *Kaiser Wilhelm der Grosse* was launched in Stettin. She quickly earned a reputation for ferocious rolling, but took the Blue Riband on her maiden voyage at 21.39 knots, starting a decade of German domination in which she was soon matched by Norddeutscher Lloyd's *Deutschland*. Both were designed to be easily converted into armed cruisers. The next Hamburg Amerika liner, the *Kronprinzessin Cecilie,* was designed to carry eight 14.99cm, four 10.4cm and two 8.64cm guns, sixteen light machine guns, two small torpedo boats and sixteen torpedoes.

Grave concern in Britain soon increased when the American banker J.P. Morgan bought Norddeutscher Lloyd and Hamburg Amerika, White Star and several other British lines, merging them with his American Line into the International Mercantile Marine Company. Afraid of losing control over their auxiliary reserve cruisers the Admiralty subsidised Cunard to build two new ships, the *Lusitania* and the *Mauretania*. A £2.6 million loan at a 2.75% interest rate and an annual subsidy of £150,000 were provided, but in return the Admiralty had to approve the ships' plans, all officers had to belong to the Royal Naval Reserve, the ships could not be sold out of Britain, and the Admiralty would control the ships in the event of war.

Kaiser Wilhelm der Grosse and *Deutschland* were very fast but at high speed they vibrated severely, causing *Deutschland* to lose her rudder on one voyage. The limits for triple-expansion engines with twin screws had been reached and a new approach was needed to achieve the Admiralty's stipulated minimum average speed of 24.5 knots. Doubts persisted about the reliability of Parson's new steam turbines, but experience with the revolutionary battleship HMS *Dreadnought* and the Cunarder *Carmania*, launched in 1903, was positive, so they were adopted for *Lusitania* and *Mauretania*. Turbines operate most efficiently at around 1,800rpm, while propellers are most effective at about 100rpm. Suitable gearboxes were not available until 1916, so as a compromise, the turbines were matched to a 180rpm propeller speed. Six turbines, four forward and two astern, were linked directly to four propeller shafts, generating 76,000shp, nearly 100 per cent more than the German liners. The turbines were driven by twenty-three boilers and 192 furnaces arranged in four huge boiler rooms directly beneath the ship's four funnels, separated by watertight bulkheads.

The engines weren't the only design challenge. If the huge boiler rooms flooded, there was not enough buoyancy to keep the ship afloat, so lateral longitudinal watertight compartments were installed outside the boiler rooms. The very large coal bunker, situated near the bow, could not hold sufficient coal for an Atlantic crossing. As the Admiralty required all vital machinery to be located below the water line, protected from enemy gunfire, additional bunkers could not be fitted in the lower hull, so the lateral watertight compartments were used as coal bunkers. The doors through which coal could be drawn were watertight but, once opened, the weight of coal prevented them being closed, making them useless as watertight compartments. During the *Titanic* enquiry in 1912, it was suggested that flooding of lateral compartments could produce a severe list, making it difficult to launch lifeboats.

With major technical issues apparently solved, the designer, Leonard Peskett, still had to find space for nearly 2,000 passengers and 850 crew and staff. Cabins for the 1,186 third-class passengers were quite spartan, but the first-class accommodation was palatial. Cabins were spacious and elegantly decorated with white carved mahogany panelling; the Regal Suites contained two bedrooms, a parlour, a bathroom and a dining room and pantry, and were modelled on Marie

Antoinette's Petit Trianon. This luxury was matched by the gilded Corinthian pillars and Rococo-panelled splendour of sumptuous dining rooms, smoking rooms, saloons, lounges, cafe verandas and reading rooms, many decorated in Louis Seize or Queen Anne style, joined by sweeping staircases that could have graced a southern antebellum mansion. The six decks needed to accommodate this luxurious floating hotel gave *Lusitania* a very high freeboard with the boat deck 18.3m above the waterline. Scale model tank tests showed this original design to be highly unstable so the beam had to be increased by 3.05m.

Despite design challenges, *Lusitania* was built in less than fifteen months, and though the banks of the Clyde had to be widened to accommodate her great length, the launch went without a hitch. After another year of fitting out, she started sea trials but soon met a serious problem; at close to her maximum speed of 26.7 knots *Lusitania* vibrated so badly that the second-class cabins near the stern could not be used. Hammer-like cavitation shocks pounding the three-bladed propellers as they approached 180rpm were magnified by resonance with the ship's framework. A bare month before her scheduled maiden voyage most second-class cabins had to be ripped out so that more steel beams and braces could be added. This did not completely solve the vibration problem, but it was reduced and *Lusitania* departed on her maiden voyage from Liverpool via Queenstown (now Cobh) to New York on 7 September 1907.

The crossing was delayed by fog and having to run in the engines carefully, and was slightly slower than the German record. On *Lusitania*'s second westward voyage, a month later, she lifted the record to 23.99 knots. In 1908, with new outer propellers with a different pitch fitted to cure the vibration, she raised the record to 24.83 knots and then, with a new captain, William Turner, to 25.01 knots. She still vibrated, however, and in 1909 all the three-bladed propellers were replaced by 5.18m diameter, four-bladed phosphor-bronze propellers like those fitted to *Mauretania*. With these she took the record to 25.65 knots, but a month later *Mauretania* set it at 26.06 knots where it remained until 1929.

With Admiralty subsidies, Cunard now had a stranglehold on the Blue Riband. Competitors no longer tried to compete on overall speed but on size, luxury and safety. Harland & Wolff built three 45,000t *Olympic*-class liners for White Star in Belfast, including Thomas Andrew's ill-fated 'unsinkable' *Titanic,* while Hamburg Amerika launched three 50,000t *Imperator*-class liners. In the meantime, *Lusitania* was refitted to allow rapid installation of twelve 15.24cm quick-firing guns. By the time this was completed, war was imminent and in August 1914 German troops marched into Belgium launching the First World War. Three months later Britain declared the North Sea a restricted British military area, cutting off German liners from the Atlantic, and followed up by blockading German ports. Exercising its rights to the Cunard ships, the Admiralty first converted *Mauretania* to a troop carrier, then, as casualties mounted, to a hospital ship, while *Lusitania* was refitted yet again and designated an express carrier for priority government cargoes. Most third-class cabins in the forward section of the ship were removed to provide extra cargo space, mainly reserved for Admiralty use.

Dancing in steerage on the *Lusitania.*

With her funnels ineffectively camouflaged in black, *Lusitania* now started the final, most controversial stage of her brief career. She was still a civilian liner and Cunard's financial responsibility, but with less passenger traffic and many fewer cabins, she was no longer profitable, though the Admiralty insisted that regular voyages were essential to maintain government supplies. In an attempt to remain solvent, Cunard reduced crossing frequency and closed one boiler room to cut coal and labour costs. With her cruising speed reduced to 18 knots, *Lusitania* still carried some, mainly wealthy, passengers but also, controversially, a wide range of war materials deemed vital to the expanding Allied war effort. The United States was still officially neutral, so these had to be disguised by falsifying cargo manifests.

Germany answered the British blockade by declaring the seas around the British Isles a war zone. The German fleet was not strong enough to enforce this with surface ships, but U-boats were another matter, and their activities abruptly increased. At first the 'cruiser rules' were followed; suspect ships were boarded and, if war materials were found, crews were removed and the ships were sunk. Britain responded by disguising armed 'Q ships' as harmless merchant vessels. After losing several U-boats, Germany abandoned cruiser rules and declared that all ships in the war zone were liable to be sunk without warning. Despite the clearly increased hazard *Lusitania* continued to run the gauntlet to Liverpool, on one occasion disguised by flying the Stars and Stripes.

Shortly after the flag episode, Captain Turner took *Lusitania* out to New York in April 1915 and on 1 May started her return journey. The omens were not good; immediately before her departure the German Embassy in Washington placed a notice in *The New York Tribune* warning that passengers would travel at their own risk, as any ship flying an Allied flag would be subject to attack. Despite this warning 1,265 passengers took the chance, amongst them 159 American citizens, including Alfred Vanderbilt and a contingent of nurses bound for the battlefields of France. There was a crew of 694, but of these only forty-five were seamen. *Lusitania*'s departure appeared normal, but there was widespread foreboding about the U-boat threat, particularly as the American tanker *Gulflight* had just been torpedoed in the Irish Sea. However, most people believed that even with one boiler room closed, *Lusitania* was fast enough to outrun any U-boat, and the Admiralty had promised that she would be escorted by the cruiser HMS *Juno* over the most dangerous sector from the Fastnet Rock, off the south-west Irish coast.

The first four days passed without incident, though during this time, twenty-three ships were sunk by U-boats around the British Isles. The Admiralty knew that two U-boats were active off Ireland, *U-30* off the north coast and *U-20* close to *Lusitania*'s planned course along the south coast. On 5 May *U-20* sank the schooner *Earl of Latham* south of the Old Head of Kinsale and attacked the White Star *Arabic* off Queenstown, and next day sank two Harrison Line freighters near the Coningbeg lightship off Co. Wexford. During the night of 6 May Captain Turner received several cautionary telegrams and, altering *Lusitania*'s course well south of the Fastnet, ordered the watertight bulkheads closed (apart from the coal access hatches). The Admiralty failed to inform him that, concerned by the U-boat threat, they had ordered HMS *Juno* back to Queenstown.

Early on 7 May several more Admiralty warnings of U-boats off the Fastnet and the Coningbeg lightship were received, but these were already out of date. *Lusitania* was now well past the Fastnet and rapidly closing on the Irish coast near Kinsale, while *U-20* was no longer off the Coningbeg. At 2 p.m. *U-20*'s commander, Kapitänlieutenant Walther Schwieger, was watching *Lusitania* through her periscope as she steamed on a steady course towards the lighthouse at the Old Head of Kinsale. Her defensive zigzag course had been temporarily abandoned so that the third officer could confirm her position by a

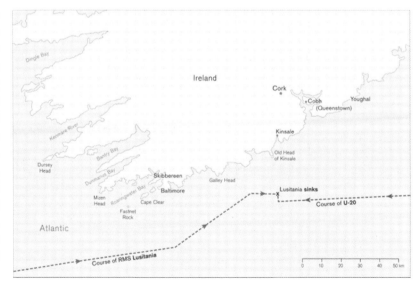

four-point fix. Moments later she turned to starboard, presenting a perfect torpedo target at about 600m range. Schwieger immediately launched a torpedo. The wake was sighted by a lookout at the last minute, but at 2.10 p.m. the torpedo struck *Lusitania*'s starboard side, just abaft the foremast. An initial small explosion was followed instantly by a much larger one, which blew a huge hole in the hull. The starboard bunkers flooded immediately and within minutes *Lusitania* was listing and down by the head with extensive fire and flooding near the first boiler room. Captain Turner quickly realised that the ship could not be saved. There were enough lifeboats for all on board, but with the rapidly increasing starboard list the port side boats swung inboard and, in the chaos and confusion, could not be launched. The starboard boats were launched, but several capsized or were smashed on the ship's side as they were lowered. The steep slope of *Lusitania*'s deck increased, then suddenly eased as *Lusitania*'s bow hit the bottom, 88m below. The hull pivoted as her stern sank and at 2.28 p.m. the great liner disappeared beneath the surface.

Hundreds of passengers were trapped on the sinking ship, but many were alive in the cold 11°C waters, though few were wearing life jackets. Vice Admiral Coke in Queenstown immediately ordered HMS *Juno* to the rescue, but almost as soon as she cast off his order was countermanded by the Admiralty, afraid that she also would be torpedoed. It would be several more hours before fishing boats from Kinsale could reach the site; by then hypothermia had done its work and many of those in the water were dead.

The survivors and the bodies were collected and brought back to Queenstown; 1,201 of the 1,962 people on board were lost (including three Germans arrested on board as *Lusitania* left New York). Amongst the dead buried in a mass grave at Queenstown during the next few days were 108 of the 159 American citizens on board. As the dead were buried, the public enquiries started. At the Board of Trade enquiry the Admiralty attempted to place all the blame on Cunard and Captain Turner, but the judge found that their ambiguous instructions, delayed, inaccurate telegraph warnings, and precipitate withdrawal of HMS *Juno* were major factors in the disaster.

Britain had already grown accustomed to dreadful death tolls from the bungling battlefield incompetence of the First World War, but the disaster triggered widespread outrage against the 'dastardly Germans' for sinking an 'unarmed' civilian ship, and the British Government seized the opportunity to re-ignite the faltering home fires of nationalistic fervour. With propaganda machinery in high gear, *Lusitania*'s role in carrying war materials was successfully concealed for many years. The exact cause of the second deadly blast, which caused most of the damage and probably destroyed the watertight bulkhead of the main coal bunker, is still hotly debated. It has been attributed to ignition of coal dust, but it is hard to believe that the 1,248 cases of 7.62cm shrapnel shells stored at the torpedo's impact point and 4,297 boxes of .303 rifle ammunition in the hold immediately above played no role.

British fury, which led to attacks on anyone and anything sounding even vaguely German, was matched by outrage in the United States about the American citizens lost but, contrary to popular myth, did not precipitate America's entry into the First World War. The trigger was

U-boat commander.

the infamous Zimmerman telegram nearly two years later, helpfully decoded and passed on by British cryptographers. This promised American territory to Mexico in return for an alliance with Germany and finally pushed President Woodrow Wilson into his pivotal declaration of war on 6 April 1917, which played such a vital role in ending the war with an armistice the following year.

References

Ballard, R., and Spencer, D., 1995, *Exploring the Lusitania*, Madison Publishing, Toronto.

Hickey, D., and Smith, G., 1981, *Seven Days to Disaster*, G.P. Putnam's Sons, New York.

Hoehling, A.A., and Hoehling, M., 1975, *The Last Voyage of the Lusitania*, Longmans, Green & Co., London.

Kludas, A., 2000, *Record Breakers of the North Atlantic: Blue Riband Liners 1838–1952*, Chatham Publishing, London.

Peeke, S., Jones, S., and Walsh-Johnson, K., 2002, *The Lusitania Story*, Leo Cooper, Barnsley.

Preston, D., 2002, *Lusitania: An Epic Tragedy*.

Ramsay, D., 2001, *Lusitania: Saga and Myth*, Chatham Publishing, London.

Simpson, C., 1972, *The Lusitania*, Longmans, London.

16 BLUENOSE AND A 'RACE FOR REAL SAILORS'

Bluenose:	two-masted Grand Banks schooner designed by William Roué, built by Smith & Rhuland, Lunenburg, Nova Scotia, to win the International Fishermen's Trophy; launched in March 1921.
Tonnage:	288t
Length:	34m
Beam:	8m
Draught:	5m
Sails:	eight, total area 1,036m^2
Crew:	15
Career:	1921: under command of Angus Walters, defeated *Elsie* of Gloucester, Mass. Many subsequent victories but in 1930 lost to *Gertrude L. Thebaud* of Gloucester in Lipton International Fishermen's Trophy. 1931: beat *Gertrude L. Thebaud* in re-match. 1938: won the final International Fishermen's Trophy Race against *Gertrude L. Thebaud*. 1942: sold to West Indies. 1946: wrecked off Haiti with freight of bananas.
Bluenose II:	replica launched at Smith & Rhuland, Lunenburg, 1963, with Angus Walters at helm. Tourist promotion vessel, currently under renovation in Lunenburg.

Some ships have a magic ingredient that cannot be explained by objective appraisal of the lines of their hulls, the design of their rigging, or, for more recent ships, the characteristics of their engines and power trains. *Bluenose* was a magical schooner; even in her later years, tired and waterlogged after a hard career of fishing on the Grand Banks of Newfoundland, she could dig deep into secret reserves and thrash her newer rivals, specially designed to beat her. She was truly a 'witch in the wind'.

The legend of *Bluenose* started formally in 1920, but its roots were planted much earlier. When John Cabot 'discovered' Newfoundland on the *Matthew* in 1497, some 500 years after Leif Erikson's longboats landed at L'Anse aux Meadows, he sailed through shoals of cod so plentiful they could 'be taken … with fishing baskets' and fishermen

were 'hardly able to row a boat through them'. Demand for fish in Europe, which had to be eaten by the faithful on the myriad saints' days, was immense and fishermen from Portugal, Spain and France soon flocked to the Grand Banks. Supply seemed unlimited but nineteenth-century wars in Europe sent prices for salt cod skyrocketing and ships from harbours all along the coasts of New England, Nova Scotia and Newfoundland soon joined in.

The relatively shallow Grand Banks extend some 450km into the Atlantic, east and south of Newfoundland. (Map, see p. 111) They were amongst the richest fishing grounds in the world, nourished by nutrients from the cold Labrador current dropped where it meets the warm Gulf Stream. An area of dense fogs, icebergs, floating pack ice and frequent savage storms, it is a perilous place for fishermen. Initially men fished from their ships with long lines of baited hooks. They caught a lot of fish but not enough to satisfy the ship owners – you couldn't fit enough men along the side of a schooner, so in the mid-nineteenth century methods changed. The fishing area could be covered much more efficiently if fishermen were sent off in small rowing boats to bring fish back to the schooners. There wasn't much space on schooners' decks, so special flat-bottomed 'dories' were invented; up to a dozen could be stacked there until needed. In the right conditions dories were fairly safe, but the conditions weren't often right. Dories, usually rowed by two men, with their kilometres of long lines, thousands of hooks, tubs and bait, would usually stay away all day, but some might be away for a week, returning so full of fish that water was sloshing over the gunwales. Blinding gales could sweep in without warning, plastering the little boats with ice and snow; all too often, heavily laden dories would be swamped or overturned, dumping their crews into the freezing water where even the few who could swim would quickly die. At other times dense fog would roll in making it almost impossible for the dorymen to find their way back to their schooners. Even aboard ship life was very dangerous and many crewmen were lost at sea. It was an exceptionally hard way to make a living with a horrendous death toll, but there were few job options along the east coast and, in the cynical accounting of the trade, crews were dispensable.

Crews were paid with a share of the catch and competition was fierce – to reach the fishing grounds, to fill their holds and to win the race back to port for the premium prices gained by the first to arrive. Skippers and crews had fierce pride in their ships and in themselves so competition for bragging rights, particularly between the Nova Scotian schooners out of Lunenburg and the Americans from Gloucester, Massachusetts, was intense. Informal races back from the Banks soon started and even some formal races, as during Gloucester's 250th anniversary celebrations in 1892. This race was held in a howling gale, but the trigger for the 'Race for Real Sailors' was the 1920 competition for the America's Cup. When the original *America* thrashed the best British yachts in 1851 before a disgusted Queen Victoria, she started one of the most hotly contested and long lasting of global sports contests. Successive wealthy British yachtsmen spent fortunes attempting to regain the ugly 'Old Mug'; by 1920 Sir Thomas Lipton had poured a lot of tea-drinking profits into four of an eventual five challenges (which earned him a trophy as 'the best of all losers'). The 1920 challenge started well with Lipton's *Shamrock IV* winning two races before losing three in a row to *Resolute*. However, when the organisers and owners called off the deciding race because the wind was too strong – a terrible 23 knots – they earned the scorn of every fisherman from Gloucester to St John's. They all felt that working fishermen with their big 'saltbankers' could put on a much better show. Senator William Dennis, owner of the *Halifax Herald* newspaper, soon announced a Halifax Herald North American Fishermen's International Competition Trophy, 'for the fastest schooner in the Nova Scotia and New England fishing fleets'.

By 1920 saltbankers had evolved from a diverse ancestry to rather similar and extremely seaworthy two-masted gaff-rigged schooners between 36.5m and 45.7m in length with 36.5m-high masts and around 836m^2 of sail. The rules laid down that the competitors must be working fishermen and the boats no longer than 44.2m overall length (possibly to eliminate the fastest American challenger) and 34.1m on the waterline, using customary rig and working sails and

with at least one season's fishing on the Grand Banks behind them. On 11 October nine Canadian ships faced off in an elimination contest out of Halifax harbour, round a triangular course at sea, then back to finish in the harbour. In winds from 18 to 25 knots, the 56km course race took just over five hours to complete, with Tommy Himmelman's *Delawana* the winner. Just over a fortnight later *Delawana* was comprehensively beaten by the Gloucester schooner *Esperanto*. Her captain, Marty Welch, born in Digby, Nova Scotia, went home with the Halifax Trophy and $4,000 in cash. This was not what the Nova Scotians had expected and they immediately laid plans to avenge the insult the following year.

Esperanto had beaten the pick of the Canadian ships, so clearly a new schooner had to be built to win back the trophy. Every shipyard along the coast was alerted; almost every shipyard designed ships,

Fishing off the *Bluenose*.

mostly built from moulded half models rather than from drawings. For centuries ships had been built along the coast. Built of green timber and sailed hard in all weathers, fishing schooners usually didn't last very long. Heavy wet cargoes quickly took their toll and ships' timbers worked hard in the rough seas – care was needed in schooners' bunks to avoid painful nips between working planks. There wasn't much time to pick a designer; a new boat would have to be in the water by the end of March 1921. The design chosen was drawn by Bill Roué, manager of his family's ginger ale factory in Halifax, who had taught himself to design boats while working as a teenage grocery clerk. His breakthrough came in 1907 when he designed *Babette* for the commodore of the Royal Nova Scotian Yacht Squadron. By 1920 Roué was a well-known member of the Squadron who had designed the fast racing yacht *Zetes*, renowned for her ability to beat into the wind.

Roué quickly produced drawings for an enlarged version of *Zetes*, but these were for a boat 36.5m on the waterline, and had to be cut down to 34.1m. Within three weeks, Roué had new drawings ready and Smith and Rhuland's Shipyard in Lunenburg was contracted to build the soon-to-be-named *Bluenose* for $35,000, twice the usual cost of a fishing schooner. On 18 December 1920 the Governor General of Canada visited Lunenburg to hammer the first spike into *Bluenose*'s keel. At lunch one toast in fine old West Indies rum led to another and by the time the dignitaries set out for the shipyard, the noisy procession resembled a Mardi Gras parade, to the disgust of the local Temperance Society. Encountering some difficulty in focusing, His Excellency took three unsuccessful swipes at the spike before a helpful aide hammered it home.

Work went ahead under the beady eye of Captain Angus Walters, part owner and skipper of the new challenger. Born in 1881, Walters had been at sea since he was 13 and by 1920 was one of the most successful and respected skippers on the Grand Banks. At the helm of *Gilbert B. Walters,* he was favourite to beat *Delawana* in the 1920 elimination race until his foretopmast broke under the press of sail. Walters was destined to skipper *Bluenose* throughout her racing career in one of the legendary maritime partnerships, like Woodget on the *Cutty Sark* or Nelson on the *Victory*. If there was magic in *Bluenose*, then Angus Walters was the magician who could conjure it up. He was also a hard man, 'an aggressive, unsportsmanlike and abusive man but a prime sailor', who knew what he wanted. As the

keel and ribs of Roué's vision gradually emerged from the frozen piles of birch, spruce, oak and pine, Walters was not entirely happy with the beautiful racing hull drawn by Roué. It was sharp and slender, 43.6m long, with huge overhangs fore and aft, and a keel that was only 15.2m long, but Walters also wanted a good working boat and insisted on raising the fo'c'sle deckhead by 45cm. This changed *Bluenose*'s lines, giving her rather chubby bow 'cheeks', which earned rude comments but gave greater buoyancy and made her much less likely to bury her bowsprit. This kept her dry and gave her an uncanny ability to beat to windward. Even with changes, the work went quickly and on 26 March 1921 after only ninety-one days' work, the slender black hull slipped into Lunenburg harbour. A fortnight later on 15 April with 35.6m-high Douglas fir masts stepped to set her 1,036m^2 of sail and fully ballasted, she set out for bait in Newfoundland and then for the Grand Banks.

It was soon clear that *Bluenose* was a seriously fast ship, but her career nearly ended abruptly. Seven days out of Lunenburg, on a black Atlantic night, she was nearly cut in half by a square rigger that ignored her bell; her crew had to take to the dories before someone on the square rigger eventually woke up. After that, all went well, and by September she was back in Lunenburg as the season's 'highliner' with the largest catch of more than 100 schooners. On 8 October, newly scraped and painted, she was in Halifax for the Canadian elimination races. Eight schooners started the first race in a gentle breeze and then hit dense fog before the wind freshened to 20 knots to provide a decent work-out. *Bluenose* won easily, beating to windward 'like a scared rabbit', and in the second race finished fifteen minutes ahead of her nearest rival, *Delawana*. Two weeks later, she faced *Elsie* from Gloucester in Halifax harbour; on 21 May the previous champion *Esperanto* had hit the sunken *State of Virginia* off Sable Island, sinking in thirty minutes.

The first championship race started in a 25-knot wind, which freshened to 35 knots. Carrying a big balloon sail, *Bluenose* romped away; when *Elsie* also set a balloon, her foretopmast carried away. The 'unsportsmanlike' Walters lowered his own balloon to level the odds, but *Bluenose* still won easily. In the second race, in a light wind *Elsie* led away, but on the windward leg *Bluenose* surged ahead and by the finish was almost 5km in front. She could now carry the coveted No. 1 on her mainsail as International Fishermen's Champion. The 1922 races, pitting *Bluenose* against Clayton Morrisey on the *Henry Ford*, started as a bit of a fiasco, because of the introduction of 'yachting rules'. In very light winds both schooners failed to complete the first two races in the stipulated six hours; the first was declared void but on the insistence of both captains, the second, which the *Ford* won, was allowed. The *Ford* led at the start in the third with winds over 25 knots, but *Bluenose* hauled her in to windward and crossed the line ahead. In the deciding fourth race held in 40-knot winds, the champion won easily after the *Ford,* carrying too much sail, lost her topmast.

Bluenose could be beaten in the right conditions, but her legend was established in the following year's races against *Columbia,* considered by Angus Walters to be the best of all her challengers. She was designed by W. Starling Burgess, one of the finest American designers of his day, specifically to beat *Bluenose.* She was a very beautiful schooner with a high bow, but she was also a real working saltbanker. She blew away the opposition in the American elimination contest and on 29 October 1923 lined up against *Bluenose* off Halifax. In a 17-knot breeze the two schooners were only inches apart round the course; forced towards the Three Sisters Ledge with *Columbia* to windward, Walters had to bear up, snagging *Columbia*'s forestay and jib. *Bluenose* actually towed *Columbia* for several minutes then took off like a scalded cat to cross the finish line eighty seconds ahead. Three days later, *Bluenose* led the second race the whole way, finishing nearly three minutes ahead, but the series collapsed in acrimony when *Columbia*'s captain, Newfoundland-born Ben Pine, claimed that the Lunenburger had passed on the wrong side of a marker buoy and the race committee awarded the race to *Columbia.* Uttering several choice profanities, Walters took *Bluenose* off fishing. The series was declared a draw and the prize money was shared, but *Bluenose* still carried No. 1 on her sail.

Eight years would pass before the next Fishermen's Championship race as Walters refused to race unless his winning share from 1923 was paid. *Bluenose* and *Columbia* never raced head to head again. *Bluenose* continued to earn her keep the hard way in a fishing industry that was changing rapidly as the saltbankers were replaced by motor trawlers, a trend hastened by several bad years for the schooner fleet. In April 1926 *Bluenose* was caught in a savage north-east hurricane south-west of Sable Island, a low crescentic sandy island, 42km long but only a kilometre wide, lying some 300km south-east of Halifax. Surrounded by shifting poorly charted sandbanks, it is one of the worst marine hazards along the east coast, and has caused at least 350 shipwrecks. When the storm broke, *Bluenose*'s anchor cable parted when she was in only 20m of water and she was driven towards the sand bars where heavy waves were breaking. The situation was desperate, but Angus Walters had himself lashed to the wheel, sent everyone else below and for eight hours fought single-handed to keep her off until the wind hauled round to the north-west; when the storm subsided sand could be shovelled off *Bluenose*'s deck.

> Don't let anyone tell you that grown people can't pray, because I heard them that night. The men sat at the galley table and each man had his galley compass in front of him. And they looked at the compass and said 'We're not going to survive this'. But we did survive. Captain Angus Walters was lashed to the wheel for eight hours. He was one of the bravest men who ever sailed the Seven Seas. I owe my life to that man and that good ship. And Angus Walters said that only the Bluenose could have survived that gale where we were.
>
> (Crewman Clem Hiltz, cited in Getson, 2006)

Bluenose wasn't the only saltbanker in trouble in 1926. In August another hurricane swept over the banks; two Lunenburg schooners were lost with all hands, while others lost crewmen and three escaped by the skin of their teeth by sailing right over the Sable Island sand bars before limping into harbour with their deck gear in tatters. The next year was even worse as another hurricane on 24 August, this time a Category 2 hurricane with sustained winds of 83 to 96 knots and gusts to 109 knots, savaged the banks. The *Joyce M. Smith, Mahala, Uda Corkum* and *Clayton Walters* from Lunenburg disappeared with all hands – eighty-two men dead. Another four fishing boats sank with the loss of thirty-three lives and sixteen more were driven ashore, while eight of the ten Newfoundland schooners on the Grand Banks were also lost. This time *Bluenose*'s cable held and though she lost all her deck gear, she rode out the storm, but *Columbia* went down with all hands somewhere west of Sable Island.

There weren't too many saltbankers left by 1931 when the next International Fishermen's races were held. This time the American challenge came from Boston with a beautiful little schooner, the *Gertrude L. Thebaud.* Skippered by the redoubtable Ben Pine, she had actually beaten the rather weather-beaten *Bluenose* for the Lipton Cup off Gloucester in 1930. However, her victory was unconvincing and everyone felt that the issue had to be settled properly. This time *Bluenose* was well prepared and lightly ballasted; she was ahead in the light winds of the first race when time ran out and won the second handily. In final race in 20-knot winds, the two ships were within touching distance for 22km before *Bluenose* sailed away to windward to win by twelve minutes.

By 1932 the Great Depression was in full swing; it was nearly impossible for a saltbanker to earn her keep legitimately and with the opportunities presented by prohibition, more than a few opted for rum running from the West Indies. However, *Bluenose,* now featured on the Canadian 50-cent stamp, and her rival were celebrities and both ships were invited to the World's Fair in Chicago. In 1935 *Bluenose* was also invited to cross the Atlantic to take part in the Spithead Naval Review for the Silver Jubilee of King George V. This trip was nearly a disaster; leaving Falmouth, *Bluenose* ran into a ferocious hurricane, which Walters described as much worse than the 1926 Sable Island storm:

> Wind hauled WSW with hurricane force … vessel labouring very hard and terrific sea running … At 9 p.m. a terrible sea hit vessel, heaving her on her beam ends; breaking foregaff, foreboom, smashing boats … throwing cook stove over on side. Tons of water going below doing other damages, causing vessel to leak.
>
> (Angus Walters' log book, 16 September 1935, cited in Getson, 2006)

A week after the three-day hurricane, she limped into Plymouth with a leaking, damaged hull that took a month to repair before she could face the voyage back to Lunenburg.

By now *Bluenose* with her strained, hogged hull had more than earned honourable retirement, but the New Englanders were still smarting about the 1931 verdict and another challenge arrived in Lunenburg. Angus Walters wavered; *Bluenose* was still the darling of Canada and now featured on the Canadian 10-cent coin, but no one was prepared to provide the $10,000 he needed to restore her to racing condition. Her timbers were water-logged and even with 50 per cent less ballast than when she was launched she was low in the water with a water line 60cm longer than when she was launched. However, an American promise of $8,000 to bring the old champion out of retirement shamed the Canadian Government into providing $2,500 and the Nova Scotia Government $1,000.

This time there would be five races over short courses off New England. Again there was squabbling over the rules, but on 9 October 1938 the contestants faced off. It was a sportswriter's dream; like an aged heavyweight champion struggling off the canvas to face a young, fit opponent, the 18-year-old veteran would duel with the young, fast upstart. The first race was close but *Thebaud* came in the winner after *Bluenose*'s bowsprit cracked on the windward leg. *Bluenose* won the second by a decisive eleven minutes, but protests were flying over her lengthened waterline. To bring her back within the rules a lighting plant and tanks weighing 5t had to be stripped out to lighten her. Ironically, this improved her performance; she followed *Thebaud* over the start line but soon overhauled the American boat to finish more than six minutes ahead. The fourth race in 25-knot winds should have been a gift for *Bluenose*; she was well ahead when her backstay broke, endangering her mast. By the time she recovered *Thebaud* had sailed off to win by five minutes. Everything now rested on the final race. On 26 October with 15–18-knot winds *Thebaud* crossed the line in the lead with *Bluenose* just behind. Walters to windward soon edged ahead, gradually stretching out his lead, whispering 'Just one more time, old girl, just one more time'. There was never more than three minutes gap as *Bluenose* raced up Boston harbour with her lee rail awash, but even a broken halyard block just before the finish couldn't stop her and, still champion, she sailed across the line and into history, two minutes and fifty seconds ahead of *Thebaud*.

The country that has kept *Bluenose* on its coins for more than eighty years should have found space to keep its idol as a museum ship in a place of honour, like *Cutty Sark* or *Constitution*, but Canada failed. After several changes of ownership, she wound up in 1943 with the West Indies Trading Company carting cod to Havana. For a year or so she gradually deteriorated in Caribbean waters under a succession of skippers while her new owners mixed with the glitterati in Havana. One night in January 1946, by then registered in Honduras and carrying a load of bananas, she foundered on a reef off Haiti.

Seventeen years later, money was at last found to build a replica, and this time Angus Walters drove in the first spike. On 23 July 1963, with both Walters and Bill Roué in attendance, *Bluenose II*, slipped into Lunenburg harbour from Smith and Rhuland's yard. *Bluenose II* is a fine ship, though after forty-nine years she badly needed the comprehensive rebuild completed in Lunenburg in 2012. She looks almost identical to her idolised ancestor, a fast sailer and one that can weather a hurricane, but she's never been tested on a race course or the fishing banks. Only two real saltbankers still survive as museum ships: *Duxton* in Mystic, Connecticut, launched in 1921, and *Theresa E. Connor* in Lunenburg, launched in 1938.

References

Backman, B., and Backman, P., 1975, *Bluenose*, McClelland and Stewart Ltd., Toronto.

Cameron, S.D., 1984, *Schooner: Bluenose I and Bluenose II; the Dramatic Story of Canada's Two Great Sailing Ships*, McClelland and Stewart-Bantam Ltd., Toronto.

Chapelle, H., 1973, *American Fishing Schooners, 1825–1935*, W.W. Norton, New York.

De Villiers, M., 2007, *Witch in the Wind: the True Story of the Legendary Bluenose*, Thomas Allen Publishers, Toronto.

Darrach, C., 1985, *Race to Fame: the Inside Story of the Bluenose*, Lancelot Press, Hantsport, Nova Scotia.

Getson, H-A., 2006, *Bluenose: the Ocean Knows Her Name*, Nimbus Publishing, Halifax.

Roué, J.E., 1995, *A Spirit Deep Within: Naval Architect W.J. Roué and the Bluenose Story*, Lancelot Press, Hantsport, Nova Scotia.

17 THE NORTHWEST PASSAGE AND THE RCMP SCHOONER *ST ROCH*

St Roch:	ice-strengthened wooden police schooner, launched at Burrard Shipyard, Vancouver, May 1928.
Tonnage:	193.43t
Length:	31.76m
Beam:	7.55
Draught:	3.96m
Engine:	Union diesel, 150hp;
Sails:	gaff-rigged with three sails on two masts, total area 226m^2
Hull:	6.99cm fir planks on thirty-three 17.8cm Douglas fir frames, with 3.8cm Australian ironbark ice sheath
Crew:	14
Career:	1928: maiden voyage to Herschel Island. 1929: first Arctic winter in Amundsen Gulf under Commander H.A. Larsen, lengthy sledge trips. 1934: major refit, enclosed bridge. 1940–41: eastwards traverse of the Northwest Passage in two seasons from the Beaufort Sea to Davis Strait, wintering in Prince of Wales Strait. 1943: refit in Halifax, larger deckhouse and 300hp engine. 1944: single season traverse of Northwest Passage to Vancouver, eighty-six days, 13,277km. 1950: first ship to circumnavigate North America, via the Panama Canal.

Ever since Marco Polo fascinated Europe with accounts of the fabled wealth of Cathay and the Spice Islands, merchants have dreamed of a short sea route for trade with the Orient. Bartholomew Diaz' voyage around the Cape of Good Hope in 1488 opened a sea route to Asia, but it was a long and dangerous one. Four years later Columbus showed that it was possible to sail far westwards without falling off the edge of the world and raised the tantalising prospect of a shorter, faster, westerly sea route through the islands of the Canadian Arctic – the holy grail of the Northwest Passage! This triggered a search for the elusive passage, which lasted for nearly 500 years. In 1497, only five years after Columbus' first voyage, Henry VII of England financed the first search, by Giacomo Caboto (John Cabot) on the tiny caravel *Matthew*. Caboto didn't get anywhere close to the Passage but did discover the extraordinarily productive fishing grounds of the Newfoundland Grand Banks. During his next voyage, the *Matthew* disappeared without trace, the first of many ships to be lost in the quest for the passage.

Imaginative European cartographers were soon showing a northern strait on their maps, which they named the Straits of Anian and the quest gathered momentum. Sir Francis Drake sought a western entrance in 1579 on the *Golden Hind*, and in 1592 the Greek pilot, Juan de Fuca, claimed to have sailed from the Pacific to the North Sea, but it wasn't until 1728 that the Dane, Vitus Bering, sailing with the Russian Navy, found the real western gateway to the passage (now the Bering Strait). Meanwhile, from the east, Martin Frobisher explored the Baffin Island coast during three expeditions from 1576–78, and John Davis followed with three voyages from 1585–87, mapping eastern Baffin Island and the Davis Strait, which separates it from Greenland. All possible routes to the west were blocked by ice, but Frobisher titillated his London backers with what turned out to be valueless 'gold-bearing' black rock, while Davis' discoveries opened up a highly profitable whaling industry. The merchants' fascination with the Northwest Passage persisted and Henry Hudson soon followed, finding his way into the cul-de-sac of Hudson Bay where he was abandoned by a mutinous crew in 1611. The Dane, Jens Munk, wintered in the same dead end in 1619–20 with the *Einhörningen* and *Lamprenen*, losing all but three of his sixty-four men to scurvy. Two English expeditions in 1631–32, Thomas James on *Henrietta Marie* and Luke Foxe on *Charles*, also carried out futile searches, though Foxe did find one feasible entry through the shallow Foxe Basin. More significant was the 1615 discovery of the real eastern gateway, Lancaster Sound, by the brilliant navigator, William Baffin, pilot on Robert Bylot's *Discovery*.

Over time, interest in the Northwest Passage waned, though temporarily revived by the tale, probably mythical, of the British *Octavius*, which allegedly entered the passage from the west in 1762, became trapped in ice and was found intact with the frozen bodies of her crew close to Greenland by the whaler *Herald,* thirteen years later.

It was Whitby whaler William Scoresby's discovery of a Siberian stone harpoon head embedded in a whale in the Davis Strait in 1815 that revived interest and stimulated the Second Secretary of the Admiralty, John Barrow, to offer a government reward of £20,000 for the first ship to traverse the passage to the Pacific. This started a deluge of British naval expeditions throughout the Canadian Arctic archipelago during the following fifty years, starting with John Ross and William Edward Parry on the *Isabella* and *Arabella* in 1818. Parry came very close to the true passage in 1819–20 when he passed through Lancaster Sound and wintered at Melville Island, but it wasn't until 1851 that the final link (then impassably blocked by ice) was proved by Robert McClure, exploring from the west on *Investigator*. *Investigator* became permanently trapped in the ice, but over three years McClure and his crew made their way east and in 1854 were rescued by Sir Edward Belcher on HMS *Resolute* who reached them through Lancaster Sound. *Investigator* and *Resolute* were amongst a flock of ships that searched for Sir John Franklin's 'lost' 1845–47 expedition with his ships, HMS *Erebus* and *Terror*. The mysterious fate of the Franklin expedition is largely responsible for the enduring mystique of the Northwest Passage. In 1854, relics of the Franklin expedition were found by John Rae during an overland search, when he also discovered another feasible passage to the west, through the narrow Rae Strait separating King William Island from the Boothia Peninsula. The Franklin mystery was partially solved when the wreck of HMS *Erebus* was discovered by the Canadian Victoria Strait Expedition in September 2014.

Discovery of either the 'true' Northwest Passage or the shallow, tortuous Rae Strait route did not cause much excitement at the time. Both routes were blocked with ice for all or most of the year and to provide a feasible trading route ships would have to be able to pass both ways in a single season. It was another fifty years before anyone tried to navigate either route; this was one of the greatest of all polar travellers, Norwegian Roald Amundsen, in 1903. Amundsen's approach was totally different from earlier expeditions; instead of a large ship and crew, he brought only five companions on the little shallow-draughted 47t herring schooner *Gjøa*. Barely escaping his creditors, he left Norway in June and passing through Lancaster Sound, reached Rae Strait in October. There he moored *Gjøa* for the winter in a fine natural harbour on King William Island now known as Gjøa Haven. (Map, see p. 161) He remained there for two years studying Inuit travel methods and sledging throughout the archipelago, before completing the journey to the Beaufort Sea in 1905. With *Gjøa* anchored at Herschel Island, Amundsen skied 800km alone to Eagle, Alaska, to telegraph the news, and then skied back again. He put the invaluable experience gained to excellent use six years later, becoming the first person to reach the South Pole.

Gjøa's voyage technically solved the age-old quest for a navigable Northwest Passage but didn't really change much; the voyage had not been completed in one season and Rae Strait was too shallow for most merchant ships. However, it did cause the Canadian government to worry about Norwegian threats to sovereignty over the Arctic archipelago, as some islands had been discovered by Otto Sverdrup, and it began to take administrative responsibility more seriously. The German Antarctic expedition ship *Gauss* was bought and, renamed the *Arctic*, was sent north on four 'flag-waving' voyages just before the First World War. Commanded by Joseph-Elzéar Bernier, she travelled 48,000km and spent three winters at remote Arctic communities but failed to navigate the Northwest Passage, though she reached Melville Island in 1910. In the 1920s, worried about Danish sovereignty threats as well, Canada established seven Royal Canadian Mounted Police posts in the eastern Arctic to administer post and customs offices and to police 2000km of coastline. Initially chartered ships including *Arctic* were used to supply the posts, but when she was scrapped a new ship, the *St Roch*, was commissioned.

The proposal for *St Roch* was novel; not only would she patrol and supply police posts and communities but, frozen in during the winters, she would act as a base for long RCMP sledge patrols throughout the archipelago. This required a nimble, shallow-drafted ship able to negotiate tortuous, poorly charted channels and strong enough to stand up to winter ice pressure. Designed by Vancouver naval architect, Tom Halliday, *St Roch*'s lineage stretched back to the famous Norwegian, Colin Archer, who designed the revolutionary *Fram* in 1892 for Fridjof Nansen, to drift while frozen in towards the North Pole. *Fram* was extremely strong, but small and 'basin' shaped so that she would be squeezed up rather than crushed by ice pressure. *Fram* was very successful, returning from Nansen's expedition unscathed and serving Otto Sverdrup during another four-year Arctic expedition, before being used by Amundsen on his successful South Pole expedition. *Fram* was retired in Oslo in the 1920s (and eventually brought ashore in a museum, together with *Gjøa*), but similar design concepts were used in building the *Maud*, which Amundsen used for several unsuccessful attempts to reach the North Pole before selling her to the Hudson's Bay Company to cover debts. Halliday was familiar with and influenced by *Maud* when he designed *St Roch*.

St Roch was launched in Vancouver in May 1928. She was small but powerfully built with an outer ice-resistant sheath of Australian ironbark, massive Douglas fir frames and 29cm square internal ice beams fastened with heavy galvanised iron fittings. The keel, stem and sternpost were extremely dense, hard Australian ironbark, as was the rudder, which could be winched up on deck for protection against ice. The bow was also protected by a 0.95cm thick iron plate. She was a two-masted auxiliary schooner fitted with a 150hp diesel engine, but her range was restricted as she could only carry about 23 tons of fuel, and motoring she used nearly a ton per day. She could carry additional fuel in drums on deck but also had to depend on supplies cached at strategic locations. She was originally intended to rely primarily on sailing and also carried a crow's nest on her 19m mainmast for ice navigation.

St Roch soon became known to Inuit communities throughout the Arctic as 'Umiarjuaq' ('The Big Ship'), but she was very small for the complex duties planned. There was accommodation for eight men in a small fo'c'sle and another five around the main cabin/saloon aft; the captain was housed in a tiny cabin in the deck-house, 'barely big enough to get undressed in'. Her nominal cargo capacity was about 80t, but she frequently carried up to 150t with a deck cargo including fuel drums, sledges, kayaks, sledge dog teams and, on several occasions, Inuit families being transported between Arctic communities.

St Roch set out on a brief maiden Arctic voyage in June 1928, commanded by an old Bering Sea whaling captain, William Gillen. All the crew were police officers but only three had seagoing experience. Crossing the Bay of Alaska, they quickly learned her foibles; with a round bottom and a blunt bow, she pitched, rolled and leaked and under sail 'just seemed to lean forward, buried her nose and refused to answer the helm', behaving like a demented porpoise. According to the mate, Henry Larsen, '*St Roch* was, and remained, the most uncomfortable ship I have ever been in'. However, she was seaworthy and once the general seasickness wore off, she was cleaned up to impress the US coastguard in Alaska with her crew adorned in RCMP full dress regalia.

Once into the Beaufort Sea, *St Roch* proved her ability, twisting and turning through narrow leads amongst the ice floes to reach Herschel Island. Contact with many remote Inuit communities of the High Arctic was just beginning and few had any resistance to diseases like tuberculosis, smallpox and influenza. When *St Roch* arrived an influenza epidemic was raging, which had caused many deaths, so precautions had to be taken to avoid spreading the disease to other vulnerable communities. However, her journey eastwards was abruptly interrupted when she ran hard aground on an uncharted reef at 6.5 knots. It took a strong west wind and unloading most of the cargo before she could be freed, allowing her to continue to Cambridge Bay where Amundsen's old *Maud* was being used as a radio station (she sank there in 1932). There a man accused of murder and two women witnesses (both widowed by the murder) were picked up for transport on the return journey to Herschel Island for a court appearance.

Back in Vancouver, Henry Larsen was appointed as *St Roch*'s new captain. Born in Norway, he had served in square-riggers as a 15-year-old and had first wintered in the Arctic in 1924. When he joined the RCMP in 1928, he started an association with *St Roch* that would last for more than eighteen years, make them both famous, and raise Larsen to the highest ranks of the RCMP. In late August, *St Roch* left Vancouver for her first Arctic winter, at Langton Bay on Amundsen Gulf. It started badly as she was driven ashore when her anchors dragged during a gale. She had to be completely unloaded to get off, but by late October she was safely frozen in. With the dogs tethered ashore on long spans, a canvas-covered wooden framework was installed over the deck, and a snow block wall was built up around the hull for insulation and wind protection. She immediately started to function as a central police post for Inuit from the surrounding communities while Larsen and his men began making regular sledge trips. The first, a 'short' trip of 480km, introduced them to the difficulties of travelling in blizzards with poorly trained dogs, but with help from Inuit neighbours they gradually learned how to travel safely in the Arctic winter. It was July the following year before the ice cleared sufficiently for *St Roch* to return to Herschel Island and then to Vancouver.

St Roch stayed in Vancouver for eight months while repairs and modifications were completed. The main modification was to fit a new, slightly larger deckhouse and a small radio shack. In June 1930 she returned to the Arctic where she would remain for the next four winters, setting a pattern for the next decade. Each winter was spent frozen in at a protected anchorage at Kogluktualuk, on Coronation Gulf and in summer she ranged from Herschel Island as far east as Gjøa

Haven. *St Roch* became the effective face of Canadian government, bringing supplies to remote police posts, carrying mail, ferrying Inuit children to school and invalids to hospital, registering births, deaths and marriages, enforcing wildlife regulations, searching for overdue travellers, and investigating 'deaths by misadventure'. Larsen made many long dog-sledge journeys, becoming expert in Inuit travel methods. He used an 'ujjuk' (sledge) with runners covered by mud for improved glide, and drove his dogs in single file with the 'Nome' centre trace characteristic of the western Arctic. Supplies for dogs and men had to be supplemented by fish and seal and Larsen's lead dog, Houdini, also developed an uncanny knack for finding the critical patches of snow suitable for building igloos.

Back in Vancouver in 1934, an open navigating bridge above the pilot house and an engine-room telegraph were added to *St Roch*, while some crew members including Larsen took the opportunity to get married; at the time RCMP members had to complete seven years of service before being allowed to marry. *St Roch* resumed her Arctic career in the severe winter of 1935–36 when she even had great difficulty in reaching Herschel Island. Larsen had to spend most of his time in the crow's nest, searching for navigable leads through the heavy pack ice. Often having to blast with gunpowder to make progress, they eventually reached Cambridge Bay where there was a major measles epidemic, which caused many deaths. Over the next years she continued her routine, though very varied, duties until 1940. The question of Canada's Arctic sovereignty had subsided during the 1930s when the Canadian government paid Otto Sverdrup $67,000 to settle any Norwegian claims, and though Knud Rasmussen and Greenland Inuit claimed hunting rights on Ellesmere Island, they received little backing from the Danish government. During the Second World War German attacks on Greenland posed a more serious sovereignty threat so, in early 1940, Larsen was ordered to undertake a secret mission with *St Roch* to traverse the Northwest Passage from the Beaufort Sea to Davis Strait.

St Roch left Vancouver on 23 June 1940. Heavily laden with her decks completely covered with coal sacks, fuel drums, small boats and crates of provisions, and very little freeboard, she was nearly submerged in bad weather. Larsen intended to complete the traverse in one season, reversing Amundsen's route through Rae Strait, but the pack ice was so heavy that it took a month to cover the 640km from Point Barrow to Herschel Island. They didn't reach Cambridge Bay until mid-September and, with new ice forming, it was too late to attempt Rae Strait. *St Roch* retreated to Prince of Wales Strait for the winter, which provided an opportunity for sledge trips to the western archipelago not previously patrolled by the RCMP. It was late July 1941 before the ice allowed *St Roch* to continue her voyage. Despite continued bad weather they reached Gjøa Haven in late August. The weather was still bad and though they got through Rae Strait, they became stuck in pressure ice north of King William Island, where *Erebus* and *Terror* were trapped during the Franklin expedition, and had to spend the next winter at Pasley Bay. Again they made many sledge trips, including one seventy-one day, 1900km journey to southern Boothia Peninsula for Constable Albert Chartrand's funeral, who died of a heart attack during the winter.

By late August 1942 *St Roch* just managed to force her way through Bellot Strait between Boothia Peninsula and Somerset Island, carried in heavy pressure ice before a strong current. They had serious trouble with a cracked cylinder but in mid-September they broke out into Davis Strait, to complete the first eastwards traverse of the Northwest Passage. *St Roch* still had to run the gauntlet of the many icebergs concentrated along the western side of the strait, one of which damaged her railing – if its shape had been slightly different, it would have sunk her. Short of power with her damaged engine she had to take refuge in western Newfoundland during a storm but finally docked in Halifax in October, almost forty months after leaving Vancouver.

Both *St Roch* and *Gjøa* had negotiated the Northwest Passage through the single season ice of Rae Strait, but this is far too shallow for merchant ships. The Northwest Passage had been conquered, but the dream of a short trade route to the Orient was as remote as ever. *St Roch* underwent a major refit in Halifax; her 150hp diesel engine was replaced by a 300hp unit and a much larger deckhouse was fitted, increasing accommodation to fifteen. To make room for the new deckhouse, the main mast with its long boom was removed, her rig was changed from schooner to ketch and the total sail area reduced to 105.8m^2. The pilot house was also raised to give a clear sight line over the bow, and larger fuel tanks, a gyro compass and a new battery room were added.

It was difficult to get the refit completed with the wartime rush in the Halifax dockyards, but by the end of July 1944 *St Roch* was ready to return to Vancouver. This time Larsen headed further north to the 'real'

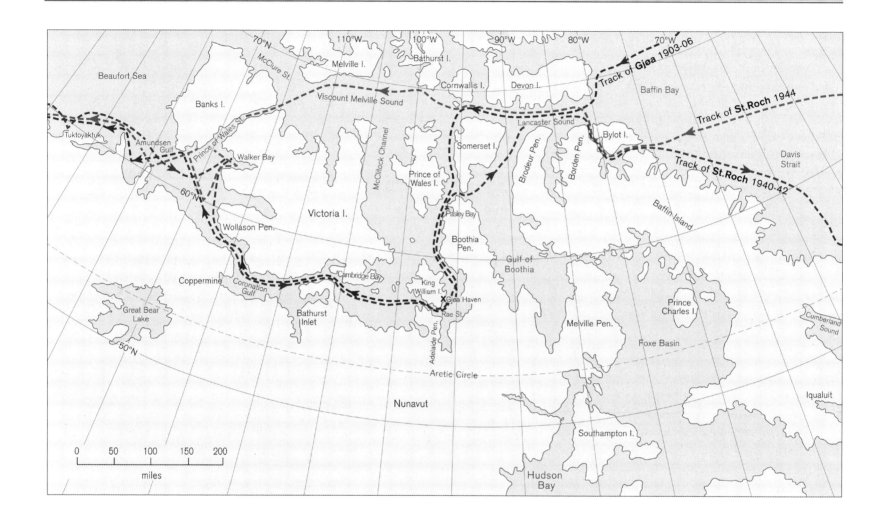

Northwest Passage through the McClure and Prince of Wales Straits where, instead of light single-season ice of Rae Strait, *St Roch* would face much heavier multi-year polar ice driven by strong currents from the Arctic Ocean. Even in Davis Strait, the ice was so heavy that they had to head almost to the Greenland coast before turning west into the archipelago. They were joined by the seven-person Inuit Panippakussuk family from Pond Inlet, together with their seventeen huskies, who accompanied them all the way to Herschel Island, living in a tent on top of the deckhouse. Along Lancaster Sound, they visited the graves of some of Franklin's men on Beechey Island, the remains of the yacht

Mary left on Devon Island by Sir John Ross in 1854 for any survivors of the Franklin expedition, and a large canned food cache left by Captain Kellett of HMS *Resolute* in 1853, for the same purpose. Soon they reached unexplored waters where the heavy blue ice of McClure Strait defeated Bernier in the *Arctic*. Very gradually *St Roch* worked her way west then turned south into more open water in Prince of Wales Strait. Her progress was excellent until they reached Herschel Island, but then they faced heavy pack ice all the way to Point Barrow. In late September they finally passed through Bering Strait and on 16 October docked in Vancouver, eighty-six days and 13,277km from Halifax.

The real Northwest Passage had finally been conquered and in a single summer; the tough little police ketch that Larsen referred to affectionately as his 'ugly duckling' had finally overcome the formidable ice, which defeated the pride of the Royal Navy 100 years earlier. *St Roch* would make two more Arctic voyages, but her duties could now be carried out more effectively by aircraft and in October 1948 she was laid up in Vancouver. However, in 1950 Larsen, by then RCMP inspector for the complete Arctic region, obtained permission to bring her east through the Panama Canal to Halifax, to become the first ship to circumnavigate North America. Then, after one more voyage, to Labrador, she was permanently retired and was sold to the City of Vancouver. In 1954, after returning through the Panama Canal, she became the central focus of a maritime museum in Vancouver.

The deep, navigable channel proven by *St Roch* vindicated the confidence of sixteenth-century cartographers who first showed a western Arctic passage to the Orient but did not immediately stimulate any trade. Local shipping in Arctic Canada increased sharply after the Second World War, but most was only made possible by the powerful American and Canadian coastguard icebreakers developed during the war. In 1968 the discovery of oil at Prudhoe Bay in northern Alaska provided a new incentive for trade, and the Humble Oil Company commissioned conversion of the massive 115,000t, 43,000shp oil tanker SS *Manhattan* (the largest merchant ship in the American fleet) to an ice breaking tanker. Her 19.8m bow was replaced by a 38.1m icebreaking bow, increasing her overall length to 306.4m, and a 13.81cm thick ice belt was added around her hull. She set off north accompanied by the Canadian coastguard icebreaker *John A. Macdonald*, and helped at times by Canadian coastguard icebreaker *Louis St Laurent* and US coastguard icebreakers USCGC *Northwind* and *Staten Island*. The object was to traverse the shortest Northwest Passage to the Beaufort Sea, between Banks and Melville Islands through McClintock Channel, but even with the assistance of icebreakers and spotter helicopters, she was defeated by the 6.7m high, 30.5m thick ice in McClure Strait. However, she did manage to trace *St Roch*'s course through Prince of Wales Strait to reach Prudhoe

Bay and load one symbolic barrel of oil before her return journey. It was a pyrrhic victory, however, as she was badly damaged and the experiment was an economic failure.

More than fifty years later, regular commercial traffic through the Northwest Passage remains a pipe dream, but because of the dramatic impact of climate change and widespread disappearance of sea ice throughout the Arctic, this will probably soon change. In 1977 the Belgian steel yacht *Williwaw* successfully traversed the passage, a voyage that has now become almost commonplace for yachts and even small cruise liners. In 2000, the RCMP vessel *Nadon,* renamed *St Roch II* for the occasion, repeated her historic voyage from Halifax through Prince of Wales Strait to Herschel Island in a mere three weeks. At last, in September 2013, the Danish bulk carrier, *Nordic Orion,* managed to follow *St Roch*'s route through the Passage, to deliver a 73,000t cargo of metallurgical coal from Vancouver to Finland, 13,000t more than she could have carried on the longer route through the Panama Canal.

References

Berton, P., 1988, *The Arctic Grail: The Quest for the Northwest Passage, 1818–1909*, Viking, New York.

Delgado, J.P., 2003, *Arctic Workhorse: the RCMP Schooner St Roch,* Touch Wood Editions, Ltd., Vancouver

Larsen, H.A., with Sheer, F.R., and Omholt-Jensen, E., 1967, *The Big Ship*, McClelland and Stewart, Ltd, Toronto.

Larsen, H.A., 1945, *Reports and Other Papers Relating to the Two Voyages of the R.C.M. Police Schooner 'St Roch' Through the Northwest Passage*, The King's Printer, Ottawa.

McGoogan, K., 2005, *Lady Franklin's Revenge*, Harper Collins Publishers, Ltd, Toronto.

Tranter, G.J., 1944, *Plowing the Arctic*, Hodder and Stoughton, Ltd, London

Williams, G., 2003, *Voyages of Delusion: The Quest for the Northwest Passage*, Yale University Press, New Haven.

18 ALTMARK: THE 'HELL SHIP' THAT WASN'T

Altmark:	fleet tanker for Kreigsmarine, launched Howaldtswereke, Kiel, 13 November 1937.
Tonnage:	10,847t
Length:	178.25m
Beam:	22m
Draught:	9.3m
Engines:	four MAN nine-cylinder diesels, 22,000shp
Speed:	21.1 knots
Range:	200km at 15 knots
Armament:	three 15cm guns, two 3.7cm AA guns, four 2cm AA guns, eight machine guns
Crew:	90–208
Career:	attached as supply and prison ship for German merchant raider pocket battleship *Admiral Graf Spee* in South Atlantic and Indian oceans. December 1939: after the Battle of the River Plate made her way north towards Germany. Detected in Norwegian waters by RAF aircraft; intercepted by Royal Navy ships and boarded by HMS *Cossack* under Captain Philip Vian; prisoners freed. Returned to Germany, renamed *Uckermark*. Served as scout ship for German battleships *Scharnhorst* and *Gneisenau*. November 1942: destroyed by an accidental explosion in Yokohama, Japan.

On 16 August 1939 a slender grey warship slipped her moorings in Wilhelmshaven and headed north along the Norwegian coast before turning west between the Faroes and Iceland, then south into the Atlantic. It was still two weeks before German troops would invade Poland launching the Second World War, but naval chessmen were already moving into place. The *Admiral Graf Spee* resulted from careful analysis of naval strategies that were successful during the First World War. The Kaiser's expensive battle fleet never seriously affected the war's outcome, but Britain was nearly defeated by the attacks of U-boats and raiders like the *Emden* on merchant shipping. The German battle fleet was scuttled by their crews at Scapa Flow in 1919 and strict 10,000t displacement limits on German battleship construction were placed in the Treaty of Versailles to ensure that German naval strength could not approach that of other major naval powers. The 1922 Washington Naval Arms Treaty sought to prevent another arms race by limiting the size of all battleship fleets, but cruiser numbers were not capped, though they were restricted to 10,000t displacement and 20.3cm maximum gun calibre. In the late 1920s Germany was not yet ready to transgress the Washington Treaty by building big battleships like *Bismarck* and *Tirpitz*. However, the First World War had shown that a very effective naval campaign could be based on a merchant raiding campaign by sinking ships but also by rapidly shifting location, spreading uncertainty and tying up enemy naval resources in extended fruitless searches. This could be particularly effective against island powers like Britain, which depend on supplies and manpower from colonies around the world.

Emden's successful First World War raiding career ended only because she was not sufficiently powerful to overcome the ships that eventually tracked her down. The Reichsmarine planned to avoid this fate by building powerful, fast independent warships to prey on isolated merchant ships in remote waters. These would be sufficiently well armed to outgun, or sufficiently fast to outrun, any Allied warship encountered. However, Germany was constrained by the Washington Treaty limits so a new type of ship, initially called 'Panzerschiffe' had to be developed. These were 186m long, 21.69m beam and 7.25m draught, which, allegedly conforming to the 10,000t displacement limit, actually displaced 16,410t when fully loaded. The three Panzerschiffe ships built were the first warships with welded hulls, which saved considerable weight. Powered by eight MAN diesel engines delivering 52,050shp, they had a top speed of 29.5 knots and range of 19,000km at 20 knots. Armament was very powerful with six 28cm guns in triple turrets, eight 15cm guns in single turrets and eight 14cm torpedo tubes. They were soon dubbed 'pocket battleships' in Britain, though they were not as heavily armoured as true battleships

Deutschland was laid down at Deutsche Werke in Kiel in 1929 and commissioned in 1933; *Admiral Scheer* was commissioned in Wilhelmshaven in 1934 and *Admiral Graf Spee* in Wilhelmshaven in 1936. All three took part in 'non-intervention' patrols during the Spanish Civil War where *Deutschland* was bombed by Republican bombers, while *Admiral Scheer* shelled Almeria in reprisal. *Deutschland* and *Admiral Graf Spee* were both deployed to stations for merchant raiding before war started. This was simple for *Deutschland* in the North Atlantic close to her supply base, but *Admiral Graf Spee*, sent to the remote South Atlantic, had to be re-supplied and refuelled by another ship. *Graf Spee*'s 'mother ship' was the *Altmark*, a 20,858t displacement, 178.25m-long oil tanker with a top speed of 21.1 knots and operating range of 23,200km at 15 knots.

Altmark was commissioned into the Kriegsmarine, captained by a former Hamburg-Amerika Line captain, Heinrich Dau, and immediately set out for the South Atlantic. She sailed via Port Arthur, Texas, to pick up 15,000 tons of diesel, then, despite American suspicions, was allowed to leave on 19 August, allegedly for Europe, but actually to rendezvous with the *Graf Spee*. En route she was repainted yellow to conceal her identity, her name was changed to *Sogne* and she started to fly the Norwegian flag. On 1 September, just after the war started, the two ships met at 24° 25′N, 36° 15′W, north-west of the Cape Verde Islands. Despite a heavy swell, ammunition, supplies and diesel oil were transferred to the *Graf Spee*, which moved some crew to *Altmark* and then went to her operating station.

On 27 September, after narrowly avoiding the British heavy cruiser HMS *Cumberland*, *Graf Spee*'s captain, Hans Langsdorff, was ordered to commence attacks on Allied shipping. Three days later, the first victim, 5,050t freighter *Clement*, was sunk by gunfire off the Brazilian coast, after the crew had been taken off. Langsdorff, a humane and principled officer who earned the respect of all prisoners captured during the next few months, was meticulous in adhering to the rules of war and the crew were sent ashore in Maceió, Brazil. On 5 October, the 4,650t *Newton Beach* was captured but not sunk; with nearly 1,000 crew, *Graf Spee* was extremely crowded so Langsdorff planned to use the freighter to carry captured crew. When the 4,220t *Ashlea* was sunk on 7 October, her crew were initially housed on *Newton Beach*, but Langsdorff soon decided that this would greatly increase the hazard of detection and decided to sink her. To spread confusion and undermine the credibility of any reports, *Graf Spee* masqueraded as the *Admiral*

Scheer, known by Allied intelligence to be refitting in Germany. Despite the ruse a massive hunt started, with cruisers *Berwick* and *York* off the West Indies, battlecruiser *Renown* and aircraft carrier *Ark Royal* off Freetown, *Shropshire* and *Sussex* off Capetown and Force G consisting of heavy cruisers *Cumberland*, *Exeter*, and light cruisers *Ajax* and *Achilles* off the South American coast. However, *Graf Spee* vanished like a will-o'-the-wisp, and although *Altmark*, spotted by one of *Ark Royal*'s aircraft, had a narrow shave, she managed to pass herself off as the American tanker *Delmar*.

Graf Spee's next victim was the 8,196t *Huntsman* en route to Freetown with a crew of eighty-six on 10 October. There was no room for prisoners on *Graf Spee*, so Langsdorff left her with a prize crew until he met *Altmark* on 14 October. He then informed Captain Dau that all the captured crew would be transferred to the tanker. *Altmark* was completely unprepared for a role as a prison ship, but store rooms on four decks were cleared and sparsely furnished with carpets and jute from *Huntsman* in place of bedding. Food supplies were also insufficient for the more than 150 prisoners now on board, though some stores were taken from *Huntsman* before she was sunk. On 22 October, *Graf Spee*, now masquerading as a French warship, sank the 5,300t *Trevanion* and transferred her crew to *Altmark* on 28 October. Langsdorff knew that British and French warships were scouring the South Atlantic, so to spread confusion *Graf Spee* was camouflaged as the British battlecruiser *Renown* with a fake second forward turret and second funnel. He then moved into the Indian Ocean and sank the 700t tanker *African Star* in the Mozambique Channel, before returning to the South Atlantic, transferring more captives to *Altmark* on 26 November. Then there was a problem; the next victim, 10,441t refrigerator ship *Doric Star*, managed to send a radio message out before being subdued by gunfire. Her captain, William Melville-Evans, also succeeded in smuggling an Atlantic magnetic variation chart with him into captivity. On 4 December, 7,983t freighter *Tairoa*'s operator also sent out a message before a shell from *Graf Spee* knocked out his radio. Most of the crew were transferred to *Altmark* on 6 December, bringing her prisoner count to 299, in addition to her 133-man crew.

Time was now running out for the *Graf Spee*. At sea continuously for nearly four months, often manoeuvring at high speed, her engines badly needed maintenance and her bottom, fouled by weed, reduced her top speed to 24 knots. Captain Langsdorff decided to make one last sweep into the shipping lanes off Rio de la Plata, before heading back to Germany. On 7 December, the 3,895t freighter *Streonshalh* carrying wheat from Montevideo to Freetown was sunk, bringing the total tonnage sunk to 50,089t, without any loss of life, but the net was tightening. On 13 December off the Rio de la Plata, *Graf Spee's* lookouts sighted masts, which Langsdorff, with his Arado spotting aircraft unserviceable, mistakenly identified as belonging to a cruiser and destroyers escorting a convoy. In fact it was part of Force G, heavy cruiser *Exeter* and light cruisers *Ajax* and *Achilles*; after receiving the message from the *Doric Star*, Commodore Henry Harwood had a hunch that Langsdorff could not resist the rich pickings of ships from Buenos Aires and Montevideo, and headed for Rio de la Plata with his depleted force (*Cumberland* was undergoing maintenance in the Falkland Islands). By the time Langsdorff realised what he was up against, it was too late to avoid action.

The Battle of the River Plate didn't last long. *Graf Spee* first concentrated her large guns on the *Exeter*, knocking her out of action with severe damage in the first half hour. Well outgunned and damaged, *Ajax* and *Achilles* courageously continued to harry the raider, and though Harwood called off the action after another fifty minutes, they inflicted significant damage on *Graf Spee.* The damage was not mortal but had to be repaired before *Graf Spee* tried to fight her way back to Germany. Fatefully Langsdorff entered

Transfer of prisoners to the *Altmark.*

Montevideo rather than Buenos Aires where neutrality rules might have been bent by the more sympathetic Argentinian government. As it was, after disembarking the remaining prisoners, Langsdorff was forced to leave within four days, regardless of whether or not repairs had been completed. The Admiralty used this time to convince him that the two damaged light cruisers had been joined by the *Cumberland* and the *Renown*, though, in fact, neither could reach Rio de la Plata until 19 December. Still unable to verify reports by aircraft, Langsdorff felt that it would be suicidal to face the augmented force with a damaged ship, and decided to scuttle *Graf Spee* outside Montevideo harbour on 17 December. The crew were transferred to Buenos Aires where Langsdorff committed suicide two days later

Captain Dau's position was now very difficult; *Altmark* was totally isolated without support in the South Atlantic with minimal armament and engines badly needing maintenance before she could attempt to return to Germany. The Admiralty now knew about *Altmark* from the prisoners freed in Montevideo and for every kilometre of the way she would have to evade British warships, ordered by the First Lord of the Admiralty, Winston Churchill, to 'scrub and search' the Atlantic. With 299 prisoners on board, she was extremely overcrowded and short of supplies. In the bare steel 'flats', prisoners endured miserable conditions, without proper bedding or washing facilities and survived on a monotonous, subsistence diet. Discipline was strict, but Dau was not a hard-bitten Nazi and *Altmark* was not a 'hell ship' or 'slave ship' as subsequently portrayed in the British press. Rations were as good as possible under the circumstances, for most of the time quite liberal exercise was allowed on deck, and medical attention was provided.

With engine maintenance urgently needed and fully aware of prowling British warships, Dau decided to head far south of Gough Island to hide in the stormy seas, bad weather and poor visibility of the Southern Ocean while engineers undertook the miserable task of overhauling bits of machinery on deck. The hull was also cleaned as well as possible and then repainted, with the identity changed again, first to *Haugesund* and then to *Chiriqui.* Conditions were dreadful in the uninsulated flats where dripping condensation soaked all the improvised bedding materials, and bad weather limited deck exercise.

It was 24 January before *Altmark* was ready to attempt the long run back to Germany. Over the next month she dodged her way northwards up the Atlantic, steering well clear of even remote islands like Tristan de Cunha and Fernando do Noronha. The 'narrows' between Recife and Freetown, where patrols from Dakar were vigilant, were particularly dangerous, but she managed to slip into the North Atlantic in early February. Dau did not know that his navigation was being tracked by the captives through a peephole and his course plotted on Melville-Evans' hidden chart, but there was no way for the

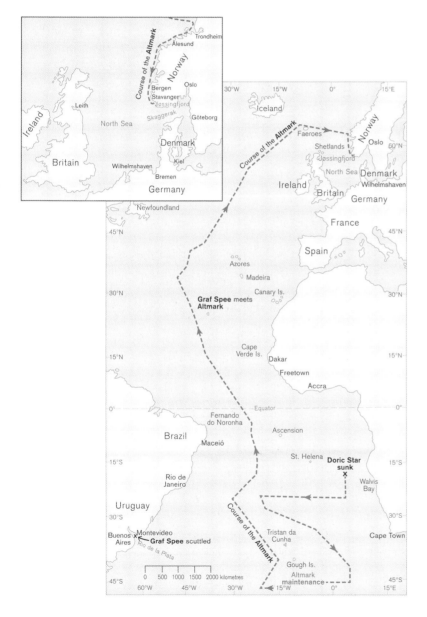

captives to get a message out to help the hunters. *Altmark* headed west to avoid the Canary Islands and the Azores, and then turned north-east between Iceland and the Faroes. It was 14 February before the Royal Navy located her when she turned up off the Norwegian coast north of Trondheim. Dau planned to sail south through Norway's neutral waters before slipping safely into the Baltic. To make this possible, all guns were removed and stowed below.

After the long lull since the battle off Rio de la Plata, events now moved very quickly. Linesøy coastguard station alerted Norwegian naval defence to *Altmark*'s arrival and she was soon shadowed by the motor torpedo boat *Trygg*. She was boarded off Trondheimfjord, but Dau convinced the Norwegian officer that she was a simple tanker and not liable to inspection. She was allowed to continue south, but the Norwegian naval defence district commander, Rear-Admiral Tank-Nielsen was not satisfied and ordered another boarding by the *Snøgg* when she reached Ålesund. Dau again evaded inspection, but *Snøgg* escorted *Altmark* south towards the strategic Bergen Defence Area where she was joined by the destroyer *Draug*. She was boarded again by *Snøgg*'s officers off Sognefjord, but despite a tremendous clamour from the prisoners, she was allowed to proceed before being halted again by destroyer *Garm*, with Tank-Nielsen himself on board. Again the prisoners kicked up a noisy cacophony but were driven back by fire hoses, while *Altmark*'s winches were turned on to drown the noise. Despite his strong suspicions, Tank-Nielsen was overruled by Oslo and *Altmark* was allowed to continue south, shadowed by several torpedo boats.

As soon as the Admiralty learned of *Altmark*'s arrival, an interception force was ordered out of Rosyth under command of Captain Philip Vian. This included cruisers *Arethusa* and *Penelope* and destroyers *Cossack*, *Sikh*, *Nubian*, *Intrepid* and *Ivanhoe*. They were still unsure of *Altmark*'s precise location as they fanned out across the North Sea, but on 16 February, despite poor visibility three RAF Lockheed Hudsons from Thornaby sweeping low over south-west Norway identified *Altmark* near Jøssingfjord. Shortly afterwards *Arethusa*, *Ivanhoe* and *Intrepid* intercepted and ordered her to halt. The order and attempts to board by *Ivanhoe* were ignored and *Altmark* managed to dodge into Jøssingfjord, still shadowed by Norwegian torpedo boats *Skarv* and *Kjell*, though ice prevented her reaching the head of the fjord.

By this time Vian had arrived with the 1,870t destroyer *Cossack*, in time for a standoff with the Norwegian ships, which prevented him pursuing *Altmark.* A flurry of diplomatic cables between Oslo, London and Berlin followed, arguing about the rights of the two belligerents in Norway's neutral waters. In the meantime Vian assembled a boarding party on *Cossack* and at 10 p.m. she steamed past the Norwegian ships into the fjord. As she approached with her searchlight focused on *Altmark,* Dau ordered his ship astern to ram her, but *Cossack* grappled and thirty-three men managed to board the tanker. After a short, intense exchange of fire, in which seven German crew were killed, the boarding party captured *Altmark*'s bridge. Opening an entry to the flats, someone yelled: 'Are there any Englishmen down there? Then come on up, the Navy's here.' The freed prisoners were quickly transferred to *Cossack* and by 11.55 p.m. the very overcrowded destroyer was on her way to Leith, where she received a tumultuous reception the following day.

The brilliantly executed rescue triggered a frosty exchange between British and Norwegian governments about the legality of the action in neutral waters, while Germany protested vehemently about the 'brutal murder' of civilian German seamen. However, the raid, which conjured images of Lord Cochrane's (prototype for Horatio Hornblower and Jack Aubrey) exploits in the previous century, exploded the boredom of the 'phoney war' and the British media moved into overdrive with headlines like 'Nazi Slave-Ship Feels the Nelson Touch!' The rescue was certainly a triumph for Captain Vian who ultimately rose to the rank of Admiral of the Fleet, but in the light of the atrocities revealed after the war *Altmark* was not a hell ship and Heinrich Dau was no Nazi 'gauleiter'. One result was to convince Hitler that he couldn't rely on Norway to cooperate in shipping Swedish iron ore down the coast to Germany, and he immediately started to plan Operation Weserübung. Less than two months later, on 9 April, German forces invaded Norway and Denmark, gaining many new bases from which ships of the Kriegsmarine, including both *Deutschland* (renamed *Lutzow*) and *Admiral Scheer* could prey on Allied convoys to Murmansk. *Altmark* managed to make her way back to Germany and, renamed *Uckermark*, resumed support of merchant raiders, before being destroyed in Yokohama in September 1940 by an accidental explosion, which also sank the merchant raider *Thor*, moored beside her, along with the newly captured Australian liner *Nankin*. The heroic *Cossack* was lost to a torpedo attack later in the year in the Mediterranean.

References

Frischeuer, W., and Jackson, R., 1955, *The Navy's Here*, the *Altmark* Affair, Victor Gollancz, London.

McIntyre, D., 1971, *The Naval War Against Hitler*, Charles Scribner's Sons, New York.

'Nazi Slave-Ship Feels the Nelson Touch', 1940, *The War Illustrated*, vol. 2 no. 26, 171–173 (1 March).

Vian, Sir Philip, 1960, *Action This Day*, Frederick Muller, London.

Wiggan, R., 1982, *Hunt the Altmark,* Robert Hale, London.

Williamson, G., and Palmer, I., 2005, *German Pocket Battleships*, 1939-45, New Vanguard, Osprey Publication, London.

Woodward, D., 1955, *The Secret Raiders*, Wm. Kimber & Co., London.

19 HMCS *SACKVILLE* (K 181) AND THE BATTLE OF THE ATLANTIC

HMCS *Sackville*:	Flower-class corvette, launched at St John Shipyard, New Brunswick, May 1941.
Tonnage:	940t displacement
Length:	60.5m
Beam:	10m
Draught:	3.5
Engine:	eight-cylinder triple-expansion with two Scotch boilers, single screw, 2,750bhp
Speed:	16 knots
Range:	6550km at 12 knots
Armament:	one Mk IX 10.2cm, one Mk VIII 2lb, two 20mm Oerlikons, four depth-charge throwers, two depth-charge rails, forty depth charges, one Mk 3 Hedgehog
Crew:	85
Career:	Battle of the Atlantic, joined the Mid Ocean Escort Force, May 1942. July 1942: on escort with convoy ON 115, severely damaged *U-43* and *U-552*. January 1943: four-month refit. Took part in thirty convoys and escorted 1,316 ships. 1944: modernisation, Galveston, Texas. May 1944: Escort Group C-2. July 1944: altered to loop layer. 1946–52 in reserve. 1954–82: oceanographic and biological research vessel. 1983: donated to Naval Corvette Trust, now Canadian Naval Memorial Trust. Museum ship in Halifax, Nova Scotia.

On 3 September 1939 a sombre Prime Minister, Neville Chamberlain, informed the British population that, for the second time in a generation, they were at war with Germany. Eight hours later several torpedoes slammed into the Cunard liner *Athenia* off the west of Scotland, sending her quickly to the bottom. Most of the 1,103 evacuees being carried to safety in Canada on the 13,581t *Athenia* were rescued, but the attack from the German submarine *U-30* served notice that the new war would pick up exactly where the First World War left off, when U-boat attacks on merchant shipping nearly starved Britain into defeat. In 1917–18, destruction of merchant shipping, the lifeblood of Britain, was prevented only by sailing in convoys protected by fast naval escorts. By 1939 the Royal Navy, though still powerful, was woefully short of the fast escorts needed to shepherd convoys through the dangerous Western Approaches where the U-boats lurked.

Fortunately not everyone in the Admiralty had been lulled into security by Chamberlain's naive promise of 'peace in our time', which followed his meeting with Adolf Hitler in Munich. Contingency plans were being laid. Destroyers, the greyhounds of the fleet that saved the nation in 1917, were too complex and expensive to build quickly in the numbers needed so a stopgap solution had to be found. This was a new class of ships, based on the tough little whale catchers refined over the previous three decades for the Antarctic whaling industry. Designed to survive the exceptionally hazardous Antarctic seas, whale catchers were extremely seaworthy, nimble enough to pursue whales like terriers, and could turn quickly almost within their own length. They were also abominably cramped, damp and uncomfortable.

The foremost British builder of whale catchers was Smith's Dock Company in Middlesbrough, on the River Tees, whose chief designer, William Reed, had also designed small patrol vessels during the First World War. Incorporating features from the catcher *Southern Pride*, built by Smith's Dock in 1935, Reed submitted plans for a new escort ship to the Admiralty. This would be 62.5m long, 10.1m beam, would draw 2.52m forward and displace 940t, with a powerful four-cylinder, 2,750hp triple-expansion engine driven by two Scotch Marine 'fire-tube' boilers. Carrying 230t of fuel, the maximum range at 12 knots would be 3,600 nautical miles, and the top speed 16 knots. She would be lightly armed with one 10.2cm gun mounted on a raised fo'c'sle, a 2lb anti-aircraft 'pom-pom' aft and several Lewis machine guns. The real sting in her tail to make life miserable for U-boats would be forty 136kg depth charges, launched from rails over the stern. Asdic sonar instruments, developed in 1918 to track submarines below the surface, would also be fitted.

The new ships, soon identified as 'corvettes', had to be very simple so that they could be constructed quickly even by shipyards with little experience of building naval ships. They also had to be cheap with a target price of £90,000 – as Winston Churchill said, 'nasty but cheap'. War was imminent and the first contracts were rushed through, twenty-six ships being ordered from British yards in July 1940, and another eighty by December. The first of these 'Flower-class' corvettes, HMS *Gladiolus,* was launched in January 1940 at Smith's Dock and started escort duties just before the Dunkirk evacuation in June 1940. By then supply lines to Britain were in crisis. Despite sinking *Athenia*, Germany was not ready for a full-scale submarine war in 1939 when the Kriegsmarine had only twenty-seven ocean-going U-boats. However, construction was rapidly increased and by June 1940 the situation for the Allies had taken a serious turn for the worse. U-boats operating from German North Sea bases could only just reach the western coastal waters of the British Isles, but after Dunkirk they moved to the French west coast, over 700km closer to the shipping lanes, and could range far out into the Atlantic.

At first, all odds were on the side of the U-boats. During what they referred to as their 'Happy Time' escort resources were stretched very thin and convoys of up to seventy ships covering many kilometres of ocean were sometimes protected by a single escort. There were only enough ships to provide protection up to 160km west of Ireland; there they joined incoming convoys while westbound merchant ships were left on their own for the rest of the voyage. Submerged U-boats were slow, but on the surface they could travel at 17 knots, and, attacking at night, were almost impossible to detect. Merchant ships were also harried, tracked and bombed by giant Focke-Wulf Condor aircraft, which would call in concentrations of U-boats – the infamous 'Wolf Packs' – to slaughter the defenceless ships. The carnage was appalling; in early October 1940 the eastbound convoy SC7 from Sydney, Nova Scotia, lost twenty out of thirty-four ships, and a few days later convoy HX79 from Halifax lost twelve out of forty-nine ships. Allied shipping losses mounted quickly; between May 1940 and the end of the year, 745 ships were sunk and more than 3 million tons of critical supplies were lost. At this rate of loss the Allied war effort would be crippled within months.

Long before Dunkirk, it was clear that British shipyards could not produce corvettes quickly enough, even with assistance from shipyards in still-neutral America. Yards in Canada with little experience of building anything larger than fishing trawlers soon received contracts, and the first Canadian corvette, HMCS *Agassiz*, was launched in August 1940. There were several differences between British and Canadian Flower-class corvettes, the most significant being the magnetic compasses rather than gyro compasses on the Canadian ships. These were more liable to disturbance in bad weather or from gunfire, making accurate navigation more difficult. Ships fresh from the shipyards with minimal 'working up' time, mostly crewed by new recruits and part-time sailors, were rushed into action.

By January 1941 when the first Canadian-built corvettes reached Britain, the Battle of the Atlantic was at its peak. Weapons were in short supply and the first Canadian corvettes to arrive, *Windflower* and *Trillium,* were fitted with wooden foredeck guns for the Atlantic crossing, prompting one Royal Navy signaller to ask if they were 'beating the enemy to death'. By then the war had turned into something very different from that envisaged when they were designed. Initially Allied planners expected U-boats to operate successfully only in coastal waters, but when they started to operate from bases in France after Dunkirk, the greatest danger lay far out to sea. Corvettes were seaworthy, but with their shallow draught and low freeboard, they were never intended for long ocean voyages. Reputed to 'roll on wet grass', in heavy seas they combined rolling and pitching that tested the strongest of stomachs, in a ghastly corkscrew movement reminiscent of the gyrations of a newly washed dog. Even in moderate seas the deck was almost continually awash and the fo'c'sle, where most of the forty-two crew (later increased to more than ninety) were crammed, streamed with water, particularly in action when shells had to be hoisted to the deck through open hatches. On early corvettes the galley was close to the stern so food was usually cold and often wet by the time it had been carried along the slippery open deck (which initially lacked non-slip coating) to the fo'c'sle. The open bridge was miserably exposed to waves shipped over the short foredeck, and during the savage Atlantic winters that soon followed it became thickly encrusted with ice which made handling the 136kg depth charges almost impossible.

As new corvettes started to pour out of shipyards in Britain and Canada, the balance of the conflict gradually shifted. The first ten Canadian corvettes went immediately to Britain, but as the war spread corvettes were also needed for the western Atlantic and most of the 122 Canadian corvettes eventually built (out of a total of 269 built by the Allies) served with the Canadian navy. As the scope of the growing conflict became clear, many modifications were incorporated. The galley was moved forward to the main superstructure, the short fo'c'sle was extended back to the bridge and bilge keels were added to improve stability and living conditions. More guns (real ones!) and depth charges were added, along with a raised gun platform, a monkey bridge above the chart house and eventually radar.

HMCS *Sackville* was the second corvette ordered for the Royal Canadian Navy, but the St John Shipyard, New Brunswick, was so busy with repair work that she wasn't launched until May 1941. By that time thirty-three other Canadian corvettes were in commission and

the Newfoundland Escort Force had been set up to guard the convoys in the lethal mid-Atlantic gap where the wolf packs could operate freely, beyond the range of Allied air cover. It was another eight months before *Sackville* was ready for escort duty. Her first efforts were not auspicious. In late February while rescuing survivors from a torpedoed Greek ship, the first lieutenant had to take over command from the alcoholic captain, who then had to be released as he was the only officer on board who knew how to navigate! Back in Halifax, he was discharged, and the complete crew was replaced by experienced officers and crew from HMCS *Baddeck*, which was confined to port with engine trouble.

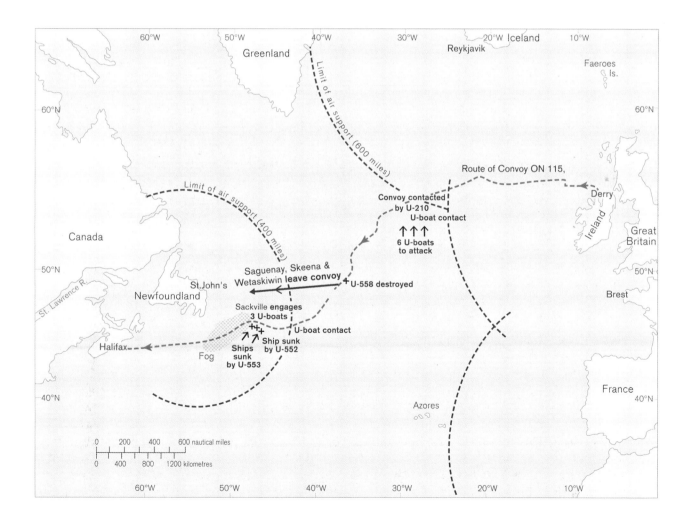

Matched with a battle-hardened crew, *Sackville* finally joined the Mid Ocean Escort Force in May 1942 with an operational sphere extended to Derry in Northern Ireland. After several uneventful convoys, in late July she had her baptism of fire with the westbound convoy ON 115. Soon after leaving Derry one U-boat was sunk by her sister corvettes, HMCS *Skeena* and *Wetaskiwin*. Short of fuel, they then had to steam directly for St John's, just before the convoy ran into a powerful wolf pack waiting in the fog-shrouded waters of the Newfoundland Grand

U-boat crew firing at the *Sackville*.

Banks. Two ships were torpedoed near midnight on 2 August, starting a two-day game of 'blind man's bluff' through fog and the glare of starshells. *Sackville* soon sighted and, with her gun blazing, tried to ram the surfaced *U-43*. The U-boat dived, but several times was driven back to the surface by depth charges. Stymied by lack of Asdic contact (which didn't work well with surfaced submarines) and primitive radar, *Sackville* repeatedly sought and tried to ram the U-boat, but even the nimble corvette could not turn quickly enough and the very badly damaged U-boat slipped away, eventually reaching port in Brittany. In the meantime several more ships were torpedoed by other U-boats, and soon *Sackville*'s radar flushed up *U-552* (which in October 1941 sank the USS *Reuben James* in the Denmark Strait). According to the U-boat's commander, Fregattenkapitän Erich Topp, *Sackville* 'came out of the fog like a gigantic wall and opened fire with every barrel'.

The range was too close for her old First World War Mark IX gun to bear easily, but she managed to blast a hole in the U-boat's conning tower. The Lewis machine guns were hopeless (the 'pom-poms' had not yet been fitted) and their bullets bounced off the U-boat's steel plates like peanuts. *U-552* was seriously damaged, but concealed by the fog, like *U-43*, she also managed eventually to limp back to Brittany.

Thanks to *Sackville* and her escort group, the balance sheet for convoy ON 115 was nearly even when the convoy steamed into St John's; two ships sunk and one damaged versus one U-boat sunk and two badly damaged. *Sackville* fought on through the autumn and winter. They couldn't avoid the never-ending atrocious weather and the nerve-jangling tension of long sleepless nights waiting for torpedoes to strike, but the escort group was lucky and successful, avoiding the heavy loss of fifteen ships each experienced by other escorts with convoys SC107 and ONS 154. By then early corvettes like *Sackville* really needed modernisation and in January 1943 she spent four months refitting in Nova Scotia, missing much of the dreadful 1943 Atlantic winter — the worst in 100 years. In the ferocious seas the tiny corvettes spent most of their time half-submerged and during one storm off the Irish coast, HMCS *Agassiz* lost her mast, her radar and most of her bridge.

Sackville emerged again in April with refurbished engines (but still with the old Scotch boilers, by then replaced on newer corvettes) and a newly reinforced bridge, armed with 20mm Oerlikon guns, which would have successfully finished off both *U-43* and *U-552* the previous August. However, she still had her short fo'c'sle and exposed well-deck with a hatch, which had to be opened for the shell-hoist during action, allowing floods of frigid Atlantic water to pour into the mess decks. She rejoined the Atlantic battle just as the tide was at last turning for the convoys. With better air cover, improved radar and new strong destroyer support groups, 100 U-boats were sunk in the first five months of 1943. In late May, Admiral Dönitz was forced to temporarily withdraw the wolf packs but by mid-September, they were back, more heavily armed with anti-aircraft weapons and acoustic torpedoes that would home in on ships' propellers.

Sackville joined the new Escort Group C-2 and in late September was involved in a savage battle off the west coast of Ireland with Wolf Pack Luether, during which the frigate *Itchen,* corvette *Polyanthus* and destroyer *St Croix* were sunk, and the stern was blown off the frigate *Lagan*. After these losses the new group was no longer viable, so *Sackville* returned to normal convoy duty, making six more crossings before the end of the year. In early 1944 her long-suffering engines gave trouble and she was at last scheduled for complete modernisation. In Galveston, Texas, she was fitted with a lengthened fo'c'sle, advanced radar and the new 'Hedgehog' mortar, which could hurl bombs out ahead of the ship while U-boat targets were still held in an Asdic beam. Still working up in Bermuda, she missed the D-day landings where corvettes played a vital role protecting landing craft fleets. She returned to convoy duty, but was soon sidelined when a major crack was discovered in one boiler. After temporary repairs in Britain, she returned to Canada on one boiler for major repairs. She was then reassigned, first as an officer training ship in Halifax and then was modified to serve as a 'loop layer' to service the long lead-cased electrical indicator cables installed off all major east coast harbours for vessel detection. Her number one boiler was replaced by a cable tank and her main gun by a cable windlass. This turned out to be a blessing; when the European war ended in May 1945 she was deemed too valuable to be sold or scrapped, unlike most of the corvettes.

Held in reserve from 1946 to 1952 during the Korean War, *Sackville* was then converted for geophysical and biological oceanographic research. Periodic modifications changed her drastically from her original 1941 form but also prolonged her career until 1982 as the only active Flower-class corvette in Canada. By then nearly forty years old, the scrapyard was clearly looming, but her guardian angel intervened again. Attempts had been afoot for some time to preserve a Canadian corvette in a maritime museum. The choice became clear in 1979 when her competitors, the *Louisburg* and the *Lachute,* were both wrecked by hurricane David in the Caribbean. Decommissioned in 1982, the task of restoring *Sackville* to her 1944 configuration as a Flower-class corvette started. The massive bridge and accommodation superstructure, fitted for her years as a research ship were removed and a painstaking search started to find authentic weapons and instruments. Bits gradually turned up across Canada, while a Vickers VII 'pom-pom' and authentic Asdic control equipment were contributed by the Irish navy, which during the 1950s consisted of three British-built Flower-class corvettes.

At last, in May 1985, the fully restored *Sackville* was dedicated as a maritime museum and a National Historic Site in Halifax, Nova Scotia. The lone survivor of the 122 corvettes built in Canada, of which thirty-four had been lost during the war while accounting for thirty-three U-boats, she would provide a permanent memorial for all the Flower-class corvettes, which adapted so magnificently to a wartime role for which they were never designed, and kept the vital supply lines open through the darkest days of the Battle of the Atlantic. Her record is also an impressive testimony to the value of the convoy system. She participated in thirty convoys and helped to escort 1,316 ships, of which only ten were torpedoed and nine sunk.

References

Dunmore, S., 1999, *In Great Waters: the Epic Story of the Battle of the Atlantic, 1939–45*, McClelland and Stewart, Toronto.

Lynch, T.G., 1981, *Canada's Flowers: History of the Corvettes of Canada*, Nimbus Publishing, Halifax.

Macpherson, K., and Milner, M., 1993, *Corvettes of the Royal Canadian Navy, 1939–1945*, Vanwall Publishing, Ltd, St Catharine's.

McIntyre, D., 1971, *The Naval War Against Hitler*, Charles Scribner's Sons, New York.

Milner, M., 1998, *HMCS Sackville*, The Canadian Naval Memorial Trust, Halifax.

Monsarrat, N., 1945, *Three Corvettes*, Cassell and Co., London.

Monsarrat, N., 1951 *The Cruel Sea*, Cassell and Co. London.

O'Connor, E., 1995, *The Corvette Years: the Lower Deck Story*, Cordillera Publishing, Vancouver.

Onions, P., My life aboard HMCS *Sackville,* www. canadasnavalmemorial.ca.

20 THE TANKER SS *OHIO* AND THE RELIEF OF MALTA

SS *Ohio*:	welded steel tanker launched by Sun Shipbuilding at Chester, Pennsylvania, for Texas Oil Co., August 1940.
Tonnage:	9,264t
Length:	156.6m
Beam:	20.7m
Draught:	8.68m
Cargo capacity:	27,000m³ oil/fuel
Engine:	Westinghouse steam turbine, 9,000shp
Maximum	19.23 knots
Crew (peacetime):	41
Career:	June 1942: turned over to Eagle Oil & Shipping Co. and British command. August 1942: under Captain Dudley Mason took part in critical Malta Convoy, Operation Pedestal. Repeatedly severely damaged by torpedoes and bombs, was eventually safely escorted into Valletta harbour with cargo of 11,500t of kerosene and fuel. Sank and split in half at mooring. August 1945: Decommissioned. September 1946: towed to sea and sunk by gunfire.

It was a submarine commander's dream. As Tenente de Vasco Renato Ferrini brought his submarine *Axum* to periscope depth at 7.55 p.m. on 12 August 1942, his eyepiece was filled by three ships, which he believed to be a destroyer, a cruiser and a large cargo ship, at a range of 1,300 to 1,800 metres. He immediately launched all four bow torpedoes, two directed straight and two obliquely. Seconds later an explosion, and thirty seconds later two more, sent blasts of flame and smoke high into the sky. Ferrini couldn't wait to assess the results; he had to submerge immediately to avoid depth charges raining down on his fragile vessel from escorting destroyers. In fact, he had scored a submariner's grand slam with all four torpedoes, seriously damaging one of the largest and most important Allied convoys of the Second World War.

Tenente Ferrini's submarine, *Axum*, was one of five submarines of the newly formed Italian 2nd Flotilla, deployed during the night of 11–12 August at the entry to the Skerki Narrows, which separate Sicily from Tunisia, to intercept the convoy as it steamed towards Malta. The convoy, Force X, was a critical operation undertaken by the Royal Navy as a last-gasp attempt to prevent the surrender of Malta. Strategically situated at the eastern outlet of the Narrows, less than 90km south of Sicily, the tiny Maltese islands had come to play a pivotal role in the Mediterranean and North African campaigns. Sitting directly across supply lines for Field Marshal Rommel's Afrika Corps, with a magnificent natural harbour in Valletta, Malta was an insufferable thorn in the side of the Axis forces. It was largely ignored before the war and Britain had allocated almost no resources to its defence; when war broke out the air defence on the islands consisted of three elderly Gloster Gladiator biplane fighters, optimistically nicknamed Faith, Hope and Charity. Malta was only thirty minutes' flying time from Italian airfields and both the Army and the Royal Air Force believed that it would be a hopeless, indefensible drain on resources, which would be bombed into submission within a few weeks. Churchill, fully aware of its strategic importance for Rommel's supplies, disagreed.

Malta was bombed incessantly. For two years a continuous stream of Italian and German aircraft pulverised the islands in nightly raids while submarines, motor torpedo boats and capital ships of Mussolini's navy throttled attempts to bring in supplies. The defiant forces in Malta maintained their attacks on the Axis supply ships, but in early 1942 Axis bombing rose to a new level. The German commander, Field Marshal Kesselring, had some 2,000 warplanes at his disposal and by early April, more than 2,000 air raids had taken place. In one month alone, 6,700 tons of bombs fell on the islands, destroying the docks and more than 10,000 houses. Most of the population were reduced to a troglodyte existence in underground catacombs while food supplies dwindled towards starvation levels. Malta urgently needed fighters to fend off the swarms of Axis bombers, and several flights of Spitfires were flown in from aircraft carriers in the western Mediterranean, but without fuel and ammunition these would be useless. Supplies continued to drop towards the critical level that would soon force Malta to surrender.

By mid-1942 the Royal Navy's resources had been stretched to breaking point by the Battle of the Atlantic and the suicidal Murmansk convoys mounted to meet Stalin's insatiable demands for armaments, but if Malta fell, Egypt and the Suez Canal could not be defended. Two convoys, one from Gibraltar and one from Alexandria, were hurriedly assembled in early June 1942 to try to force their way through to the islands. Impeded by minefields and harried non-stop by bombers, torpedo bombers and Italian naval units, both convoys soon lost warships and critically scarce cargo ships, including the large, modern tanker *Kentucky*. Only two freighters from Gibraltar reached Valletta, while no ships at all from the eastern convoy got through. Malta was still defiant, but the perilous situation was desperate and in secret, it was recognised that, without further supplies, it would have to surrender no later than 7 September. There was barely enough time to arrange one last convoy – it had to succeed!

Operation Pedestal was one of the most important operations of the war, and the Royal Navy was scoured to assemble a strong warship escort that might have a chance of fighting its way through to Valletta. Fortunately the Murmansk convoys had been temporarily suspended after the disastrous losses of convoy PQ 17 at the beginning of July, freeing up some vessels. Cargo ships were almost as scarce, particularly large, modern vessels that could keep up with the warships and maintain a convoy speed of 16 knots during the dash for Malta. Eventually thirteen fine ships were collected on the Clyde; registering an average of 9,809t, all were capable of at least 16 knots. As they arrived each was modified with the addition of anti-aircraft and machine guns. Most important, however, was the fourteenth ship, the tanker *Ohio*. No tanker large and fast enough could be found in the British merchant fleet and it took a direct appeal from Churchill to President Roosevelt to make the *Ohio* available, which many in America felt should be saved for the Pacific war. *Ohio* was a magnificent new ship, launched at Chester, Pennsylvania, for the Texaco oil company in 1940. She was large and fast with a welded steel hull and an immensely strong honeycomb structure of bulkheads, which divided her cargo space into nine large central tanks, eight large wing tanks and sixteen smaller wing tanks, and was also splendidly appointed with mahogany-lined cabins for the senior officers.

Ideal for the task, *Ohio* had arrived in Britain on 21 June. On 23 June she was turned over to the Ministry of War Transport, the Red Ensign of the Merchant Navy was hoisted and a British crew under Captain Dudley Mason of the Eagle Oil Company took over. She was immediately brought into a dockyard to be fitted with anti-aircraft guns, minesweeping paravanes and parachute and cable rocket launchers, while the engines were modified to make them less vulnerable to bomb-blast damage. The fourteen merchant ships assembled off Gourock in the Firth of Clyde and on 2 August set sail in four columns, to be joined at sea by naval ships from all around the British Isles. The largest escort force of the war under the overall command of Vice Admiral Sir Neville Syfret included the battleships HMS *Nelson* and HMS *Rodney* with their armament of 40.6cm guns, five aircraft carriers, seven light cruisers, twenty-eight destroyers, thirteen corvettes, three fleet oilers and a fleet tug. Some of the ships joined at Gibraltar, while nine British submarines were also out on patrol in the Mediterranean. Vulnerable to air attack, the battleships and carriers would turn back at the entry to the Skerki Narrows, leaving the vital Force X with four light cruisers and eleven destroyers to shepherd the convoy over the last and most dangerous stretch to Valletta, assisted by a Malta escort group of four minesweepers and seven motor launches.

As the convoy raced down the Atlantic, the merchant ships rehearsed complex emergency manoeuvres, particularly the rearrangement from four to two columns, which would be necessary to pass through the Skerki Narrows. By the time Gibraltar was reached through fog on 9 April they had almost reached naval efficiency. Refuelling so many warships under cover of darkness at Gibraltar was a nightmare, impossible to keep secret from enemy agents watching from Algeciras on the Spanish coast, but early on 10 August, the convoy cleared the Straits and reassembled in four columns. Led by the cruisers *Nigeria*, *Cairo* and *Manchester*, they were protected by a screen of eleven destroyers, 5.5km ahead. *Nelson* and *Rodney* covered the rear of the convoy with the cruiser *Kenya*, protected by a screen of seven small Hunt-class destroyers, 5.5km behind, while the aircraft carriers were out on the wings.

Initially all went well, though several German aircraft had to be chased away, but in the late afternoon a French civilian aircraft flew over the convoy and radioed its course and composition. This delighted the Axis command and its forces were alerted, with one set of U-boats and Italian submarines off the Algerian coast, more moving towards the Narrows, minefields and E-boats protecting the channel and numerous bombers and torpedo bombers ready to take off. The first torpedo attacks came early on 11 August and at lunchtime the first hits sank the aircraft carrier *Eagle*. Many submarine sightings followed as the convoy took evasive action and increased speed to 16 knots. By sunset a horde of Junkers 88 bombers and Heinkel 111 torpedo bombers arrived but were driven off by a ferocious barrage of anti-aircraft fire. They returned at dawn the next day and the freighter *Deucalion* was hit. From then on ships' gun crews would remain in constant action amid a non-stop cacophony of bomb blasts and tracer fire. One destroyer was soon damaged ramming an Italian submarine, while Stuka dive bombers blew the stern off another and badly damaged the flight deck of the carrier *Indomitable.*

As the sun went down on 12 August, the convoy approached the Narrows and, still under air attack, started the complex reorganisation into two columns, while the big ships of Syfret's Force Z turned back for Gibraltar. (Map, see p. 165) Meanwhile the *Axum,* which first sighted the convoy in mid-afternoon, having completed its careful stalk, was waiting, and at 7.55 p.m. Tenente Ferrini fired his torpedoes. Almost as soon as they were fired cruiser *Nigeria,* the convoy's flagship, slewed round with her rudder jammed and took on a 15° list as her engine room flooded. Seconds later a second cruiser, *Cairo* (mistaken by Ferrini for a destroyer), erupted as she was hit by two torpedoes, one of which blew off her stern. Scarcely had the water settled before a huge fireball exploded from the *Ohio,* as the fourth torpedo buried itself beneath her bridge, blowing a gaping 7m by 8m hole in her side. Confusion was immediate as *Nigeria* with her rudder jammed circled slowly to port while the doomed *Cairo*'s crew was rescued by the destroyer *Ashanti,* which then sank her. The loss of the *Nigeria* and the *Cairo* was a major blow to the convoy; these were the ships designated for aircraft control so fighter support could no longer be vectored in from Malta.

Attacks continued unabated and within two hours the freighters *Brisbane Star, Empire Hope* and *Clan Ferguson* were hit by torpedoes, while another crushed the bows of the cruiser *Kenya,* though she could still continue at 25 knots. Later in the night torpedo boats attacked and the cruiser *Manchester,* struck amidships by a torpedo, joined the list of cripples, soon to be followed by the freighters *Glenorchy, Wairangi, Almeria Lykes, Santa Elisa* and *Rochester Castle.* The convoy was in chaos with nearly three-quarters of the merchant ships now crippled or sunk, but despite the huge hole beneath her bridge, *Ohio* managed to get under way again, first limping towards the Tunisian coast in an attempt to reach Malta independently. Impeded by torn plating, she could no longer be steered from the bridge and had difficulty keeping course, and soon had to be helped back to the shattered convoy by the destroyer *Ledbury.* She rejoined just in time to see the freighter

Waimarama immediately ahead of her explode in flames. With kerosene leaking from her tanks, *Ohio* was like an incendiary bomb waiting to ignite. Several bombs blew her temporarily completely out of the water, and as she made an emergency turn to port, another bomb burst open her bows, which quickly filled with water. Despite the efforts of Spitfires and Beaufighters from Malta, non-stop waves of enemy bombers homed in on the shattered convoy. As the only tanker, *Ohio* was the prime target for repeated attacks by Stuka dive bombers, interspersed by a damaged Junkers 88, which crashed upside down on her foredeck, blowing out the boiler fires.

Rocked by repeated explosions, *Ohio*'s engines kept stopping and the lighting failed in her engine room. Struggling on, she slowed to 2.5 knots, dropping further and further behind the remnants of the convoy, though the freighter *Dorset,* set ablaze by bombs, with the destroyer *Bramham* in attendance, was still in sight. Eventually two bomb blasts in quick succession knocked out both *Ohio*'s port and starboard boilers. Dead in the water, she was unable to steer until an emergency block and pulley was rigged. She was now only 96km from Malta and the destroyer *Penn* passed a cable to try to tow her in, but the big tanker, almost awash and now drawing over 11.3m, would only circle lazily to port. Throughout the afternoon, still under continuous bomber attack, they tried to get her moving, but it was near sunset before they had any success, when the minesweeper *Rye* from Malta arrived to help. While their ordeal dragged on, three of the freighters, *Port Chalmers, Melbourne Star* and the damaged *Rochester Castle,* finally slowly made their way into Valletta's Grand Harbour. There were cheering crowds and bands playing, but without the tanker with the vital fuel for the air defence, the success was a hollow one. Meanwhile, 95km away, the blazing *Dorset* finally sank. Despite the help of Spitfires from Malta, bombers continued to get through, hitting *Ohio* again and stopping the tow. With the cable reattached after two hours the little convoy managed to crawl on again for a while at a meagre 4 knots until the cable parted again just after midnight.

The exhausted crews were dead on their feet, and rested aboard the escorts until the sun rose again on 14 August, when a large group of volunteers, many from the sunken freighters, reboarded *Ohio. Penn* and *Rye,* now joined by the destroyer *Ledbury,* gingerly took up station on either side of *Ohio*'s battered hull, and lashed together with cables, the strange little convoy started out again, crawling like a wounded spider across the calm sea in the bright sunshine. Luckily most of the bombers had now refocused their attention on the escort vessels racing west towards Gibraltar, but even without their unwelcome attention, there was no certainty that the mortally wounded tanker would hold together for the last few kilometres. Gradually the speed was worked up to 5 knots until Captain Mason warned that the shattered tanker would break apart. By afternoon the Maltese coastline could be seen on the horizon, but they still had to thread their way along a narrow, tortuous channel through the minefields. It was almost impossible to manoeuvre the deadweight of the loaded, largely submerged tanker round the channel's 140° turns; *Ohio*'s momentum dragged the destroyers towards the minefields, but as night fell tugs arrived from Valletta to help. Painfully slowly they inched along the channel until, at dawn Valletta's harbour master arrived and, with tugs attached, *Ohio* with her decks almost awash slowly moved past the harbour boom and the cheering crowds to tie up at Parlatorio Wharf.

The magnificent, brave *Ohio* would never sail again. As the last fuel was hurriedly pumped out of her tanks, she settled slowly onto the bottom of the Grand Harbour where she continued to serve a useful function as accommodation for forces for the rest of the war. But her stubborn refusal to sink and the almost incredible courage of her crew had lifted Malta's siege and changed the course of the war. The forces of Malta would continue to torment Rommel's supply lines and two months later, the Afrika Korps, starved of fuel, would be forced to start their long retreat westwards from El Alamein. *Ohio* was spared the indignity of the scrapyard; in September 1946 her hulk was towed to sea and honourably sunk by gunfire.

References

Bragadin, M.A., 1957, *The Italian Navy in World War II*, United States Naval Institute, Washington.

Hill, R., 1975, *Destroyer Captain*, William Kimber, London.

Shankland, P., and Hunter, A., 1963, *Malta Convoy*, Fontana Books, London.

Smith, P.C., 1970, *Pedestal: The Convoy that Saved Malta*, William Kimber, London.

Pearson, M., 2011, *The Ohio and Malta*, Pen and Sword Books, Barnsley.

Woodman, R., 2000, *Malta Convoys, 1940–43*, John Murray (Publishers) Ltd, London.

21 USS *INDIANAPOLIS* (CA-35) AND THE SACRIFICE OF A SCAPEGOAT

USS *Indianapolis*:	Portland-class heavy cruiser, New York Shipbuilding Co., launched 7 November 1931.
Tonnage:	9,800t
Length:	190m
Beam:	20m
Draught:	5.28m
Engines:	eight White Foster boilers and turbines, 107,000shp
Speed:	32.7 knots
Crew:	1,196 (wartime)
Armament:	nine 22.8cm guns in three turrets, eight 12.7cm AA guns, eight 1.27cm machine guns, two OS2U Kingfisher catapult floatplanes.
Career:	intended as fleet flagship, served as state ship for President F.D. Roosevelt, notably 1936 state visit to Brazil, Argentina, Uruguay. Extensive Second World War service in Pacific, flagship for Fifth Fleet: New Guinea, Battle of the Aleutians, Gilbert & Marshall islands, western Caroline and Marianas, Battle of the Philippine Sea, Iwo Jima, Okinawa, ten battle stars; severe damage from 'kamikaze' plane. Refit in US then carried 'Little Boy' A-bomb to Tinian. 30 July 1945: torpedoed and sunk by Japanese submarine *I-58* with immediate loss of some 300 lives; over 550 of the survivors died during the four days before rescue arrived.

The United States Navy entered the Second World War with the worst disaster in its history. On 7 December 1941 without declaring war, Japanese aircraft attacked the United States Pacific Fleet at Pearl Harbour, Hawaii, sinking or damaging eight battleships, three cruisers, three destroyers, an anti-aircraft training ship and a minelayer, and killing or injuring 3,684 servicemen. Designed to sap morale and deter American action in Southeast Asia, the attack had precisely the opposite effect. Forty-four months later, a fortnight before the war ended, the Navy suffered another disaster with ripple effects still felt, more than seventy years later. On 30 July 1945 the heavy cruiser USS *Indianapolis*, en route from Guam to Leyte in the Philippines, was torpedoed by a Japanese submarine and sank twelve minutes later,

ultimately resulting in the deaths of more than 880 of its crew of 1,196. The *Indianapolis* was the last US Navy ship to be sunk during the war, but it was the horrible fate of many who escaped the sinking, and the subsequent post-war enquiry that have made the case notorious.

Launched in New York in 1931 and already an old ship by 1945, *Indianapolis* was still a powerful, effective 9,800t warship. She was 190m long and generating 107,000shp, had a top speed of 32.7 knots. A main battery of nine 22.8cm calibre guns and eight 12.7cm anti-aircraft guns gave her a serious sting, and she also carried two OS2U Kingfisher floatplanes. She was not an obscure or unimportant ship but had been a prominent flagship for the Navy and acted as ship of state for President Franklin Roosevelt on several occasions, including a 1936 goodwill tour to Brazil, Argentina and Uruguay.

Indianapolis started her distinguished war record with a taskforce that bombarded Japanese-held ports at Salamaua and Lae, New Guinea, then successfully attacked Japanese fortifications at Kiska Island in the Aleutian Islands and supported landings on Amchitka. In August 1943 she joined the Fifth Fleet as flagship for Vice Admiral Raymond Spruance and fought with General MacArthur's forces along the islands of the western Pacific, winning ten battle stars. She provided fire support for invasions of the Gilbert and Marshall Islands, bombarded enemy installations in the Western Carolines and the Marianas Islands and participated in the 19 June 1944 Battle of the Philippine Sea – the 'Marianas Turkey Shoot' – when 426 Japanese aircraft were shot down. After overhaul in the United States, *Indianapolis* returned to the western Pacific early in 1945, assisting in bombardments of the Japanese mainland and Iwo Jima, and providing fire support for the invasion of Okinawa during which she shot down six enemy aircraft before receiving a direct *kamikaze* bomb strike, which blew two holes in her keel. Despite severe damage she managed to cross the Pacific for repairs near San Francisco. The repairs were expected to take four months, but in early July her captain, Charles McVay, was suddenly ordered to terminate the refit abruptly.

The surprise termination was so that *Indianapolis* could carry out an urgent and very secret mission. Though Japanese forces had bitterly contested every inch of ground, by July 1945 the eventual outcome of the war was not in doubt. From large runways constructed at Tinian, Guam and Saipan, B-29 Superfortresses were pounding Tokyo and other major Japanese cities with devastating bomb attacks. However, a final invasion of the Japanese mainland, anticipated for November, would be immensely difficult and was expected to cost half a million American casualties. Unknown to all but the scientists involved and a few top politicians, over the previous six years more than $2 billion and intense research effort had been concentrated on the Manhattan Project to develop an atom bomb. On 16 July 1945 this was successfully tested at Alamagordo, New Mexico. Faced with the possibility of huge casualties in a war that could continue for many months, President Truman decided to authorise deployment of the bomb against Japan.

Though no one on board *Indianapolis*, including Captain McVay, was aware of the real nature of her secret mission, this was to race across the Pacific to deliver the first atomic bomb to bombers waiting at Tinian airfield. On 15 July, even before the successful New Mexico test, a large wooden crate and a black metal canister containing the atom bomb nicknamed 'Little Boy' and critical fissile uranium-235 were delivered under tight security to *Indianapolis*. Early the following morning, mooring lines in San Francisco were cast off and despite the incomplete repairs and a crew that included many new recruits, *Indianapolis* left swiftly on her secret mission. In heavy weather she steamed at close to maximum speed to reach Pearl Harbour in a record seventy-four and a half hours. After refuelling she continued, anchoring off Tinian early on 26 July, and completing the 8,000km voyage in a mere ten days. Within hours the mysterious cargo had been unloaded (the components of Little Boy were actually assembled in the hold of Superfortress *Enola Gay* en route to her target at Hiroshima six days later).

Indianapolis was ordered to leave immediately for Leyte, via Guam, for training with the Fifth Fleet under Admiral McCormick before joining Task Force 95 under Admiral Oldendorf off Okinawa. Unbeknownst to anyone, the first seeds of a disaster had been sown; the message to Oldendorf, which specified no arrival date, was filed, while the message to McCormick was misdirected and not decoded. In Guam on 27 July, McVay cleared *Indianapolis*' 2,080km, three-day voyage along the 'Peddie' route to Leyte with the convoy routing officer at the Naval Operating Base. The voyage would be at the 'Standard Speed of Advance', below 16 knots, and McVay was informed of Captain Naquin's decision that no destroyer escort would be available. Cruisers were relatively lightly armoured and particularly vulnerable to torpedo attacks, but the Peddie route, now relatively remote from the active battle zone, was considered to be reasonably safe. *Indianapolis* carried no sonar equipment, but it was assumed that her great speed would allow her to outrun any submarines. McVay was not informed that submarines of the Japanese Tamon Group were known to be active along the Peddie route; this information came from the highly secret ULTRA decoding of intercepted Japanese messages and, though not available to the routing officer, was known to Captain Naquin. The six Tamon Group submarines were the most formidable in service during the war, 3,688t (submerged), 106.7m long, carrying ninety-four crew, armed with six *kaitens* (manned suicide torpedo craft) and nineteen torpedoes, and capable of 17.7 knots (surface). Nobody informed McVay that a US destroyer had been sunk between Okinawa and Tinian by a *kaiten* from the Tamon Group on 24 July.

Indianapolis left Guam on 28 July and by evening on the 29th was halfway to Leyte. Her orders specified zigzagging during daylight and in good visibility at night, at the 'discretion of the Commanding Officer'. She had been zigzagging by day, but as night fell the weather deteriorated and with poor visibility this was suspended. Shortly before midnight she was detected by sonar equipment on Tamon Group submarine *I-58*. On surfacing, her commander, Lieutenant-Commander Mochitsura Hashimoto, saw and misidentified her as an Idaho-class battleship at about 16km range. Submerging swiftly, Hashimoto tracked her approach and, at 12.04 a.m. on 30 July, at a range of 1,500m, launched six torpedoes. Two torpedoes hit *Indianapolis*, one on the starboard fo'c'sle, blowing off 20m of her bow and destroying a high-octane fuel tank causing an instant blaze. Moments later the second struck close to the bridge, penetrated her armour belt and destroyed the boiler rooms and the powder magazine in a massive explosion, which knocked out all communication from the bridge. The ship, still travelling at 12 knots with one propeller turning, scooped up a huge amount of water through the gaping bow. This smashed through successive bulkheads and caused a 15° list, which quickly increased to 60°. It was clear that *Indianapolis* could not be saved and at 12.13 a.m., McVay gave the order to abandon ship.

McVay's first thought was to send out an emergency radio message, but the phone link had been destroyed and, in the flaming chaos, he couldn't contact either radio shack. In the remaining few minutes he was preoccupied trying to make sure that men going over the side were wearing lift vests. *Indianapolis* was equipped with two 7.93m motor whaleboats, which were not damaged by the explosions, a number of floating nets and thirty-five cork and canvas life rafts, but in the rush of departure from San Francisco few had been provided with provisions and water. Fortunately 2,500 kapok life vests had been delivered to the ship just before departure. In the event, many men jumped into the oil-covered water without life vests, there was no time to launch the whaleboats and only twelve of the life rafts could be cleared

before *Indianapolis* rolled on her side and sank, three minutes after the abandon-ship order and twelve minutes after the first torpedo struck.

Astonishingly, nearly three-quarters of the crew managed to escape the explosion, fire and confusion of the rapid sinking, but they were in desperate straits. In the dark, men were spread over several kilometres of rough, oil-covered ocean. No one knew how many had survived or exactly where they were; some were seriously injured, some couldn't swim and at least half were without life vests. Many were far away from any of the twelve life rafts, which in any case were designed to carry only twenty-two men each. With no certainty that SOS signals

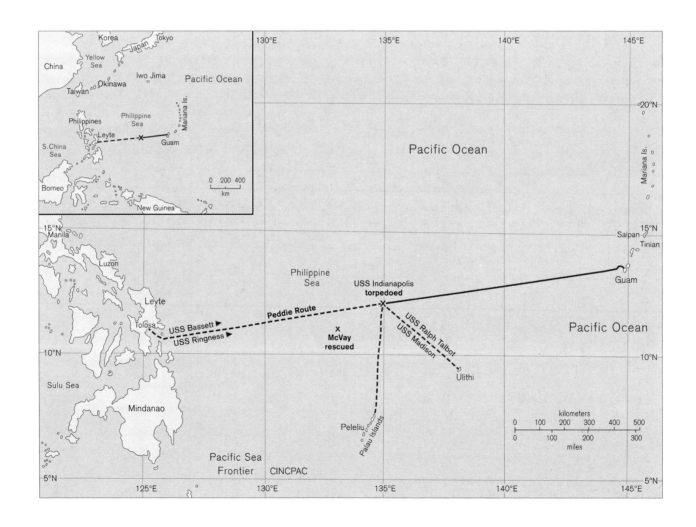

had been transmitted and the position of *Indianapolis* known, the only immediate hope was that emergency measures would be triggered when she failed to arrive as scheduled in Leyte early on 31 July.

The survivors soon began to float southwards at differing rates, progressively spreading out. Some of the more experienced crew started gathering survivors into groups, trying to support those without life vests and get them close to life rafts or floating nets. Captain McVay, initially alone in the water, found two empty life rafts and started to collect isolated stragglers. As the sun rose over the debris and oil-covered sea, temperatures quickly shot up to around 40°C and soon thirst, sunburn and the blinding glare were added to the survivors' miseries. The heads of the men in life vests were scarcely above water, particularly those with inflatable vests which began to leak. As the day wore on the most severely injured and those in shock started to die, and soon hundreds of sharks homed in on the scent of blood. Initially they attacked only those already dead, but by the morning of 31 July, they started to attack the living as well, particularly those isolated or at the edge of the larger groups.

In Leyte, the failure of *Indianapolis* to arrive had not been noticed; in the confusion of hundreds of invasion vessels, ships were assumed to have arrived unless contrary information was received; a specific directive (10CL-45) stated that the arrival of combatant ships should not be reported. Both Admirals McCormick and Ohlendorf in their respective commands were expecting *Indianapolis* but were unaware of specific arrival dates. No alarm was sounded for the dwindling number of survivors already in the water for more than forty hours, which would stretch to eighty hours before any relief appeared. Despite the warm sea, many men were becoming hypothermic while others, succumbing to dreadful thirst, drank seawater and slipped into violent fits, delirium and comas before dying. Shark attacks on both living and dead continued throughout the night, terrorising the hallucinating, shrinking groups of men.

On the morning of 2 August a Lockheed Ventura PV-1 bomber commanded by Lieutenant Chuck Gwinn was on submarine patrol at 900m over an area stretching 800km north of his base on Peleliu when he spotted something on the surface. Descending to 90m for a bombing run, he could suddenly count thirty men in the water. He radioed an immediate report then continued searching and soon counted many more. At 12.45 p.m., having fixed the position at 11°54′ N, 133°47′E, he sent a second message urgently requesting

a rescue vessel. By then his superior, Lieutenant-Commander George Atteberry, had requested dispatch of a large Consolidated Catalina PBY-5A seaplane, and was himself heading for the site in his own Lockheed Ventura. The second message was also received by the commander of the Marianas, Vice Admiral Murray, on Guam who immediately ordered two destroyers to depart at top speed. Lieutenant Adrian Marks heard Atteberry's message and took off in a Catalina from Peleliu on his own authority, arriving at the site at 3.20 p.m. By then the Philippine Sea Frontier office at Tolosa on Leyte had finally woken up to the fact that *Indianapolis* had not arrived and at last were starting to coordinate rescue operations.

As ships and several B-17 Flying Fortresses converged on the site Marks completed a risky sea landing, bouncing along the surface in his Catalina, and started to pick up survivors. Three hours later another Catalina arrived, while overhead, Atteberry's Ventura guided the big seaplanes towards the survivors, scattered over kilometres of ocean. By midnight, the first destroyer, the *Cecil J. Doyle* (diverted by its captain, Graham Claytor, on his own initiative), arrived followed by the high-speed transport *Bassett* and destroyers *Ralph Talbot* and *Madison*. It was not easy to pick up the enfeebled, hallucinating survivors and many had to be convinced that the rescuers were not Japanese warships. It was difficult to find all the scattered men, and McVay's small group wasn't picked up by the *Ringness* until 10 a.m. on 3 August, 186km from where *Indianapolis* had sunk. By mid-afternoon the last men had been rescued, though the search continued until 8 August. Only 321 of *Indianapolis*' crew of 1,196 had survived; four more would die within a week.

Even in the euphoria that followed the destruction of Hiroshima by Little Boy on 6 August and Nagasaki on 9 August, which would end the war within days, the magnitude of the disaster had penetrated to the highest echelons of the Navy. Admiral Nimitz ordered a court of enquiry in Guam, which concluded by 20 August. Disciplinary action was ordered for some lower-ranking officers for incompetent decoding of the notification to Admiral McCormick's staff of the expected date of *Indianapolis*' arrival in Leyte and failure to report her failure to do so, but no blame whatsoever was assigned to those who could have warned Captain McVay of the real threat of submarine activity or sundry other blunders. The major blame and a recommendation for court martial was assigned to McVay for failure to zigzag and to send out an SOS, ignoring clear evidence that two emergency messages had been received. Admirals Nimitz and Spruance both disagreed in writing with the court martial recommendation, but they were overruled by the chief of naval operations, Admiral King.

The *Indianapolis* was the only one amongst 436 ships of the US Navy lost during the war whose commander faced a court martial. This was convened in December 1945 to consider two charges: failure to abandon ship in a timely manner, which was quickly dropped, and failure to zigzag. Despite clear evidence of the poor visibility and testimony from Lieutenant-Commander Hashimoto of *I-58* that zigzagging would not have affected the result (corroborated by the expert, highly decorated American submarine commander Captain Glynn Donahue). McVay was convicted of 'hazarding his ship by failing to zigzag'. No blame was attached to any of the naval procedures in place and the court was not made aware of a report to Admiral King that blamed the navy for failure to make full use of the information on submarine activity from the ULTRA decoding.

Letters of reprimand or admonition were sent to four officers of the Philippines Sea Frontier at Tolosa; all were subsequently withdrawn. Captain McVay was demoted in permanent and temporary rank. Although he was released from arrest and restored to duty by the Secretary of the Navy, his naval career was effectively ended. Almost immediately he started to be plagued by hate mail from some of the families of men who had died, accusing him of murder. This sentiment was not shared by those who attended and applauded him at a first reunion of survivors at Indianapolis in 1960. Though surprised and gratified by this reception, the disaster continued to prey on his mind and in 1968 he committed suicide at his home in Connecticut. This might have ended the case but other survivors, concerned about the rank injustice to McVay, petitioned to have it reopened. In response, the Navy acknowledged no miscarriage of justice, but thanks to the efforts of a Florida schoolboy, Hunter Scott, and declassification of the ULTRA reports of submarine activity (which had not been released to McVay nor to his court martial), the Senate Armed Services Committee eventually convened hearings in 1999. One year later Congress passed an amendment exonerating Captain McVay of culpability for the loss of USS *Indianapolis*. In the view of former US submarine commander, Bill Toti, 'he should never have been prosecuted in the first place'.

References

Hashimoto, M. (trans. E.H.M. Colgrave), 1954, *Sunk: The Story of the Japanese Submarine Fleet, 1941–1945*, Henry Holt & Co., New York.

Helm, T., 2001, *Ordeal by Sea, New American Library*, Penguin-Putnam International, New York.

Kurzman, D., 1990, *Fatal Voyage: the Sinking of the USS Indianapolis*, Atheneum, New York.

Lech, R.B., 1982, *The Tragic Fate of the USS Indianapolis: the Navy's Worst Disaster at Sea*, Cooper Square Press, New York.

Nelson, P., 2002, *Left for Dead*, Delacorte Press, New York.

Newcomb, R.F., and Maas, P., 2001, *Abandon Ship: the Saga of USS Indianapolis and the Navy's Greatest Sea Disaster*, Harper Collins Publishers, New York.

Toti, W.J., Commander, *U.S. Navy, 1999, The sinking of the Indy and responsibility of command*, Proceedings, Naval Institute, Vol. 125 (October).

22 SS *FLYING ENTERPRISE*: THE FIGHT FOR SURVIVAL THAT MESMERISED TWO CONTINENTS

SS *Flying Enterprise*:	welded steel-hulled Type C1-B freighter launched as SS *Cape Kumukaki* under the US Maritime Commission Emergency Shipbuilding Program by Consolidated Steel Corporation, Wilmington, CA., January 1944.
Tonnage:	6,710t
Length:	120.83m
Beam:	18.31m
Draught:	8.4m
Engine:	two Westinghouse steam turbines giving 4,000hp
Speed:	14 knots
Crew:	48 + 10 passengers.
Career:	1947: sold to Isbrandtsen Shipping Co., New York. 21 December 1951: left Hamburg for New York under Captain Kurt Carlsen with mixed cargo and ten passengers. 25 December: disabled and listing in Atlantic storm west of Ireland. 28 December: SOS transmitted. 29 December: crew and passengers evacuated by SS *Southland* and USS *General A.W. Greely*. Captain Carlsen remained aboard. 2–3 January 1952: joined by USS *John W. Weeks* and tug *Turmoil*. 4 January: *Turmoil*'s mate Dancy joined Carlsen. 5 January: taken in tow by *Turmoil*, 560km from Falmouth. 10 January: tow parted 76km from Falmouth; Carlsen and Dancy abandoned ship, which sank at 4.10 p.m.

Some ships simply vanish without trace. Others, like the *Titanic* or the *Lusitania*, betrayed by bad luck or bad judgement, surrender and sink quickly with huge loss of life in a glare of publicity that can generate years of controversy. In maritime history, however, there are very few ships that can match the *Flying Enterprise*'s epic battle for survival, beset by hurricane winds and hammered by violent rogue waves in an Atlantic winter storm, nearly 500km off the Irish coast. Listing so far to port that waves could wash across her rail, pouring in through the massive crack that split her hull, and abandoned by all but her stubborn Danish captain, Kurt Carlson, *Flying Enterprise* seemed sure to sink within hours. But neither she nor her captain would give up so easily; for almost two weeks she fought back, being towed ever closer to safety in Falmouth, Cornwall. At first her ordeal was just one more SOS message amongst the hundreds that pour in from the Western Approaches every winter, but Carlson's lone heroic fight to save his stricken ship captured the imagination of every reporter on both sides of the Atlantic. Grainy black and white photos plastered across newspapers caught the essence of his epic struggle, strangely enhanced by the absence of television cameras. All along the coasts of the Atlantic listeners clung to their radios for more than a fortnight for each static-ridden bulletin from far out in the storm-lashed Western Approaches.

Flying Enterprise was an unlikely candidate for celebrity status. She was one of 5,549 vessels built under the Emergency Shipbuilding Program of the US Maritime Commission during the Second World War to counter the disastrous losses inflicted on Allied merchant shipping by the Nazi U-boat campaign, which threatened the flow of essential supplies and war materials across the Atlantic. Many of these, 2,755, were the unloved and unlovely 'Liberty' ships. The programme was developed under the 1936 United States Merchant Marine Act introduced to subsidise construction of fifty merchant ships per year to revitalise the aging American merchant fleet. Construction was increased to 100 ships per year in 1939 and 200 in 1940. In 1940, Britain, with rapidly escalating losses to U-boats, ordered sixty tramp steamers from US shipyards under the Lend-Lease programme. The order was for Ocean–class ships with riveted steel hulls and coal-fired triple-expansion reciprocating engines, following an obsolete, but well-tested design that originated in Sunderland in 1879. The Liberty ship programme, started in 1941, followed the same basic design, but coal-fired boilers were replaced by two oil-fired boilers and, crucially, riveted steel hulls were replaced by welded steel hulls. Welded hulls reduced labour costs by a third and drastically shortened the time required to build ships. The first Liberty ship, SS *Patrick Henry*, launched in September 1941, took 246 days to build, but this dropped to an average forty-three days, and by 1943, three Liberty ships were being completed every day. In a famous publicity coup, SS *Robert E. Peary* was launched four days, fifteen hours and twenty-nine minutes after her keel was laid.

The Liberty-ship design was simple: the rather ugly hull, designed to minimise the use of curved plates, which slowed production, was 134m long, 17m beam and 8.5m draught. There were two full-length decks and five large holds with a capacity of about 9,104 tons, accessed through large hatches. Wartime loads frequently greatly exceeded the nominal capacity with heavy deck cargoes. The large holds were ideal for war materials; a Liberty ship could carry 2,840 jeeps or 440 tanks, and many were also used as troop carriers. Oil-fired boilers and the triple-expansion engine provided 2,500hp, a speed of 11.5 knots and a range of up to 36,000km A crew of thirty-eight to sixty-two was carried with twelve to twenty-five naval armed guards. Most Liberty ships carried several guns and up to six 20mm machine guns. They weren't designed for combat but could give an attacker a nasty reception; SS *Stephen Hopkins* even took on and sank the German commerce raider *Stier* in 1942.

Liberty-ship construction was a triumph of industrial logistics, masterminded by Henry J. Kaiser, responsible for construction of the San Francisco Bay Bridge and the Hoover Dam. Most existing US shipyards were fully extended with naval construction in 1940–41, but eighteen identical new shipyards were hurriedly built along the east, west and Gulf coasts. Parts were fabricated at factories throughout the country and moved to the shipyards for rapid assembly in 250t shipments. The programme's success depended greatly on recruitment of many workers, most of whom were women without industrial experience; this became famous as the Rosy the Riveter programme, though most women were actually trained as welders. Welded hulls had been introduced for German pocket battleships in 1929, but this was their first use for ordinary merchant ships.

Liberty ships were controversial from the start and President Franklin Roosevelt initially didn't help by describing one as 'a dreadful looking object', though he soon got behind the project, designating 27 September 1941, as Liberty Fleet Day. It is generally believed that Roosevelt was responsible for their popular name, quoting Patrick Henry's 1775 declaration 'give me Liberty or give me death' and promising that the ships would bring liberty to Europe. They came in for much criticism, but without them victory in 1945 would not have been possible. They were criticised for being too slow and vulnerable to U-boat attack, but much more serious was the tendency of their welded hulls to split apart without warning. Around 30 per cent of Liberty ships suffered cracked hulls and at least three were lost at sea when they suddenly split in half. The concern was given particular point when a welded ship, the *Schnectady* (not a Liberty ship), suddenly split in two while moored alongside a quay. Suspicion initially focused on the welding and inexperienced welders, but the main cause was eventually identified after the war as brittle fracture of steel when subjected to low Atlantic sea temperatures. Steel is ductile at high temperatures, but becomes brittle and vulnerable to spontaneous fractures at low temperatures; the fractures can propagate at the speed of sound (343m per second). The critical temperature for the transition from ductile to brittle varies, depending on the steel type and the stress to which it is subjected. Fracture mechanics was a young science in the 1940s, but subsequent research has shown that the Liberty ship problem was partly caused by use of 'rimmed steel', cheaper and more widely available than other grades. More appropriate 'welding steel' did not appear until after the war. However, minute flaws in welding at key points like hatch corners may also have acted as 'stress risers', generating cracks that could spread almost instantaneously, not being isolated by the size of individual plates as on a riveted ship. Wartime overloading almost certainly contributed, and brittle fracture can also be generated by suddenly increased stress by, for example, very large waves.

Despite the cracking problem and other hazards of war, only about 200 Liberty ships out of 2,755 built were lost during the war. Even so concerns about their durability led to development of the larger, faster and less stiff 'Victory' ships and increased production of the more sophisticated C1 ships, which were originally designed before the war. C1 ships had more robust scantlings and carried their own equipment gear to load and unload holds, but were more expensive and took longer to build. Only 194 were produced under the Emergency Shipbuilding Program compared with 530 Victory ships. In 1951 *Flying Enterprise*, a C1-B ship, was comparatively new, launched as SS *Cape Kumukaki* in January 1944. She was sold to the Isbrandtsen Shipping Company of New York in April 1947, joining a fleet of eleven other steamers. Her captain, Kurt Carlsen, was a highly experienced old-school sailor, born in Denmark in 1914, who served his apprenticeship on square riggers, becoming an able seaman at 18. He earned his Danish master's licence in 1936 and his US master's ticket in 1947.

Flying Enterprise left New York in November 1951 and, a typical tramp steamer that took on cargo wherever it could be found, both unloaded and loaded cargo in Rotterdam, Antwerp and Bremen in early December before completing her cargo in Hamburg for the return voyage to New York. There is some uncertainty about her precise cargo – several different manifests apparently exist – but it was certainly varied, including 1,270t of pig iron, 890t of African coffee, 800 bales of peat moss, 5t of carpets, twelve Volkswagen cars, sixty-five birdcages, 260 bags of grass seed, twenty-five barrels of onions, 447t of jute rags and 17t of animal hair from India, together with Chippendale and Louis Quatorze furniture, assorted other antiques, several hundred typewriters and bags of registered US mail. She also carried 30t of naphthalene and an undisclosed amount of zirconium, apparently destined for the first American nuclear submarine, USS *Nautilus*, then being developed.

Flying Enterprise sailed on the evening tide from Hamburg on 21 December with ten passengers on board, bound for New York. By Christmas Eve she was butting through 'confused' seas in the English Channel against a westerly breeze gusting to Beaufort Force 6–7. Much worse was in store; on Boxing Day, she was off the south-west coast of Ireland; with dire weather forecasts streaming in, Carlsen reduced speed to 4 knots and then hove-to as the wind climbed to a full Force 12 hurricane. The term 'perfect storm' had not been invented but this is what was brewing up along the whole west coast of Europe. From Stornoway in the Hebrides to Cape Finisterre in Spain, winds approached 160km/h, interspersed with much stronger gusts. All over the Western Approaches, ships were in trouble; SOS signals streamed in to the rescue services and many ships foundered with loss of life.

It didn't seem that the weather could get worse, but it did; off to the south-west of Ireland at 50° 41′N and 15° 26′W, the *Flying Enterprise* was being hammered by giant waves. (Map see page X) Early on 27 December, she was suddenly thrown on her side by a massive wave and sharp bangs like gunfire echoed through the ship – her hull had cracked! The crack ran right across the deck aft of hatch three; about 4cm wide just in front of the bridge, it thinned to a hairline fracture down the sides towards the waterline, but it worked open and closed as *Flying Enterprise* hung up between wave crests. Within minutes the bosun and crew fought their way out to winch the crack tight with cables and wooden blocks, then hurriedly built a wooden frame across the crack and poured in wet cement to seal it.

The damage was serious, but the urgent action had staved off the immediate peril; the ship returned to an even keel and the pumps could easily handle the water leaking in. Carlsen was still confident that he could reach a safe harbour, but the hurricane continued unabated and two days later the second shoe dropped. Rogue waves were scarcely known at the time, but it was a rogue 20m-high wall of water that hit *Flying Enterprise* on 28 December. It tore off deck fixtures, crushed bridge windows and the starboard lifeboat and threw *Flying Enterprise* on her side in a 25° list from which she did not recover. Throughout the ship, fittings were torn loose as the cargo shifted down to the port side. Carlsen immediately tried to bring her head round to face the waves, but in minutes the engine cut out and the helm wouldn't respond. Now the situation was truly desperate; without power, the pumps were useless and, realising that the ship would have to be abandoned, Carlsen radioed urgently for help. *Flying Enterprise* was now well out into the Atlantic at 49°20′N, 17°20′W, nearly 500km south-west of the Fastnet Rock.

Despite the violent storm, half a dozen ships quickly changed course, radioing that they were on their way to help. Just after midnight, the British freighter *War Hawk* sighted the *Flying Enterprise*, and the American *Southland* and the British *Sherborne* arrived a few hours later. *Flying Enterprise*'s list to port was getting steadily worse, increasing to 60° and occasionally rolling to 80°. By no means sure that his foundering ship would survive until morning, Carlsen marshalled the passengers in lifejackets on the starboard side, ready to jump at a moment's notice. No rescue could be attempted in the dark so they spent the night huddled in a passageway near the bridge. By morning, the wind temporarily eased to Force 4, and with three more ships arriving, the Norwegian *Westfal Larsen,* the German *Arion* and the 13,000t American troopship USS *General A.W. Greeley*, oil was dropped to calm the waves and the rescue started. It was ominously difficult and lifeboats from *Sherborne* and *War Hawk* both quickly capsized, but eventually boats from *Southland* and *Greeley* managed to get close enough to help the passengers and crew as they jumped in pairs into the sea. Hauling the soaked, exhausted, oil-smeared survivors into the lifeboats and the long journey back to the ships were desperately dangerous tasks; it took over six hours of intense effort, but the only casualty was a middle-aged man who died in a lifeboat.

The successful rescue of fifty people in the appalling conditions was more than enough to secure a place in maritime history, but *Flying Enterprise*'s saga had barely started. Kurt Carlsen was still on board and, still optimistic about saving her, refused to leave his ship. Isbrandsten in New York had called in the powerful tug *Oceaan* from Rotterdam, but with well over 1,000km to steam, it would take at least a day to reach the stricken ship. On the way, believing that *Flying Enterprise* had been abandoned, she diverted to help her sister tug, 836t *Zwartse Zee,* which was in desperate trouble with a tow and with lives at stake off the coast of Brittany. Meanwhile the *Greeley* with the survivors on board had to head for port, so the destroyer USS *John W. Weeks* was ordered out from Bordeaux to relieve her. Already storm-battered before her departure, she was soon heading into a Force 8 gale and couldn't get to the *Flying Enterprise* until 2 January. Nearly every rescue tug in Western Europe was busy; the much less powerful *Abeille 25* from Calais tried to help, but had to turn back. On New Year's Eve, after seven days at sea, the 1,136t, British Bustler-class tug *Turmoil* successfully brought the crippled Shell tanker *Mactra* in from west of the Fastnet safely to Falmouth and two days later she set off for *Flying Enterprise.*

Even with the *Greeley* standing by, a kilometre off, the 'dark nights of the soul' that Kurt Carlsen endured are almost impossible to imagine, alone on the *Flying Enterprise,* without power and with waves crashing over the steeply sloping decks, and bulkheads in imminent danger of collapsing to send her straight to the bottom. Even the emergency radio packed up, but Carlsen had a small portable shortwave battery set and, laying a wire aerial out onto the deck, he managed to establish contact with the *Greeley.* Despite the constant danger, he settled down on a couch in the radio shack, and apparently slept with one hand on the floor to warn him in case the water rose too high.

As dawn arrived Carlsen's ordeal continued; with the wind rising again to a full gale, he had to scour the darkened ship's passages for any kind of food. Eventually the *John Weeks* got close enough to pass food and hot coffee across on a thin line, but the list was getting steadily worse and No. 3 hold, directly forward of the crack, was now completely flooded. Despite heading straight into the gale, *Turmoil* was making good time, and at 11 p.m. on 3 January, she finally reached the *Flying Enterprise.* Immediately, lit up by searchlights, she tried to pass a towing cable to Carlsen. This would first require attachment of a light leader line, which would be used to draw in a 7.6cm manilla messenger cable, and finally a 12.7cm wire hawser. Wedged against the *Flying Enterprise*'s steeply canting stern and clinging by one hand, with a superhuman effort Carlsen managed to get the heavy cable secured, but as it was drawn back to *Turmoil,* the shackle split. Early the following morning, with winds gusting to 60km/h and the *Flying Enterprise* being pounded by 6m waves, they tried again, but the leader fell short. It took a long time to gather things together for another

attempt; this time Carlsen laboriously made his way along the wet, almost vertical deck to the bow. Several times the leader fell short, but in the late afternoon, after seven failed attempts, they succeeded. Carlsen made the line fast, but as the heavy cable was drawn across, the leader snapped. After several more attempts, *Turmoil*'s captain, Dan Parker realised that the exhausted Carlsen had to have help if he was to make the tow fast. With dusk coming on, *Turmoil* manoeuvred dangerously close to *Flying Enterprise* and, as the ships touched momentarily, the tug's mate, Kenneth Dancy, jumped across onto the freighter.

Even with two men to draw in and secure the leader, the next attempt failed, so they settled down to wait for dawn. By 9 a.m. on 5 January, the wind dropped slightly, and this time Carlsen and Dancy managed to get the wire hawser aboard and properly shackled to a bollard. The long 560km tow to Falmouth could now start, but, listing at 70° and down by the head with her shattered rudder high in the air, *Flying Enterprise* couldn't steer and was a most recalcitrant client. On *Turmoil,* Captain Parker ran out an unusually long 600m of hawser and as he increased the tension, the big freighter gradually started to move. As the ships got under way, the tow required a very delicate touch on *Turmoil*'s big winch; *Flying Enterprise* would suddenly sheer off, sometimes at right angles to the hawser as water sloshed around in her holds. Parker had to play her gently like a salmon fisherman to prevent the hawser snapping. Very gradually he increased speed until the freighter was moving at about 3 knots. Meanwhile, dangerously short of fuel, the *John W. Weeks* was now replaced by another destroyer, USS *Willard Keith,* to maintain Carlsen's communication link with the world. It also managed to pass some food to the freighter including a large tin of butter, which Carlsen and Dancy used to grease the hawser to prevent chafing.

With *Turmoil* delicately playing her, with Captain Parker trying to anticipate each of her wild swings, *Flying Enterprise* edged her way slowly towards the north-east. Meanwhile the attendant flotilla grew, joined by the British tugs *Dextrous* and *Englishman,* the Trinity House ship, *Satellite,* and the French tug *Abeille 25,* while the air above buzzed with aircraft hired by the news media. For several days the weather held and by 8 January the convoy passed the Scilly Isles and *Flying Enterprise*'s funnel could be occasionally sighted with powerful binoculars from Land's End. Falmouth started to prepare a great civic reception, but it was too soon to celebrate; by late afternoon, their luck ran out. The wind started to rise again and, early on 9 January, reached Force 7 and, with 3m waves, the hawser suddenly snapped.

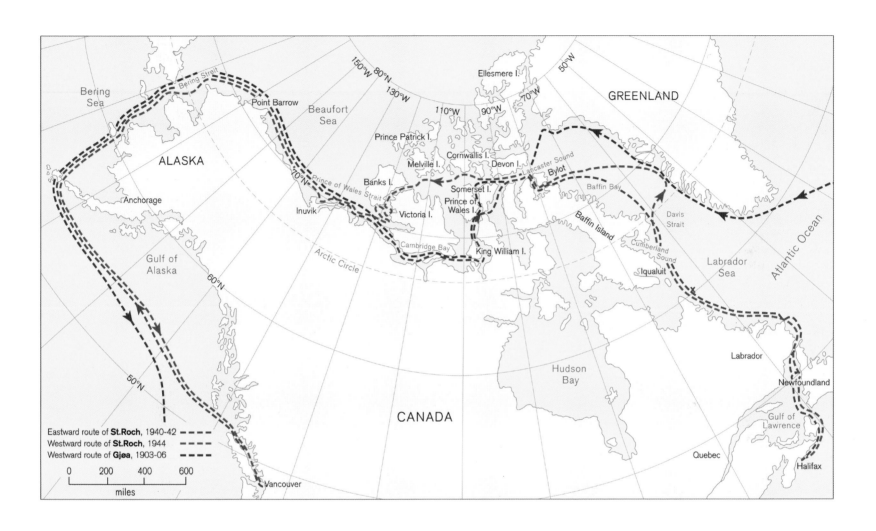

Bering
Sea

ALASKA

Anchorage

Gulf of
Alaska

50°N

Point Barrow

Beaufort
Sea

70°N

Prince of Wales Strait

Inuvik

Victoria I.

Cambridge Bay

Arctic Circle

60°N

150°W 80°N

130°W

Prince Patrick I.

Melville I.

Banks I.

110°W 90°W

Cornwallis I. Devon I.

Somerset I.
Prince of
Wales I.

King William I.

Ellesmere I.

70°W

Lancaster Sound
Bylot

50°W

GREENLAND

Baffin Bay

Baffin Island

Cumberland
Sound

Iqaluit

Davis
Strait

Labrador
Sea

Atlantic Ocean

CANADA

Hudson
Bay

Labrador

Newfoundland

Gulf of
Lawrence

Quebec

Halifax

Eastward route of **St.Roch**, 1940-42
Westward route of **St.Roch**, 1944
Westward route of **Gjøa**, 1903-06

0   200   400   600
miles

Vancouver

Fugitive German prison ship *Altmark* discovered off southern Norway by RAF Lockheed Hudson bombers, 16 February 1940.

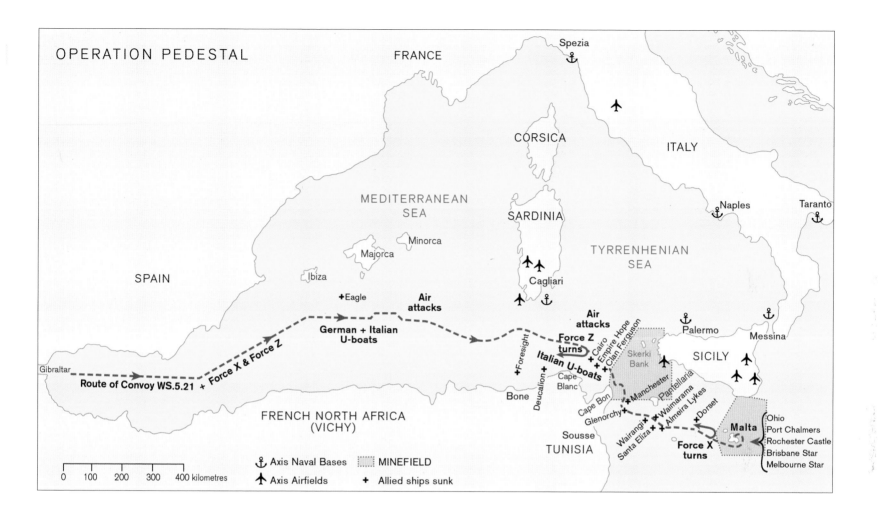

OPERATION PEDESTAL

FRANCE

Spezia

CORSICA

ITALY

MEDITERRANEAN
SEA

SARDINIA

Naples

Taranto

TYRRENHENIAN
SEA

Minorca

Majorca

SPAIN

Ibiza

+Eagle

**Air
attacks**

Cagliari

Palermo

Messina

**German + Italian
U-boats**

+Foresight

**Air
attacks**

**Force Z
turns**

+Cairo
+Empire Hope
+Clan Ferguson

Skerki
Bank

SICILY

Gibraltar

Route of Convoy WS.5.21   + **Force X & Force Z**

+Deucalion

Italian U-boats

Cape
Blanc

Bone

Cape Bon
+Glenorchy

+Manchester

Pantellaria

Dorset
+

+Waimarama
+Almeira Lykes

FRENCH NORTH AFRICA
(VICHY)

Sousse

TUNISIA

+Wairangi
+Santa Eliza

Malta

**Force X
turns**

Ohio
Port Chalmers
Rochester Castle
Brisbane Star
Melbourne Star

| 0 | 100 | 200 | 300 | 400 kilometres |

⚓ Axis Naval Bases   ▥ MINEFIELD

✈ Axis Airfields   + Allied ships sunk

Austin Dwyer
ASMA

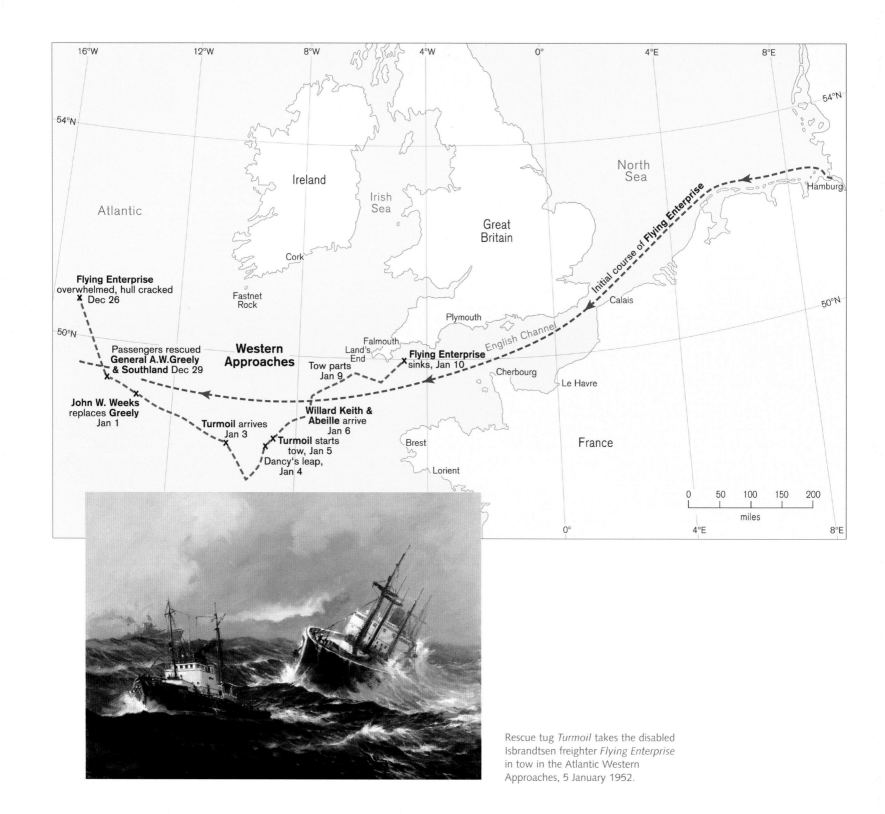

16°W   12°W   8°W   4°W   0°   4°E   8°E

54°N

Ireland

Irish
Sea

North
Sea

Atlantic

Great
Britain

Hamburg

Initial course of Flying Enterprise

Cork

Flying Enterprise
overwhelmed, hull cracked
✗ Dec 26

Fastnet
Rock

50°N

Plymouth

Calais

50°N

Passengers rescued
**General A.W.Greely
& Southland** Dec 29

**Western
Approaches**

Falmouth
Land's
End

Tow parts
Jan 9

Flying Enterprise
✗ sinks, Jan 10

English Channel

Cherbourg

John W. Weeks
replaces **Greely**
Jan 1

Turmoil arrives
Jan 3

**Willard Keith &
Abeille** arrive
Jan 6

Turmoil starts
tow, Jan 5
Dancy's leap,
Jan 4

Le Havre

Brest

France

Lorient

0   50   100   150   200

miles

0°   4°E   8°E

Rescue tug *Turmoil* takes the disabled
Isbrandtsen freighter *Flying Enterprise*
in tow in the Atlantic Western
Approaches, 5 January 1952.

British Antarctic Survey research/supply ship *John Biscoe* unloading stores off Base E, Stonington Island, February 1963.

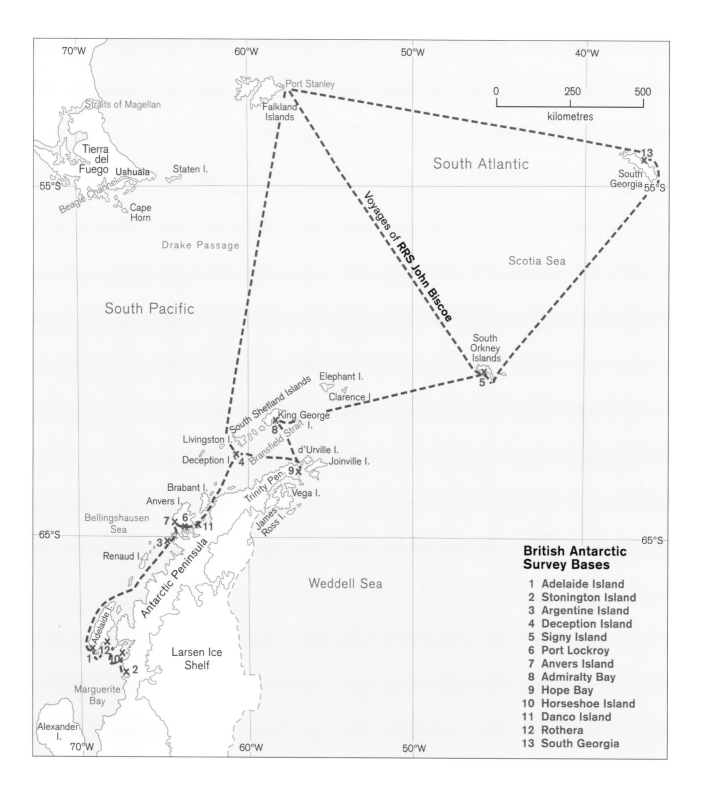

70°W   60°W   50°W   40°W

Straits of Magellan

0   250   500

kilometres

Port Stanley

Falkland
Islands

South Atlantic

13

Tierra
del
Fuego

Ushuaia   Staten I.

South
Georgia

55°S

55°S

Beagle Channel

Cape
Horn

Drake Passage

Voyages of **RRS John Biscoe**

Scotia Sea

South Pacific

Elephant I.

South
Orkney
Islands

Clarence I.

South Shetland Islands

5

King George
I.

Livingston I.

8

Bransfield Strait

Deception I.

4

d'Urville I.

Joinville I.

Brabant I.

9

Anvers I.

Trinity Pen.

Vega I.

Bellingshausen
Sea

7 6

11

James
Ross I.

65°S

65°S

3

Renaud I.

Antarctic Peninsula

Weddell Sea

**British Antarctic
Survey Bases**

Adelaide I.

Larsen Ice
Shelf

1   Adelaide Island
2   Stonington Island
3   Argentine Island
4   Deception Island
5   Signy Island
6   Port Lockroy
7   Anvers Island
8   Admiralty Bay
9   Hope Bay
10   Horseshoe Island
11   Danco Island
12   Rothera
13   South Georgia

12

1

10

2

Marguerite
Bay

Alexander
I.

70°W   60°W   50°W

RRS *John Biscoe* working through moderate pack ice off the coast of Adelaide Island, Antarctica. (Rorke Bryan)

RRS *John Biscoe* attempting to avoid icebergs in the Bellingshausen Sea, Antarctica. (Rorke Bryan)

Great Lakes ore carrier *Edmund Fitzgerald*, en route from Superior to Sault Ste Marie in distress during a storm south of Caribou Island, Lake Superior, 10 November 1975.

Before another hawser could be attached, Carlsen and Dancy would have to cut the broken remains of the hawser off the bollard with a hacksaw. Hour after hour, clinging to the wet deck with waves washing over them as the big freighter drifted slowly eastwards, settling lower and lower in the water, they sawed away at the heavy hawser until a 12m wave washed them down onto the submerged port rail. By dawn on 10 January a full gale was blowing and the end was in sight. An RAF helicopter attempted to reach the ship but was repeatedly driven back by the gale. In the early afternoon, Carlsen and Dancy heard explosions as the watertight bulkheads gave way and knew that it was time to leave. Barefoot and in lifejackets, they crawled out along the almost horizontal funnel while *Turmoil,* dangerously close to the sinking ship, lowered a rope ladder. Dancy jumped first but, mistiming a wave, fell 8m to the water. Finally, the stubborn, courageous Dane jumped and, after nine eternal minutes both men managed to grasp lifebelts hurled from *Turmoil* and were hauled up to safety. They were just in time; ten minutes later *Flying Enterprise*'s stern went under and at 4.11 p.m. her bow finally disappeared. The escorting flotilla sounded their sirens in a final salute, and then set off for Falmouth where *Turmoil* docked to a hero's welcome at 8 p.m.

Carlsen could hardly have been prepared for the maelstrom of publicity that greeted him. As far as he was concerned, he was no hero but simply a captain who had lost his ship. Not only did he apologise publicly but both he and Dancy refused all opportunities to gain commercially from their ordeal. Even to a world not yet grown completely cynical about self-seeking celebrities, this was something new and the papers had a field day. From Falmouth, Carlsen was shepherded to a public dinner and reception at Grosvenor House in London, where he was conferred with the Knighthood of Dannebrog by King Frederik of Denmark. Public adulation continued when he eventually reached New York on 17 January, where he was saluted by the sirens of every ship in the harbour, followed by a ticker tape parade up Broadway. He continued to insist that he was simply a seaman who had done his best to save his ship, but he was awarded with Lloyd's Silver Medal for Meritorious Service while Kenneth Dancy received a Medal for Industrial Heroism by the *Daily Herald* newspaper. However, he was still a captain who had lost his ship and he had to face a United States Coastguard court of enquiry, convened while he was still aboard *Flying Enterprise*. The court of enquiry was appropriately rigorous, but Carlsen had nothing to fear; the official verdict exonerated him from any blame for the loss of his ship, and he soon received a new command from Isbrandtsen – the *Flying Enterprise II*!

However, the story of the *Flying Enterprise* was too good to evade the attention of conspiracy theorists and rumours still continue to swirl, sixty-four years later: Why did Captain Carlsen stay so stubbornly with a ship that was clearly on its way to the bottom? Why did the United States Navy put no fewer than three warships at risk in the stormy Atlantic for an ordinary merchant vessel? Why was the strategically important zirconium being shipped on an ordinary merchant ship? Why did *Turmoil* try to tow her all the way to Falmouth when a shorter tow to Cork or Brest might have brought her to safety? What was the 'secret' cargo carried by *Flying Enterprise* and did Carlsen stand to benefit personally from salvage rewards? In 1960 the Italian salvage firm Sorima did retrieve some $210,000 of her cargo, originally valued at about $800,000, but apart from the general recognition that zirconium, not listed on the manifest, was being carried, no answer was found to any of these questions. The *Flying Enterprise* is now one of the most important dive sites in the British Isles, but despite many visits it seems unlikely that anything will be added to the extraordinary story of an extremely brave seaman doing exactly what he had been trained to do.

References

Bishop, L., 2005, Captain Carlsen and the Flying Enterprise, www.deepimage.co.uk.

Brookes, E., 1957, *Rescue Tug: the Story of the Flying Enterprise and the Salvage Tug Turmoil,* E.P. Dutton and Company, New York.

Delaney, F., 2006, *Simple Courage: a True Story of Peril on the Sea*, Random House, New York.

Elphick, P., 2006, *Liberty: the Ships that Won the War*, Naval Institute Press, Annapolis.

Kafod-Hansen, M., 1952, *Kaptajn Carlsen*, Samlarrens Forlag, Copenhagen.

Lane, F.C., 1961, *Ships for Victory: a History of Shipbuilding Under the US Maritime Commission in World War II*, The Johns Hopkins Press, Baltimore.

Sawyer, L.A., and Mitchell, W.H., 1981, *From America to United States: The History of the Long Range Merchant Shipbuilding Programme of the US Maritime Commission*, World Ship Society, London.

23 RRS *JOHN BISCOE*: ANTARCTIC WORKHORSE

RRS *John Biscoe*:	ice-strengthened Antarctic research/supply ship, launched in 1956 by Fleming & Ferguson, Paisley, for Falkland Island Dependencies Survey (now British Antarctic Survey).
Tonnage:	1,584t
Length:	67.07m
Beam:	12.2m
Draught:	5.6m
Engines:	two eight-cylinder diesel electric, 1,450bhp
Speed:	11 knots
Range:	30,000km
Capacity:	521m^3 hold, two 10t derricks
Crew:	33 crew, 34 base personnel.
Career:	1956–57: maiden supply voyage to British bases on the Antarctic Peninsula and neighbouring islands. 1957: additional strengthening to frames. 1957-91: annual research and supply voyages to British Antarctic Survey bases. 1975: established Offshore Biological Programme. 1979: modified for research; 3t bollard-pull bow thrusters, additional laboratory space, 10m stern gantry and 2t crane to handle trawl gear and 9,000m cable. 1991: replaced by RRS *James Clark Ross*. 1994: sold to Fauza Shipping, Tartous, Turney, renamed *Fayza Express*. 2004: scrapped, Allagra, Turkey.

Aptly described by Alan Gurney as having 'a sheer line so remarkable it looked as if hewn with an axe by a palsied, cross-eyed, demented naval architect', even her designers could not have called the RRS *John Biscoe* beautiful. She looked like the work of a do-it-yourselfer, combining bits from two different assembly kits. From the stern to bridge her sheer line was fairly orthodox, with some 4.5m freeboard; from her quarters she looked like a rather dumpy merchant vessel, with an ugly square deckhouse stuck out close to the stern. However, forward of the bridge, her sheerline dropped abruptly to a very low well deck with less than 2m freeboard, then rose again to a sharply-raked icebreaker bow where two bow anchors nestled into large, square recesses. Her bizarre appearance was exacerbated by a large crow's nest on her foremast, 10m above the deck, testifying to her identity as an ice navigation ship.

I first set eyes on the *John Biscoe* at the end of a Southampton quay, having walked past the majestic *Queen Mary* on one side and her equally magnificent sister *Queen Elizabeth* on the other. She not only looked strange, but exceedingly small. I was eagerly anticipating my new job with the Falkland Island Dependencies Survey, but *John Biscoe* looked much smaller and more vulnerable than the mail boat *Cambria* on which I had crossed the Irish Sea the previous night in a Force 12 hurricane. The Irish Sea can be malevolent, but I was convinced that it would be nothing compared to the Drake Passage and the full fury of the Southern Ocean. The small red, snaggle-toothed ship did not look reassuring, but she was much tougher than she looked; she not only took everything she met in her stride on that voyage but continued to do so for another thirty years, to become the longest serving of any Antarctic ship.

John Biscoe was launched in 1956, the first British ship designed for Antarctic service since Captain Scott's *Discovery*, launched in Dundee in 1901. Britain became involved in Antarctica with Captain James Cook's circumnavigation in 1772–75 with the Whitby barque, HMS *Resolution,* and in 1820 one of the first to sight the Antarctic continent was the Royal Navy's Edward Bransfield, Irish commander on the brig *Williams*. Britain's lengthy squabble with Argentina over the Falkland Islands, or Islas Malvinas, soon started, but for nearly 100 years Britain largely ignored Antarctica. James Clark Ross's expedition with HMS *Erebus* and HMS *Terror* in the 1840s opened the way for later exploration and there were intermittent brief visits by government-sponsored expeditions and private whalers and sealers, but it wasn't until the dramatic race for the South Pole by Shackleton, Scott and Amundsen in the early twentieth century that Antarctica really caught the public imagination. By then European countries, gripped by nationalistic fervour, had divided up Africa, and were turning their attention to Antarctica. Expeditions from Belgium, Britain, Norway, Sweden, France and Germany quickly descended on the continent. Nothing moves the public like a dead hero and the deaths of Scott and his companions on the Ross Ice Shelf set light to British public interest in Antarctic exploration. However, it was the Norwegian, C.A. Larsen, who triggered the permanent British presence in Antarctica and establishment of the Falkland Islands Dependencies Survey.

Larsen was a well-known, successful whaling captain, but by the late nineteenth century the decline of over-hunted Arctic whale populations threatened the Norwegian whaling industry. Larsen managed to raise funds for several Antarctic voyages on the barque *Jason* in 1893 to search for new whaling grounds, and in 1905 he established the Grytviken whaling factory on South Georgia. Other Norwegian companies and the British Salvesen's and Southern Whaling Company soon followed and the modern Antarctic whaling industry was born. Whale catchers ranged far south and more factories were soon set up on the South Shetland Islands and the Antarctic Peninsula. Whaling became very profitable during the First World War and after a century of indifference, Britain started to take its claim to the Falkland Islands Dependencies (based on its contested 'first discovery') seriously. The Falkland Islands' government began to collect substantial revenues from whaling licences, which were used to fund whale population studies and management by the British Discovery Committee.

Though Norwegian whalers reaped good profits they begrudged the large licence fees collected by the Falkland Islands' government, and in the 1920s started deep-sea pelagic whaling (non-shore based) with large factory ships, which could process whales on board, operating independently far south into the Ross and Weddell Seas, beyond British control. Territorial claims and ownership of Antarctic resources quickly became very contentious as Norway, Australia, New Zealand and France staked claims over large sectors of the continent and adjacent seas, while Chilean and Argentinian claims to the Antarctic Peninsula and neighbouring islands overlapped with the Falkland Islands Dependencies. Whale products were becoming increasingly significant for production of explosives and Japan and Germany also started Antarctic whaling and in 1938–39, the Nazi-sponsored *Schwabenland* expedition attempted to claim much of eastern Antarctica by dropping swastika markers from aircraft.

Although remote from the European battlefields, Antarctica soon became entangled in the war as the fast, armed German merchant raiders, 3,144t *Thor* and 7,766t *Pingvin,* entered Antarctic waters to capture Norwegian factory ships and whale catchers. Britain was worried that Germany would establish bases on the Antarctic Peninsula to prey on Allied merchant ships in the South Atlantic with tacit support from Axis-friendly Argentinian naval forces, and organised several armed merchant cruiser voyages to dismantle Argentinian claim markers. In 1943 the British government eventually decided to establish continuously manned bases in Antarctica with the covert naval Operation Tabarin. Suitable ships were hard to find during the war, but in January 1944 the little 350t whale research ship *William Scoresby* and the 853t Falkland Islands supply steamer *Fitzroy* set up bases on Deception Island in the South Shetlands and Port Lockroy, further south along the Peninsula.

By modern standards, Operation Tabarin bases, which set the pattern for British Antarctic operations for the next fifty years, were very modest, like mountain refuge huts. Each consisted of a small, cramped wooden hut with a tarred roof, a bunkroom, living room, a kitchen with a coal-fired cooker, and a rudimentary bathroom, food store and workshop. They were built on rocky outcrops without quays where ships could unload; everything needed during the long isolated Antarctic winter – timber, cement and roofing materials for huts, crates of provisions, sacks of coal, sledges and hundreds of other essentials – all had to discharged into boats, ferried through ice floes, then carried ashore over icy, slippery rocks. Britain had no icebreakers so the bases, beyond aircraft range and inaccessible throughout the winter, had to be completely self-contained. From March to December, the outside world could be contacted only by Morse radio transmissions to Port Stanley in the Falkland Islands. The first bases were very small with five men at Deception and nine at Port Lockroy. Everyone had to turn their hand to whatever needed to be done: hut construction, carpentry, cooking, navigation, mountaineering, boat repair, sledge building, tent sewing, veterinary practice, dog-team driving, and, where necessary, medical diagnosis and treatment. The first base members were experienced naval volunteers, but the operation's ongoing success came to depend largely on many self-reliant, practical amateurs.

Operation Tabarin was primarily intended to strengthen British claims, but meteorological observations, needed for weather forecasting in the Southern Hemisphere, were also started. The first bases were on islands with little possibility for field travel, but Hope Bay base was set up on the mainland, providing access to the interior of the Antarctic

Peninsula. Neither *William Scoresby* nor *Fitzroy* were suitable as supply ships; *Scoresby* was too small and *Fitzroy*'s thin steel hull was very vulnerable to ice damage. *Eagle*, an old wooden Newfoundland sealer built in 1902, was leased but even this tough old veteran nearly sank in heavy pack ice off Hope Bay during a storm and had to retreat before unloading was completed. The men at Hope Bay, short of stores for the winter, still built a hut, started meteorological observations and began a field-surveying programme with an 800km sledge trip along the unexplored mountainous spine of the Antarctic Peninsula with two teams of huskies.

The German threat ended in 1945, but Chilean and Argentinian claims were as serious as ever, and as whaling started again, British, Norwegian and Japanese factory ships were joined by a Russian expedition and Aristotle Onassis' rogue operation, which paid no attention to internationally agreed whale management protocols. The British Government decided that Operation Tabarin should be continued as a civilian operation, the Falkland Islands Dependencies Survey (FIDS), and should expand operations far south in the 'British' sector. The object was to strengthen Britain's claim by continuous occupation, map publication and 'effective administration' by base leaders appointed as justices of the peace and postmasters. As FIDS expanded and established more bases, it could no longer rely only on Royal Navy personnel, but needed similar practical skills and experience. Over the next fifty years, most 'Fids' would be adventurous amateurs who sailed from Britain each October to reach Antarctic bases between November and late February, where they would spend the following two winters. Normally ships would resupply bases each summer and bring new personnel while maintaining a core of experienced men (it would be another fifty years before a conservative administration would accept women).

With new FIDS bases established in the difficult ice conditions south of the Antarctic Circle, suitable supply ships became critically important. Though stores and provisions were planned with some margin of safety for an additional winter in case a ship couldn't reach a base through the pack ice, regular resupply was essential for long-term operation. *Scoresby* and *Fitzroy* were still available but *Eagle*, so badly damaged off Hope Bay, had returned to Newfoundland. Very few ships were to be found; the Americans were transforming Antarctic shipping with powerful modern icebreakers but cash-strapped, post-war Britain had no money to build an icebreaker. The small, wooden-hulled

Newfoundland freighter *Trepassey* was leased as a stopgap to help the *Scoresby* and *Fitzroy*. Packed with stores, coal, building supplies and sledges, with huskies housed on their bridges, the three ships managed to relieve existing bases and establish several new ones, but this was only to be a temporary measure, which required the vulnerable *Fitzroy* to contend with the heavy Marguerite Bay pack ice well south of the Antarctic Circle. It was touch and go, particularly when *Trepassey* was badly damaged by fire off Stonington Island.

If FIDS was to survive as a permanent Antarctic operation then better ships were essential. A retired 1,190t US Navy net-laying tug built in Delaware in 1943–44 was bought for $75,000 (half the annual FIDS budget), refitted and renamed *John Biscoe* after the famous sealing captain who circumnavigated Antarctica in 1831–32. She served for nine years but failed to solve resupply problems. In her first season she was lucky to be able to follow US icebreakers *Edisto* and *Burton Island* into Marguerite Bay to resupply Stonington base at 68°11'S, but on her own the following year, couldn't get closer than 300km, forcing those on base to spend a third winter. (Map, see p. 170) The *John Biscoe* was not powerful enough and if a suitable ship wasn't found, FIDS bases south of the Antarctic Circle would have to be closed. A small Baltic freighter was purchased in 1954 and, renamed *Shackleton*, was sent south, but she nearly sank on her second voyage when a iceberg tore a hole in her hull and was not strong enough to help resupply the southern bases.

With the future of FIDS in the balance, the British government finally provided funds for a specially designed ship. The new ice-strengthened 1,584t *John Biscoe* was designed in 1954 by Graham and Woolnough of Liverpool and built by the Fleming and Ferguson shipyard in Scotland. The round-bottomed, double hull was built of low temperature, high-impact ductile steel plating to meet Lloyd's ice navigation specifications, with frames closely spaced at 30cm, a raked cutaway icebreaking bow and her propeller protected from ice by heavy fins. To cope with the absence of unloading facilities at bases she had a heavy scow and a motor launch (soon dubbed the 'Biscoe Kid'), both easily launched from her low well deck. She was not an icebreaker, but could penetrate moderate pack ice, while her two engines could give 1,450hp in emergencies.

Commanded by highly experienced Ulster ice-captain, Bill Johnston, the new *John Biscoe* left Southampton for her maiden voyage in October 1956. During the following months her capacity was fully tested; pack ice along the west side of the Antarctic Peninsula can be very difficult as big multi-year ice floes from the Bellingshausen Sea and ice avalanches from precipitous glaciers are jammed into narrow channels by powerful winter gales. Conditions vary greatly from year to year; sometimes channels are clear of ice and even cruise ships and yachts can enter, but in most years *John Biscoe* had a slow tedious battle to relieve southern bases. She could steam through light, open pack ice, but in heavy ice she had to charge floes with a bone-jarring crash as her momentum carried her cutaway bow a few metres forward until floes shattered under her weight. Grinding to a halt, she would then edge her way astern before beginning another charge. Inside, it sounded terrible as heavy floes ground their way alongside like giant can openers. Sometimes she was stuck for days manoeuvring back and forward to escape massive 60m-high icebergs out of the Bellingshausen Sea, churning their way through the pack ice like giant battering rams. Progress could be numbingly slow; in 1964, she took over a month to work her way through 160km of pack ice to relieve the Adelaide Island base on Marguerite Bay. Struggles with ice took a serious toll; during her maiden voyage her bows were damaged and many plates were bent in, so her frames had to be strengthened. Despite such wear and tear, during her long career she never suffered critical damage, though one year she got badly stuck in Marguerite Bay and had to be helped by the American icebreakers, *Glacier* and *Northwind*. Every year she returned with bent and battered plates, but she never failed the men waiting to be relieved on bases all along the Antarctic Peninsula and in 1959–60 even penetrated far south into the Weddell Sea where Shackleton's *Endurance* was crushed in 1915 to relieve the base at Halley Bay.

When FIDS became the British Antarctic Survey in 1961, the main focus gradually shifted to scientific research. In 1970 the new 4,816t *Edward Bransfield* took over most resupply duties from *John Biscoe*, which then concentrated on hydrographic surveying and biological research, setting up an important Offshore Biological Programme in 1975. In 1979 she was refitted for scientific research; her stern deck house was replaced, giving space for a 10m gantry and 2t crane to handle trawl gear and a 9,000m cable, the bridge deck was extended aft to give laboratory space, while more accommodation and 3t bow thrusters were installed.

John Biscoe continued to work as a research vessel for the British Antarctic Survey until 1991, when the new, powerful icebreaking 5,556t research vessel *James Clark Ross* was launched. She was pensioned off and in 1994 was sold to Fauza Shipping Tartous, Turkey, and, renamed *Fayza Express,* started work as a cargo/passenger vessel. She was finally scrapped in Allagra, Turkey in 2004, but she still lives on in the warm memories of a whole generation of FIDS who watched anxiously for her red hull each spring and enjoyed many convivial evenings in her wood-panelled lounge. She is survived by the Biscoe Kid, now a harbour tug in Scotland, which was one of the 1,000-strong fleet that thronged the Thames for Queen Elizabeth's Diamond Jubilee celebrations in May 2012.

References

Anon, 1956, The Royal Research Ship *John Biscoe,* Shipbuilding and Shipping Record, 88(25), 803–808.

Boult, T., 2014, *Her Home the Antarctic: The Royal Research Ship John Biscoe,* Amberley, Stroud, Gloucestershire.

Bryan, R., 2011, *Ordeal by Ice: Ships of the Antarctic,* The Collins Press, Cork.

Fuchs, V.E., 1982, *Of Ice and Men,* Anthony Nelson, Oswestry.

Gurney, A., 2000, *The Race to the White Continent,* Norton, London.

Haddelsey, S., with A. Carroll, 2014, *Operation Tabarin: Britain's Secret Wartime Expedition to Antarctica, 1944–46,* The History Press, Stroud, Gloucestershire.

Walton, E.W.K., 1955, *Two Years in the Antarctic,* Lutterworth Press, London.

24 THE SS *EDMUND FITZGERALD* AND THE GALES OF NOVEMBER

SS *Edmund Fitzgerald*:	bulk lake ore carrier, launched June 1958 at River Rouge, Michigan for Ogleby Norton Co., Cleveland.
Tonnage:	13,632t
Cargo capacity (nominal):	25,400t
Length:	222.25m
Beam:	23m
Draught:	7.6m
Engine:	coal-fired Westinghouse turbine 7,500shp
Speed:	14.2 knots
Crew:	29
Career:	carried taconite (iron ore pellets) from Duluth and Superior to Toledo, Detroit and Cleveland. Typically made seventy-five round trips per season, with a career total of 748; regular seasonal record carrier, with 27,402t single-voyage record in 1967. 1969: bow thrusters fitted. 1971–72: converted to oil-fired with automated controls. 10 November 1975: sank during severe storm carrying 26,116t of taconite, with loss of all hands.

From the bow, her deck seemed to stretch forever. When she was launched on 7 June 1958 at the Great Lakes Engineering Works, Rouge River, Michigan, the *Edmund Fitzgerald* was the longest ship on the Great Lakes and automatically succeeded to the honorary title Queen of the Great Lakes. With a length of 222.25m she was the first 'laker' built 'within a foot of the maximum length allowed for passage through the … St Lawrence Seaway', where the Welland Canal, which bypasses Niagara Falls, can accommodate ships up to 222.6m long, 22.9m wide and 7.6m deep. The 'Mighty Fitz' was actually 17.7m shorter than the *Lusitania* and much shorter than many present-day saltwater behemoths like the Royal Caribbean and Princess Line cruise ships, but her narrow beam needed to pass the locks made her seem much longer than she actually was. Passing through the locks at Sault Ste. Marie (the Soo) or the Welland canal, she presented a massive red wall of steel to onlookers and must have seemed as impregnable as a medieval fortress. However, there is no such thing as an unsinkable ship and the vicious, destructive November gales that whip Lake Superior into a maelstrom of freezing water found a chink in her armour in 1975, and sent her to the bottom, 27km off Whitefish Point, Michigan.

The North American Great Lakes, shared by Canada and the United States, are amongst the largest seas in the world, surpassed amongst freshwater lakes only by the Caspian Sea. The largest, Lake Superior, with a surface area of 82,100km^2 and average depth of 147m is bigger than Ireland, stretches 560km from the lake head at Duluth to the Soo on the Canada–United States border. In midsummer Lake Superior can seem benign, but there is no major mountain chain to protect it from the Arctic. From late November to spring violent gales sweep down from the North Pole churning its waters into a death trap with waves that can quickly encase ships in ice or drive them helpless onto the American lee shore. No one really knows how many ships have foundered on the Great Lakes since *Le Griffon* vanished with a cargo of beaver furs in 1697, but at least 6,000 ships have disappeared with the loss of some 30,000 lives. Certainly there are more than 4,750 known shipwrecks. Many of these occurred during November gales as skippers tried to squeeze in one last cargo before shipping was shut down until spring. Violent storms occur every year, but some have a special place in history. The four-day onslaught of the storm of 7 November 1913, which flattened buildings all around the Great Lakes and dumped 60cm of snow on Cleveland, was one of the most destructive ever. Winds exceeding 70 knots whipped up 11m-high waves, sank ten ships killing 235 men and drove another twenty ships ashore, including the luxury cruise ship, *Hamonic,* whose captain just managed to reach Whitefish Bay before she sank.

The first Europeans on Lake Superior were voyageurs in their great 11m-long 'Canots de Maître' or Montreal canoes with eight–ten-man crews and tons of cargo, heading west to collect beaver furs from the trading posts scattered through Rupert's Land. As fur trade outposts changed to permanent settlements commercial shipping started to develop on the lakes, which provided a much simpler transport route than the heavily forested lands along both shores. Most traffic was initially in small brigs and schooners with 15–20t cargo capacities, but the rapid industrial development triggered when the Erie Canal opened in 1825 led to demands for larger, more powerful ships and by the mid-nineteenth century, steam ships dominated traffic on the lower lakes. The rapids at the Soo where loads had to be portaged were a major constraint for Lake Superior trade, but a canal was opened there in 1855 and one year later, the first load of iron ore to leave Lake Superior (a mere 269 tons) was transported by the steamer *Octonagon* for the Cleveland Mining Company.

Rapid industrial development at Detroit, Chicago, Cleveland and Buffalo ensured expansion of the iron-ore trade, particularly once the Lake Superior and Mississippi railroad reached the lake head in 1869 and allowed ore from western mining areas like the Vermilion Range to reach the twin ports of Duluth and Superior. However, many commodities were carried over the Great Lakes: salt, gypsum, sand, slag, cement, grain, coal, lumber and potash. It was not until 1888 that iron ore became the leading freight, with an annual total of 5,063,877t. The iron-ore trade largely determined development of specialised bulk freighters on the Great Lakes. The first, the wooden 69m-long *R.J. Hackett*, built at Cleveland in 1869, was designed so that its large holds could be lined up perfectly with the iron-ore loading chutes. In 1890, Alexander McDougall launched a 'whaleback' iron-ore carrier, *Colgate Hoyt*, at Superior. Unlike other bulk carriers, this had a very pronounced tumblehome and looked like a cross between a submarine and Eriksson's Civil War USS *Monitor*. Though fast (nearly 14 knots) whalebacks became obsolete by 1898, as they could not operate with modern unloading equipment.

The biggest constraints for the ore trade were the size and depth of locks and the time taken to unload bulk carriers. In the 1870s a 300t cargo took only a few hours to load but four days to unload. One constraint was greatly reduced in 1896 when the Poe Lock at the Soo opened, stimulating John D. Rockefeller to order twelve new 145m-long bulk freighters for the Bessemer Steamship Company. The next development involved hatches with 7.8m spacing, which could operate much more efficiently with the 3.8m spaced loading chutes at Duluth and Superior. The *Augustus B. Wolvin* launched at Superior in 1904 had 83.8cm x 60cm hatches and a length:beam ratio of 10 which became characteristic for lakers (the length:beam ratio for an ocean-going freighter is typically around 7). Traditional deck beams and stanchions were also replaced by heavy transverse plate girders between alternate hatches, allowing up to 10,694 tons to be discharged in four and a half hours. The characteristic 'two island' design of earlier lakers and the *Edmund Fitzgerald* also appeared, with the main bridge and cabins at the bow, and a secondary bridge, engines and funnel at the stern. Launch of the *Augustus B. Wolvin* triggered a rapid increase in the size and number of lakers and development of the modern Great Lakes fleet.

When the *Edmund Fitzgerald* was launched at Rouge River, Michigan, in June 1958, she was the longest ship on the Great Lakes, 222.25m long, with a capacity of 25,400 tons. With three central cargo holds, separated by non-watertight bulkheads and twenty-one 3.4 x 15m watertight hatches, she was the biggest and most luxurious of the lakers. Three fo'c'sle decks had well-appointed cabins, two guest state rooms, two dining rooms, a state-of-the-art bridge and a magnificent chart room. She was one of the fastest of the lakers and soon acquired nicknames like Pride of the American Fleet and the Toledo Express. Her launch, before a crowd of 15,000, was a bit of a fiasco; the champagne bottle used for christening failed to break (as on the ill-fated cruise ship *Costa Concordia*) until the third attempt, and as she slid sideways into the water she collided with a pier and nearly capsized, drenching spectators with a huge wave and giving one watcher a heart attack. Despite these initial ill omens, the Mighty Fitz started a successful career with a maiden voyage to Silver Bay to load taconite, and several days later sailed into Toledo with a record-breaking cargo.

Edmund Fitzgerald's record-breaking maiden voyage to Toledo was followed by many over the next seventeen years. Regularly amongst the top ore carriers, she set seasonal records of over a million tons six times and in 1969, a single-voyage record of 27,402 tons. Her trips were usually from Superior or Duluth to either Toledo or Detroit and by November 1975, she had completed some 748 round trips and covered more than 1.6 million kilometres. In 1969 a diesel-powered bow thruster was installed and in 1971–72, an oil-fired boiler with automated controls was fitted. Along the way she met her share of incidents, running aground in 1969, colliding with the Canadian Steamship Lines' *Hochelaga,* and hitting a dock wall in 1970, 1973 and 1974, damaging some of her frames and her keelson. Such incidents were run of the mill for a hard-working laker and in 1975 she was still a young ship. Working on freshwater lakes, lakers suffer much less corrosion than saltwater ships and sixty–seventy-year careers are not unusual. The oldest laker currently operating, the 168.3m-long *St. Mary's Challenger,* was launched in 1906. Certainly as the Mighty Fitz loaded taconite at the Burlington Northern Railroad dock in Superior on 9 November 1975 nobody thought that her career might be drawing to a premature close.

The *Edmund Fitzgerald* had a highly experienced twenty-eight-man crew under Captain Ernest McSorley. A thirty-seven-year veteran with the Columbia Transportation Company, he became the youngest captain on the lakes in 1951, and took command of *Edmund Fitzgerald* in 1972. He had a reputation as a master who would drive his ship through the worst weather, and at 1.15 p.m., as soon as loading was complete, he cast off while the crew were still 'dogging down' the hatch cover clamps. This was absolutely critical as the *Fitz* was heavily laden drawing 8.28m with only 3.51m freeboard. With bad weather forecast, she would be shipping waves across the deck. The clamps were a concern; an inspection in October had found that some were damaged, and repairs had been scheduled for the winter layover. As soon as she cleared the Superior breakwater, the *Fitzgerald* increased to full speed on a north-east course parallel to the Minnesota coast, to clear the Apostle Islands before turning east towards the Soo. She was soon in sight of another big ore carrier, the *Arthur M. Anderson* under Captain Jesse Cooper, also headed for the Soo.

At first the two ships faced moderate easterly winds, and though winds increasing to 38 knots were predicted there was little cause for concern as the gale was expected to pass south of Lake Superior. As evening approached, with the wind and waves picking up, the forecast storm track was changed to cross the ships' course directly, bringing gales to the whole of Lake Superior. Both captains decided to alter course to the north to gain shelter from the Canadian coast. By midnight off Isle Royale, still hours away from shelter,

they were being hammered by 52-knot north-east winds and 3m-high waves. With the gale gusting from 21° off their port bows, the long lakers were twisting and quivering in a violent corkscrew motion, flexing and bending as steep, irregular waves broke over their decks. At 2 a.m. the forecast was upgraded from gale to storm with winds reaching at least 58 knots, while barometric pressure had dropped to 990.17mb. This was no ordinary storm and the incessant battering forced even the hard-driving McSorley to reduce speed, but even so the *Fitzgerald* gradually drew ahead and was lost to view from the *Anderson.*

Near the Canadian coast at mid-morning on 10 November, the ships turned south, then near midday, south-east on a course between Michipicoten and Caribou islands, directly towards the Soo. As the eye of the storm passed, the wind veered south then north-west dropping to 5 knots, but with pressure now down to 979.33mb, it would return even stronger with the full fetch of Lake Superior driving waves onto the ships' sterns. The strait between Michipicoten and Caribou is 35km wide, but there is a bad shoal, the Chummy Bank, just south of Michipicoten, and an even worse one, the Six Fathom Shoal, north

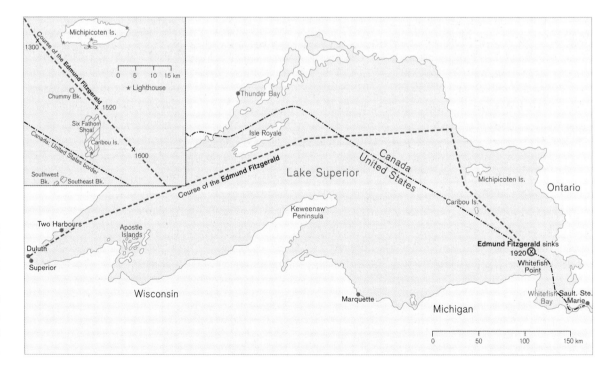

of Caribou Island. Both are inaccurately shown on the charts used in 1975, which were originally surveyed in 1916 and 1919. Some parts of the Six Fathom Shoal are now known to extend further north with maximum water depths of only 7.5m. Captain Cooper on the *Anderson* opted for a central course, but the *Fitzgerald*, now 15km ahead, headed much closer to Caribou Island, perhaps for shelter from the full force of the wind. By 2.45 p.m. she was due south of Michipicoten in steadily increasing 43-knot winds with 5m-high waves washing across the deck and heavy snow falling. During the next thirty minutes she was in the thick of where Six Fathom Shoal is now known to extend.

It is not quite clear exactly what happened, but at 3.35 p.m. McSorley called the *Anderson* reporting trouble. One of the deck railings of the *Fitzgerald* had collapsed, two ballast vents had disappeared and, with two pumps working, she was taking on water and listing to starboard. McSorley asked Cooper to shadow him down the lake and said he would reduce speed to let the *Anderson* catch up. At 4.10 p.m. McSorley radioed the *Anderson* again reporting loss of both radars and asked for help in navigation. Meanwhile the storm was getting worse; at the Soo winds were reaching 80 knots and waves were washing over the lock gates. By 6.30 p.m. the *Anderson,* south of Caribou Island and heading for Whitefish Bay, was hit by two massive 11m-high waves, with winds gusting to 90 knots and nearly 4m water depths on her deck. At 7.10 p.m. the *Fitzgerald,* 16km ahead of the *Anderson*, reported that she was holding her own; after that there was only silence and the *Fitzgerald* disappeared from the *Anderson*'s radar.

They say that Lake Superior, or Gitche Gumee as it is called by the First Nations, does not give up its dead. None of the bodies of the twenty-nine men lost on the *Edmund Fitzgerald* has ever been recovered, though a shattered lifeboat was washed up in Whitefish Bay. Despite lengthy official enquiries, no one is yet certain of the cause of the disaster. In May 1976 a remotely operated robot from US Coastguard cutter *Woodrush* took photos of the wreck lying on the bottom of Lake Superior at a depth of 150m. She was in two pieces; did she sink because she broke in two or did the force of hitting the bottom shatter her? The long narrow lakers are notoriously prone to flexing and

at least two, *Carl D. Bradley* on Lake Michigan in November 1958 and *Daniel J. Morrell* on Lake Superior in November 1966, broke in half after 'hogging' in rough seas. The loss of deck railing around 3.30 p.m. on 10 November would indicate a structural failure or stress fracture; was this related to weakness caused by earlier groundings, perhaps exacerbated by McSorley's hard driving of the heavily laden ship in bad weather, or did she ground on the Six Fathom Shoal? The July 1977 report of the Marine Board of Inquiry set up by the Coastguard decided that the most likely cause was massive flooding of the holds caused by ineffectively sealed hatch covers. This conclusion was vehemently contested by the Lake Carriers Association, which represents fifteen lake shipping companies. Despite subsequent dives on the wreck, no one really knows and Ernest McSorley cannot defend himself, but *Edmund Fitzgerald* will not be forgotten, and she probably will not be the last ship to lose a contest with the gales of November on the Great Lakes.

References

Bishop, H.E., with D. Paquette, 2000, *The Night the Fitz Went Down*, Lake Superior Port Cities, Inc., Duluth.

Hemming, R.J., 1982, *Gales of November: the Sinking of the Edmund Fitzgerald,* Contemporary Books, Chicago.

Hertel, R., 1999, *The Edmund Fitzgerald: Lost With All Hands*, Spring Lake, Michigan.

Kantar, A., 1998, *29 Missing: The True and Tragic Story of the Disappearance of the S.S. Edmund Fitzgerald*, Michigan State University Press, East Lansing.

MacInnes, J., 1997, *Fitzgerald's Storm: the Wreck of the Edmund Fitzgerald,* MacMillan Canada, Toronto.

Ramsey, R., 2009, *S.S. Edmund Fitzgerald: Requiem for the Toledo Express*, Houghton, Michigan.

Schumacher, M., 2005, *Mighty Fitz: the Sinking of the Edmund Fitzgerald*, New York.

Stonehouse, F., 2006, *The Wreck of the Edmund Fitzgerald*, 6th Edition, Avery Colour Studios, Gwin, Michigan.

25 SISTERS OF MERCY: THE TUGS *YELCHO*, *FOUNDATION FRANKLIN* AND TURMOIL

Tugs abound in almost every port in the world. Some are barely bigger than large motor boats, scurrying like sheepdogs around cruise ships, tankers and large bulk carriers in congested harbour waters, still vitally important despite the precise control which bow and stern thrusters now provide to ships' captains. Others are large, powerful, rust-streaked ocean-going vessels, able to face the worst storms anywhere in the world. All have names, but most toil in relative anonymity; only a few feature fleetingly in the news, typically when they are involved in dramatic rescues. Tugs rarely get the credit they deserve, but without them global maritime activity would be swiftly paralysed. In honour of all these obscure, vital working bees of the maritime world, this chapter tells the stories of three tugs that emerged briefly from anonymity into the full glare of media attention.

The Chilean Naval Tug *Yelcho*

Yelcho:	iron steam tug launched in 1906 at George Brown yard, Glasgow, for the Chilean Sociedad Ganadera y Industria Yelcho cargo and towing service.
Tonnage:	219t
Length:	37m
Beam:	7m
Depth:	5.5m
Engine:	350hp coal-fired compound Muir & Houston
Speed:	10 knots
Crew:	22
Career:	1908: sold to the Chilean Navy, ordered to Punta Arenas for lighthouse supply and maintenance. July 1916: ordered to tow the schooner *Emma* towards Antarctica in an attempt to rescue twenty-two members of Shackleton's *Endurance* expedition, marooned on Elephant Island; stopped by pack ice 160km from objective. August 1916: repeat attempt alone met scattered ice 60km from Elephant Island but successfully brought back all marooned men to Punta Arenas, then Valparaiso. 1945: decommissioned, tender for petty officer training school. 1958: retired. 1968: scrapped.

Yelcho was a small, unremarkable 219t vessel built in Glasgow in 1906 by George Brown & Co. for the Chilean Sociedad Ganadera e Industrial Yelcho cargo and towing service. In 1908 she was sold to the Chilean Navy and was ordered to Punta Arenas on the Straits of Magellan for lighthouse supply and maintenance in the remote southernmost part of Chile. Lacking radio, electric light and heating, she was not a sophisticated ship and seemed destined for a short, obscure, prosaic career. This changed on 12 July 1916 when she was ordered to tow the 40-year-old schooner *Emma* as close as she could to sub-Antarctic Elephant Island, off the northern Antarctic Peninsula.

By then the plight of the men from Sir Ernest Shackleton's *Endurance* expedition was worldwide news, even if overshadowed by the battlefield slaughter of the First World War. On 27 October 1915, after being trapped in the ice of the Weddell Sea for nine months, *Endurance* was crushed by inexorable ice pressure. After many more months camped on the ice, expedition members finally made their way to Elephant Island, from which Shackleton and five companions made an epic voyage to South Georgia in the 7m-long cutter *James Caird*. Then Shackleton, Tom Crean and Frank Worsley crossed the unexplored mountain core of the island to reach the Norwegian whaling station at Stromness. Immediately Shackleton set out to organise a rescue for the twenty-two men marooned on Elephant Island. The Antarctic winter was already setting in and with savage winter gales jamming pack ice into an impenetrable barrier no ship would normally attempt the 2,500km voyage. However, the situation of the men living in smoky darkness under two upturned boats on a shingle beach on Elephant Island was desperately critical as their scant provisions of seal and penguins slowly ran out.

Shackleton made a first attempt on the tiny unstrengthened British whale catcher *Southern Sky* but failed against heavy pack ice and, short of coal, had to return quickly to Port Stanley in the Falkland Islands. No suitable relief ship could reach Port Stanley from Britain before October, so the increasingly frantic Shackleton telegraphed the governments of all neighbouring countries to seek help. On 10 June the Uruguayan trawler *Instituto de Pesca No 1* set out from Port Stanley, and came tantalisingly close (40km) to the island before heavy ice forced her to turn back to Port Stanley with a worn-out engine and empty coal bunkers. Meanwhile, the British community in Punta Arenas, Chile, had raised £1,500 so that Shackleton could charter an old schooner, the *Emma*. On 12 July she was towed south by the *Yelcho* but could get no closer than 160km before the ice stopped her and she had to be towed back to Port Stanley.

It was now mid-August, the middle of the harsh Antarctic winter. The situation was desperate and the stress on Shackleton was immense; Worsley observed that 'he had not a grey hair when we started out to rescue our men the first time … now … he was grey-headed'.

Yelcho was forbidden by the Navy to enter pack ice and no better ships were available, but exercising all his charismatic charm, Shackleton managed to persuade President Juan Luis Sanfuentes of Chile to let her attempt to reach Elephant Island. No ship had ever sailed to the Antarctic in August, and it was a serious risk for the little tug with its single, unstrengthened iron hull. Commanded by Lieutenant Luis Pardo, she left Punta Arenas westwards through the Straits of Magellan, then down the coast to the Beagle Channel where she took on 300 bags of coal to add to the 72 tons already on board, then headed south into the Drake Passage on 28 August. As well as her twenty-two-man crew, she had Shackleton, Tom Crean and Frank Worsley aboard. Anticipating the worst of the weather, instead of gales and huge seas she met fog. She met scattered icebergs 96km from Elephant Island, but at 11.40 a.m. on 30 August, the fog lifted to reveal the beach camp on Elephant Island. Nervously, Shackleton watched as small figures gradually emerged until the full count of twenty-two men was complete.

The marooned men were quickly transferred and, forty-five minutes later, *Yelcho* hastily retreated northwards before the wind turned to bring the pack ice back. With forty-eight men crowded into the space intended for twenty-three, the return journey to Chile was no picnic. Frank Hurley described her as 'a veritable porpoise, diving under … the smallest seas which rake her deck … one feels apprehensive of one's safety when they … pull large flakes of rust off the vessel's plates … like all other craft, she is fitted with pumps, however, [they] don't work.' (Hurley, 1925)

Despite everything, she arrived back to Punta Arenas on 3 September to a triumphal welcome: Shackleton wrote in a letter 'everything that could swim in the way of a boat was out to meet us'. Ten days later they re-boarded *Yelcho* for the voyage to Valparaiso where some 30,000 people turned out to welcome her on 27 September:

> as *Yelcho* steamed up the lane formed by Chilean warships everything that could safely float, ferries, launches and coal barges followed … Bands blared, bunting fluttered, whistles and the sailors massed on the warships cheered

(Hurley, 1925)

Lieutenant Luis Pardo became a national hero and was immediately promoted to 'Pilot 1st Class', but, a modest man, he turned down the £25,000 reward offered. He continued to have a distinguished naval career, including a term as Chilean consul in Liverpool, until his death in 1935. He is honoured by many street names in Chile, by the Pardo School of Navigation, and by a statue on the beach at Point Wild on Elephant Island where Shackleton's men were marooned. The little *Yelcho* remained in the Chilean Navy until 1945, and then acted as the tender for the Navy's petty officer school until she was scrapped in 1968. Her name was passed to two subsequent ships of the Chilean Navy while her bow is now a permanent memorial in Chile's southernmost town, Puerto Williams.

Salvage tug *Foundation Franklin*

Foundation Franklin:	Frisky-class Admiralty tug, launched by John Lewis & Co, Aberdeen, 1919.
Tonnage:	612t
Length:	47.3m
Beam:	9.8m
Draught:	4.6m
Engine:	1,200hp triple-expansion with two coal-fired Scotch boilers
Speed	12–15 knots
Crew	31

Career:	fleet duties at Scapa Flow, Orkneys, then laid up. 1924: sold to Atlantic Towing Co., Hamburg, renamed *Gustavo Ipland*, then again laid up. 1930: sold to Foundation Marine, Montreal, refitted in Canada with extended boat deck, enclosed bridge, large salvage hold and 8t derrick. 1930–48: numerous salvage jobs along Canadian east coast and as far east as Bordeaux. 1946: converted to oil. 1948: last salvage of Norwegian freighter *Arosa*, then replaced by Bustler-class *Foundation Josephine*.

In the 199 years since John Wood's *Tug* and John Boult's *Perserverance* started work as tow boats on the rivers Clyde and Tyne respectively, many tugs have been designed for different purposes, but the stars of the tug firmament are the big, powerful, deep-sea ocean-going tugs that can carry out long-distance towing and complex salvage operations in atrocious weather conditions. Early steam-powered tugs like the 54t *Samson* launched on the Tyne in 1817 had very limited capability; Samson only produced 40hp and was only suitable for harbour operations. The inefficient engines with very high coal consumption made long-distance towing impossible. As engine efficiency improved, screw propulsion became more common and large bunker capacity was added, this changed and by the 1870s several very long tows from places like St Helena to Britain had been completed.

Almost as soon as steam tugs appeared, the Admiralty became an important client and by 1900, the Royal Navy's expanding global role significantly increased the need for ocean-going tugs. Despite this, in 1914 the Royal Navy owned only four ocean-going tugs but quickly had to meet greatly increased demand for salvage tugs for vessels damaged by submarines or minefields. This was met by requisitioning 100 civilian tugs and from 1916 to 1919 by construction of larger tugs: five 885t Stoic-class tugs, six 1,400t Resolve-class tugs, forty-six 440t Saint-class tugs and three 612t Frisky-class tugs (sometimes called Racia-class tugs). By the end of the war the Royal Navy had numerous coal-fired paddle and screw tugs capable of handling the largest warships in the fleet, which were soon surplus.

Frisky-class tugs were handsome 47.3m-long vessels with twin vertical funnels, high boat decks, open bridges and monkey bridges, radio shacks and long low towing flats with three large towing bows and thirty-one crew housed in the stern. They were excellent sea boats with 1,200hp triple-expansion engines giving a maximum speed of 15knots. Launched in 1919 HMS *Frisky* was employed in fleet duties at Scapa Flow, then laid up until 1924 when she was sold to the Atlantic

Towing Company, Hamburg, for towing on the Rhine and in the Baltic, and renamed the *Gustavo Ipland*. She was soon laid up again until 1930, then she was sold to Foundation Maritime, Montreal, renamed *Foundation Franklin* and refitted in Halifax with new crew quarters in the bow, her bridge enclosed, a large stern hold for pumps, ground anchors and salvage equipment and her main mast strengthened to take an 8t derrick boom.

It took time to carve out a position amongst her competitors on the Canadian Atlantic coast but, based in Halifax, she soon started an outstanding career as a North Atlantic rescue tug, immortalised in Farley Mowat's book *The Grey Seas Under*. Over eighteen hard years she took part in more than 100 rescue operations from Quebec City in the west to France in the east, and from Bermuda in the south to the Straits of Belle Île in the north. Not all were successful, but her rescues were legendary, saving many ships and hundreds of seamen.

Salvaging is a brutally difficult and competitive business; tugs are usually called only as a last resort by ships already in desperate straits in very bad weather, often aground on dangerous reefs in immediate danger of breaking up. Tugs must put to sea in atrocious conditions and steam flat out to the rescue location to arrive before the ship sinks or breaks up and before competitors arrive. Insurance agreements must then be negotiated with masters before work can start. Almost inevitably, salvage operations are difficult and dangerous with a high risk of failure; if they do fail, tug operators receive no payment, even if weeks of dangerous work have been involved.

Foundation Franklin's first salvage attempt was unsuccessful, and nearly ended her career. In March 1932 after a very difficult Atlantic crossing, the 5,000t Hamburg–Amerika Line freighter *Harburg* became disabled in a hurricane when her rudder stock broke, 80km south-west of Sable Island. For thirty-six hours the *Franklin* fought her way through monstrous seas, searching for the freighter, which was drifting rapidly south-eastwards. Then a particularly savage sea snapped a turnbuckle on her steering chain; without steering, she broached helplessly in the troughs of the waves. It took three hours to shorten the chain and make a new turnbuckle, and two hours more for two men, half-drowned under the stern grating, to fit the chain back on the rudder quadrant, so that the helpless tug could steer again. By then the New York tug *Willett* was also heading for *Harburg* and was much closer than the *Franklin*. As the storm intensified, both tugs had to heave to, but four days after the SOS, the *Willett* reached *Harburg* and got a line aboard, three hours before *Franklin* arrived. *Franklin* entered Halifax harbour four days later with no compensation for a voyage that nearly destroyed her.

Franklin's next salvage operation was almost as difficult but luckily was more successful. The British freighter *Firby*, carrying wheat, had run ashore in the Straits of Belle Île, 800km away from Halifax. *Franklin* took two days to reach the freighter, hard aground on a reef, surrounded by icebergs. Her bottom plates were badly torn and before any attempt could be made to tow her off, the cargo had to be jettisoned and her holds pumped out. The big salvage pumps repeatedly clogged with wet fermented grain and lost their prime, and eight days of frustrating effort were needed before she was light enough to be towed off. Late at night with a new storm rising, *Firby*'s engines running full astern and *Franklin*'s boilers close to bursting, she finally came loose with much grinding of damaged bottom plates. With 5m of water in her holds and pumps running flat out, she was dragged slowly to shelter in the lee of an island. Three days later she was beached in Frigate Harbour and made sufficiently watertight for the 1,000km tow to Quebec City. It was another ten days before the tow could start, and another four before the awkward client could be nursed through the mudbanks and narrow channels of the St Lawrence into dry dock.

Most of *Franklin*'s rescues, like 8,500t *Cordelia,* aground in Canso Strait, occurred in the dangerous coastal waters around Nova Scotia, Newfoundland and the Gulf of St Lawrence, but there were also plenty of cries for help from the open Atlantic, like the 6,000t Belgian freighter *Emile Jacqui*, which lost her rudder in a gale, 560km south-west of Halifax, just before Christmas 1934. At first her sister ship, *Henri Jaspar,* tried to steer her from astern, but with another gale rising, she eventually had to take *Franklin*'s tow. In the next seven hours with the wind rising to over 90 knots, *Franklin* herself was in real danger. Off Chebucto Head the tow parted, but she had successfully towed *Jacqui* to a good holding ground. With two anchors down, she could survive until the wind dropped and a new hawser could be attached, allowing her to be towed into Halifax. In March 1935 another of *Emile Jacqui*'s sister ships, *Jean Jadot*, also had rudder trouble in a gale, 500km south-east of Newfoundland. Initially the little US Coastguard cutter *Mendota* tried to help but eventually had to slip the tow. The *Franklin* fought desperately for two days to keep the big freighter off the lethal shoals of Sable Island, but towing became easier when the jammed

rudder finally broke off and the little tug was able to drag another rescued ship triumphantly into Halifax harbour.

Despite the U-boat threat *Franklin* was very active throughout the Second World War. At first she had to operate without an escort, but eventually Captain Harry Brushett browbeat the naval authorities into providing one. Amongst many extraordinary rescues, one that strained her to the limit was British freighter *King Edward*, which she reached 1,600km east of Halifax. When they finally docked at St John's, Newfoundland, *Franklin* had less than a 0.5t of coal dust left in her bunkers after steaming more than 4,000km in twenty days. In 1944, *Franklin* rescued no fewer than twenty-two ships, followed by another eight in 1945. Shortly after the war ended, she had to tow a huge bucket dredge from the St Lawrence to Bordeaux, a major challenge with her limited bunker capacity, even with sacks of coal stacked on her deck.

In 1946, *Franklin* was converted from coal to oil, increasing her range by 50 per cent, but despite this her future was soon threatened when Foundation Maritime purchased HMS *Samsonia*, a 6-year-old Bustler-class tug, which was renamed *Foundation Josephine*. After months of declining activity, *Franklin*'s last salvage job was in January 1948 when the Norwegian motor ship *Arosa* was disabled by mechanical problems, far out in the Atlantic at 38°20′N, 51°48′W,

Foundation Franklin towing the *Arosa*.

1,400km from Halifax. With *Foundation Josephine* under repair, *Franklin* set out to fight her way through heavy seas and a full gale, which soon progressed into a hurricane. She took nearly four days to reach the *Arosa*. In the eye of the hurricane, she managed to get a hawser aboard, then set out towards home, but with the hurricane again blowing full force from the north-west, she could tow at less than 1 knot, and it was soon obvious that her fuel would not last until Halifax. Now in trouble herself, for three days she battled westward with ice all over her superstructure and her radio out of commission, then her towing winch tore out and she disappeared from *Arosa*'s view. The Norwegian sent a new SOS and the urgently repaired *Foundation Josephine* put to sea, but it took eleven days before she could tow the big freighter into Boston. Meanwhile, with water pouring through her damaged deck, almost out of fuel and with her old engine failing, *Franklin* was in desperate peril. However, against all odds she cheated the ocean one more time and, to the astonishment of those along the waterfront, slowly emerged five days later like a spectre out of the fog at Chebucto Head fog to enter Halifax harbour.

The Admiralty Rescue Tug *Turmoil*

Turmoil:	Bustler-class rescue tug launched at Henry Robb yard, Leith, May 1945.
Tonnage:	1,136t
Length:	57.9m
Beam:	11.8m
Draught:	5.2m
Engines:	two eight-cylinder British Polaris diesels, 3,200hp
Speed:	16 knots
Range:	27,000km
Armament:	one 7.62cm AA gun, one 2lb pom-pom, two 20mm AA guns, four machine guns.
Career:	launched immediately after VE day. Chartered to Overseas Towing & Salvage. 1951: participated in search for Brazilian dreadnought *Sao Paulo* adrift near Azores. 1951–52: after rescuing tanker *Mactra* from Fastnet nearly managed to successfully tow *Flying Enterprise* in to Falmouth. 1954: retrieved stern half of tanker *World Concord* from Irish Sea to Antwerp. 1957: Rejoined Royal Navy at Ardrossan. 1961: Laid up. 1964: sold to Tsavili Salvage & Towing, Piraeus, renamed *Nisos Kerkya* then *Matsas*. 1986: scrapped.

One of the few tugs to triumphantly overcome anonymity was another Bustler-class tug and sister ship of the *Foundation Josephine,* the *Turmoil.* As in the First World War, when the Battle of the Atlantic reached its crescendo, the Admiralty faced a huge demand for rescue tugs, and again it had only four ocean-going tugs, although all were new, powerful 3,000hp Brigand-class vessels. Again civilian tugs were swiftly requisitioned, including twenty-one First World War veterans and immediate orders were placed for many new rescue tugs: twenty-one 700t Assurance-class tugs in 1939, twenty-three 788t Favourite-class in 1942, six 868t Envoy-class in 1944, and eight 1,118t Bustler-class, four built in 1941/42 and four in 1944/45.

Bustler-class tugs launched in 1942 were 1,100t, while those launched in 1945 registered 1,136t. They were the fastest and most powerful British wartime tugs. The diesel engines provided very flexible power, able to go from full ahead to stop in two–three seconds, and stop to full astern in one–three seconds. Only one was amongst the twenty-three British tugs lost during the war; HMS *Hesperia* was wrecked on the Libyan coast together with an Assurance-class tug in February 1945 while trying to keep a floating dock, which had broken its tow, off the rocks. All had excellent records, but the one that became a media star was HMS *Turmoil* because of its dramatic attempt to rescue the *Flying Enterprise*, described in Chapter 22.

Turmoil was launched on 11 May 1945, just as the war ended. Soon surplus to requirements, she was chartered to the Overseas Towage and Salvage Ltd, London. Among many assignments, she was involved in three remarkable rescue attempts. In November 1951 she was part of a massive search for the 1909 Brazilian dreadnought *Sao Paulo,* which, with eight crew aboard, broke free 280km north of the Azores while being towed from Rio de Janeiro to Britain to be scrapped. *Turmoil* joined HMS *Bustler* and ships of the US and Portuguese navies, and aircraft from Gibraltar, to scour the Atlantic, but the elusive battleship was never seen again.

Barely two months later, *Turmoil*, towing the tanker *Mactra*, disabled west of the Fastnet Rock in a severe gale, was called to help the *Flying Enterprise*, badly damaged by the same storm, which was listing and splitting in two far out in the Atlantic at 49°43′N, 14°43′W. After dropping *Mactra* at Falmouth, *Turmoil* reached *Flying Enterprise* and over the next seven days towed her 400km almost reaching Falmouth before she sank. It was a very courageous attempt but a failure for which *Turmoil* and her owners, operating with Lloyd's Open Form, received only praise.

Two years later, *Turmoil* was involved in another high-profile rescue when the 20,000t Liberian tanker *World Concord* split in half during a November gale in the Irish Sea. The stern section drifted towards the Welsh coast where the thirty-five men aboard were rescued by the St David's lifeboat, while *Turmoil* headed for the bow section with seven men aboard. Before a tow could be secured the bow drifted away, but the men were rescued by the Rosslare lifeboat. Meanwhile the unmanned stern section drifted into Cardigan Bay where *Turmoil* managed to get a wire aboard. *World Concord* was in ballast, but had not been degassed so the damaged tanks were leaking volatile, flammable gases. The shattered stern was extremely difficult to tow, incessantly sheering away to port or starboard, but *Turmoil* nursed it towards shelter along the Irish coast to enter Belfast Lough. Suddenly the wind, veering east, put her on a lee shore, making this impossible so, in the teeth of the north-easterly gale, *Turmoil* clawed off the lee shore to battle north through the narrow, dangerous North Channel. She was barely through this when the wind backed westwards, driving her towards a new lee shore. Again she fought for hours to escape to the north-west before rounding Ailsa Craig to enter the haven of Holy Loch, after towing the awkward stern section nearly 500km in two days. The missing bow section was later salvaged by the tug *Cautious*.

Roughly patched up, the two halves of *World Concord* were moved to Belfast Lough and then, with *Turmoil* towing the stern and the tug *Salveda* the bow, set off for Antwerp to be reunited. This apparently straightforward towing job turned out to be another memorable battle through incessant gales, with the ungainly stern section sheering off at right angles to the course, but after towing more than 1,600km in two weeks, *Turmoil* delivered it safely to the Scheldt; *Salveda* followed with the bow twelve days later. The halves were eventually rejoined and *World Concord* resumed her interrupted career as a tanker while *Turmoil* returned to more prosaic tasks. In 1957 she was restored to the Admiralty as *RFA Turmoil*, but after refitting at Ardrossan yard in 1961, she was laid up. In 1963 she was sold to Tsavliris (Salvage and Towage), Ltd, Piraeus, and was renamed *Nisos Kerkyra* and then *Matsas* before finally being scrapped in 1986.

References

Brookes, E., 1956, *Rescue Tug*. E.P. Dutton and Co., Inc., New York.

Hurley, F., 1925, *Argonauts of the South,* G.P. Putnam's Sons, New York and London.

Mowat, F., 1958, *The Grey Seas Under,* McClelland and Stewart, Toronto.

Shackleton, Sir E.H., 1919, *South: The Story of Shackleton's 1914–1917 Expedition,* William Heinemann, London.

Thomas, P.N., 1983, *British Steam Tugs,* Waine Research Publications, Wolverhampton.

If you enjoyed this book, you might also be interested in …

The Evolution of the Transatlantic Liner

CHRIS FRAME & RACHELLE CROSS

The Evolution of the Transatlantic Liner follows the changing form of the transatlantic ocean liner from its inception in the nineteenth century through to the present day. This book traces the major evolutions in passenger ship design and how it was influenced by changing needs and beliefs, while at the same time showcasing how these enormous ocean craft helped shape societies on both sides of the Atlantic Ocean. Using rare photography, the authors look at the way a changing world, politics and technology led to the construction of ever larger, faster and grander ocean liners. Covering great liners such as *Great Western*, *Great Britain*, *Britannia*, *Etruria*, *Kaiser Wilhelm der Grosse*, *Oceanic*, *Lusitania*, *Mauretania*, *Olympic*, *Titanic*, *Bremen*, *Normandie*, *Queen Elizabeth*, *United States* and many more, this volume is a valuable addition to your historical maritime library.

978 0 7524 7973 6

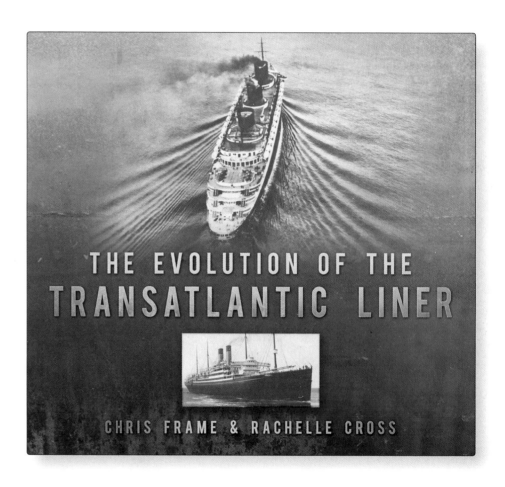